THE BEER AND WHISKY LEAGUE

THE BEER AND WHISKY LEAGUE

THE **ILLUSTRATED HISTORY** *OF THE* **AMERICAN ASSOCIATION— BASEBALL'S RENEGADE MAJOR LEAGUE**

• • •

DAVID NEMEC

MARK RUCKER, PICTURE EDITOR

L Y O N S   &   B U R F O R D ,   P U B L I S H E R S

Printed in the United States of America

Design by Howard P. Johnson

10 9 8 7 6 5 4 3 2 1

Library of Congress Cataloging-in-Publication Data

Nemec, David.
    The beer and whisky league : the illustrated history of the American Association, baseball's renegade major league / David Nemec ; photographic and archival assistance by Mark Rucker.
        p.   cm.
    Includes bibliographical references and index.
    ISBN 1-55821-285-X
    1. American Association (Baseball league : 1882–1891—History. 2. Baseball—United States—History—19th century. I. Title.
GV875.A57N46   1994
796.357'64'0973—dc20   94-27805
                                                                                           CIP

Photo credits

From the collection of Phillip Von Borries—2–3; The R.G. Potter Collection, University of Louisville Photographic Archives—18, 28; Transcendental Graphics—20, 23, 25–26, 30–32, 34–37, 42, 44–46, 48–53, 55, 56 *bottom*, 60–61, 63, 64 *bottom*, 65, 67, 72–74, 76, 81–82, 83 *top*, 84–87, 89, 92, 95–100, 111–12, 113 *top*, 114–20, 125, 126, 131, 135–37, 139–40, 148–49, 154–55, 157–58, 160, 166–170, 174, 176–77, 179, 182, 184, 186, 188–90, 192–95, 197, 199, 201, 206, 208–13, 215–16, 218, 220–24, 226–27, 229–30, 232–33, 235–36, 241, 243–46; From the author's collection—21, 29, 90, 103, 110, 129–30, 138, 152, 161, 172, 178, 181; National Baseball Library & Archive, Cooperstown, N.Y.—24, 33, 47, 54, 58, 64 *top*, 68, 71, 79, 83 *bottom*, 94, 105–6, 108, 121–24, 128, 132–33, 141–42, 144, 147, 150–51, 153, 156, 164, 173, 200, 204, 234, 238, 240, 242; From the collection of Dennis Goldstein—27, 70, 225; *Sporting Life*—39, 56 *top*, 62, 104, 134, 171, 196; From the collection of James Bready—66, 93, 102, 107; The Hillerich & Bradsby Collection, University of Louisville Photographic Archives—69; From the collection of William Loughman—113 *bottom*; *The Sporting News*—159, 198, 228, 231; From the collection of Bruce Foster—175; From the collection of Michael Olenich—191.

To Carol, who has seen enough of me to know
all the ways in which I belong back then.

"In the Country of baseball, time is the air we breathe, and the wind swirls us backward, until we seem so reckoned in time and seasons that all time and seasons become the same."

—Donald Hall

CONTENTS

ACKNOWLEDGMENTS

THIS BOOK WAS FIRST HATCHED IN MY MIND about ten years ago as a pictorial history of the American Association. At that time I didn't believe I could unearth enough material to sustain a written history, mainly because none had ever been done before. The first to suggest to me that I might be wrong was Thelma Morris, who generously took time out from her duties at the Cleveland Public Library one December morning in 1986 to shepherd me through the library's catacombs, where were moldering a welter of guides and scrapbooks from the last century that had not seen daylight in decades. To her, I and every other baseball researcher fortunate enough to discover her before her retirement will always be grateful.

In the years since, I have come to owe much also to the staff at the San Francisco Public Library for helping to turn up much of the material on microfilm that became the backbone for this book.

For their assistance, information and encouragement, I am

grateful to these baseball historians, writers, researchers and collectors: James Bready, Bill Carle, Dennis Goldstein, Scott Flatow, Frederick Ivor-Campbell, Tony Salin and Tom Hill.

For his legwork on the Columbus teams, I am grateful to my nephew Matthew Oliver.

For providing me with the space and atmosphere at Yaddo that helped this book to take shape in my mind, I am grateful to the Yaddo Corporation.

For putting his enormous knowledge of 19th-century baseball to the arduous task of fact checking The Beer and Whisky League, I am grateful to Bob Tiemann.

For his unflagging interest in the American Association, his many discoveries about the Louisville teams and, above all, for believing long before anyone else did that a book like this could one day find a home, I am grateful to Phillip Von Borries.

Mark Rucker worked closely with me on the pictorial front in *The Beer and Whisky League*. His technical expertise and his sensitivity is apparent to me on virtually every page. As can be expected in a book like this, there are a few player and team photographs of less than stellar quality for the simple reason that it is either them or nothing. On the other hand, thanks mostly to Mark's efforts, there are many photographs that we both hope will electrify readers much as they did us when we first saw them.

INTRODUCTION

THE MOST VIBRANT AND FREEWHEELING TIME in baseball history came during the ten years between 1882 and 1891, when the upstart American Association fought the National League tooth and nail for the right to co-exist as a major league. Although the Association ultimately lost the war, it won many battles along the road and in the process played a large hand in revolutionizing the game. Yet this rebel federation's profusion of achievements has gone almost unnoted. The vast majority of the American Association's leading players and executives are scarcely known today outside a small circle of historians, while their National League counterparts, like Cap Anson, Al Spalding, King Kelly, Monte Ward and Hoss Radbourn, are famous throughout the baseball community.

Since remarkably little has been written about the men and the events that shaped the American Association, the baseball detective now on the scent must ferret out original sources and then pray they are reliable. Unhappily, many have long since

been found to be considerably less than trustworthy. Pete Browning's name, for instance, was misspelled for years in record books
as well as on his tombstone. A number of the American Association's lesser lights like Al Atkinson, Henry Easterday, Ed Daily
and George Pinkney fared much the same fate. Even more confusing, at the close of the 1884 season Association officials awarded the loop batting title to Dude Esterbrook, claiming he had hit
.408. A short while later they changed their minds and decided
that Harry Stovey won the crown by hitting .404. Not until nearly a century had passed did it emerge that Dave Orr was probably
the real winner with a much less awesome .354 average.

These are just a few of the many discrepancies that have am-
bushed me over the horde of years since I first stumbled upon the
American Association when my father gave me a copy of Franklin
Lewis's history of major league baseball in Cleveland for Christ-
mas. In building a chronicle of the Beer and Whisky League, I
originally attempted to use for scaffolding only known and prov-
able facts, while keeping my own interpretations and opinions to
a minimum. Early in the hunt, though, I realized that even during
the ten years the American Association was in existence, much of
its history was *already* murky and in dispute. So I came to recognize that while it was important for me to be, insofar as possible,
accurate and objective, it was equally vital to tell a complete and
cohesive story.

But when your sources conflict wildly, as mine did, on such
basic points as on what date a hotly contested pennant was
clinched, who managed the winning team that year and whether
the team's star hit over .400 the following season or a mere .326—

well, it was sometimes a struggle to meet my pledge to myself to untangle more mysteries and leave fewer loose ends dangling in this history than in anything previously written about the American Association.

To decide which version to accept when there was a major difference of fact or opinion, my hierarchy was as follows: In most cases I went with *Sporting Life* because it seemed, in my judgment, to attract all the best writers of the time to its pages and to present the most complete and unbiased reportage on every facet of the game, both on and off the field, almost from the moment of its inception in April 1883. Yet I never found *Sporting Life* so infallible that I cared to bank my all on it. What's more, its presses did not begin to roll until nearly a year and a half after the American Association was born. To learn about the Association's infancy, I therefore relied on the local newspapers in the cities that originally housed Association franchises—Cincinnati, Louisville and St. Louis especially—and on the illuminating glances backward at the Association's early days that appeared from time to time in both *Sporting Life* and *The Sporting News*, after it joined the competition for the nickels of the sports-minded in 1886.

As adjunct sources, I combed game accounts and newspaper items in other Association and National League cities and also Henry Chadwick's scrapbooks at the New York Public Library. Lastly, I turned to numerous team histories and general histories of the game in the 19th century. All were helpful, but none was persuasive, if only because their authors pondered and chose, as did I, from conflicting original sources and always with a goal in mind that was different than mine.

No one else, it appears, has ever undertaken to tell the full, intricate and unbowdlerized story of the American Association and has aimed his research and selected his material to accomplish this task. In any event, this tale is as complete as I can make it for the moment. No doubt, even as you read these words, someone, somewhere, will mine a nugget that I missed, but that's part of the game. Even Columbus didn't get it all right. He simply got there first.

These points aside, I have always been more fascinated by how and why things happened than by what happened. Consequently, much of this history of the Beer and Whisky League dwells on the volcanic relationships and interactions among the characters who were part of its making, and I sincerely hope you will enjoy my approach.

• • •
Some 78 years after his death, the American Association's archetypal hero at last received a grave marker that gave him his due in both name and deed. Dedicated in 1984 it was financed jointly by Louisville Mayor Harvey Sloane and John A. Hillerich III, the president of the Hillerich & Bradsby Company. The Hillerich family had long owed an enormous debt to Browning, whose quest for a custom-made bat first turned them from lathing butter churns to making Louisville Slugger bats.

1881

September—Baseball men in several large cities without major league teams receive a series of cleverly crafted postcards and telegrams inviting them to meet and discuss forming a new major league.

October 10—Chris Von der Ahe, O.P. Caylor, Horace Phillips, Denny McKnight and a number of other men who are instrumental in starting the American Association gather for the first time in Pittsburgh.

November 2—The American Association holds its first formal meeting in Cincinnati and awards franchises to Cincinnati, St. Louis, Pittsburgh, Louisville, Philadelphia and Brooklyn.

1882

March 11—AA owners retract their pledge to reinstate blacklisted National League players; the Brooklyn franchise is awarded several days later to Baltimore, requiring the Maryland city to assemble a team only six weeks before the season opens.

May 2—The AA stages its first championship games at St. Louis, Pittsburgh and Philadelphia.

July 2—In an emergency meeting at Cincinnati to address rampant umpiring problems, the AA becomes the first major league to hire a staff of salaried umpires.

October 6—AA champion Cincinnati beats NL champion Chicago 4–0 in the first postseason game in history between two major league pennant winners.

October 23—Columbus Buckeyes and New York Metropolitans admitted to the AA.

November 18—Horace Phillips publicly declares that he sired the AA, opening a debate over who should receive credit for being the loop's founding father that continues to this day.

December 12—The NL discards the archaic foul-bound rule, but the AA elects to retain it, meaning that in AA games a fielder can still retire a batter simply by catching a foul hit on the first bounce.

1883

February 17—AA and NL moguls meet formally for the first time at the "New York Conference" along with a representative of the Northwestern League, and the three loops draft the Tripartite Agreement, an early form of the National Agreement.

April—A telephone connection made between St. Louis's Sportsman's

Park and downtown headquarters enables the Browns to report events on the field as fast as they occur and also to post scores of other AA games in progress on "bulletin boards."

May 1—The AA opens its first season as an eight-team loop.

September 30—The closest major league pennant race to date ends with Philadelphia claiming the AA flag by a one-game margin over St. Louis and Philadelphia drawing 330,000 fans to break all prevailing season attendance records by some 80,000.

October 27—Peace of a sort is established between the AA and the NL when both loops meet in New York to draft the game's first "National Agreement."

December 13—To combat the rebel Union Association, the AA swells to 12 teams by admitting new franchises in Brooklyn, Toledo, Washington and Indianapolis.

1884

April—The NL allows overhand pitching for the first time in spring exhibition games, but the AA continues to restrict pitchers to sidearm deliveries; the AA, on the other hand, becomes the first major loop to adopt a rule giving a batter his base if he's hit by a pitch.

May 1—The AA opens its only season as a 12-team loop.

May 19—Members of the Cincinnati and Indianapolis teams are arrested in Indianapolis for playing on the previous day, a Sunday, thereupon igniting a war between Sunday ball proponents and Sabbatarians that will last long after the AA dissolves.

July 19—After weeks of dithering, AA officials declare a June 21 game between New York and Louisville an official contest and award New York a victory that eventually helps the Mets win the pennant; this action, coming nearly a month after the fact, is but one glaring example of the sort of administrative indecision that haunts the AA all during its existence.

August 5—Virginia replaces the financially depleted Washington franchise.

October 25—Providence completes a three-game sweep over the Mets in the first NL versus AA "World's Series."

December 11—Shortly after being signed by Cincinnati, pitcher Tony Mullane is suspended by the AA for the entire 1885 season as a punishment for his constant contract jumping.

1885

April—The AA completes its spring exhibition slate by winning 15 of its 27 contests with the NL, the first time the junior loop has shown superiority in preseason interloop play.

April 18—After dropping Virginia, Toledo, Columbus and Indianapolis, the AA again is an eight-team league as it begins its fourth season.

April 29—The Mets, owned by the Metropolitan Exhibition Company, are fined by the AA for having released Tim Keefe and Dude Esterbrook in a paper transaction so they can sign with the New York NL team, which is under the same ownership.

June 6—Some six weeks after the season begins, AA moguls abolish the foul-bound rule and vote to allow overhand pitching.

October 17—A joint meeting between the AA and the NL results in a new National Agreement and the first attempt at a player salary limitation plan.

November 25—*Sporting Life* echoes the decision made by a select committee of major league officials by declaring the 1885 World's Series between St. Louis and Chicago a draw.

December 19—In a landmark decision, a Philadelphia court prevents the AA from ousting the Mets, finding for the New York team in its bid to retain its AA franchise under new ownership.

1886

March 20—AA president Denny McKnight is made to resign because of his poor handling of the Mets situation and the Barkley case.

March 27—Second baseman Sam Barkley files a legal brief that results in his successfully preventing the AA from suspending him for contract jumping.

April 25—Brooklyn beats Baltimore 11–1 in the first Sunday game ever played at Brooklyn's Ridgewood Park, but new loop president Wheeler Wyckoff throws out the result, claiming the game did not have the AA's official approval; the first Brooklyn Sunday game that counts does not occur until May 2, when Brooklyn and the A's tie 19–19 after the two clubs exhaust all six playable balls Brooklyn has on hand.

October 23—A 10-inning, 4–3 triumph enables St. Louis to beat Chicago 4 games to 2, giving the AA its only undisputed World's Series win over the NL.

November—In a series of joint meetings in Chicago, AA and NL mangates adopt a common set of playing rules that include the NL recognizing the hit batsman rule and both leagues doing away with batters being allowed to call for either high or low pitches; the NL capitalizes on the peaceful proceeding by snatching the AA's Pittsburgh franchise.

1887

April—After not paying much attention to exhibition results for several years, the NL, wanting to reassert its superiority after losing the 1886 World's Series, wins 21 of 35 preseason games with the AA.

April 16—The AA opens its sixth season with its first franchise change since 1885, when Cleveland replaces Pittsburgh.

September 5—O.P. Caylor is barred from a special AA meeting in New York, a move that permanently sours him on the AA and turns him into its archenemy.

October 26—St. Louis wins 9–2 to gain just its fifth victory in a marathon 15-game World's Series with Detroit that is both an esthetic and financial disaster for the AA.

November—Soon after the World's Series, both leagues rescind an experimental rule adopted prior to the 1887 season that counts walks as hits and also a rule giving a batter four strikes instead of three.

November—On the heels of the Brown's embarrassing World's Series loss, Chris Von der Ahe begins selling and trading many of his star players, leading observers to conclude that he is acting in a pique to break up his team.

December 28—In the wake of the Browns' breakup, *Sporting Life* predicts the AA will soon fold and draws up several different ways in which the NL can reform prior to the 1888 season and include the AA teams it would like to absorb.

1888

January 16—Kansas City replaces the defunct New York Mets as the AA's eighth team.

April—Chris Von der Ahe's vastly revamped St. Louis Browns win five straight games versus defending World's Series champion Detroit in spring exhibition play, but O.P. Caylor makes light of it in his new baseball paper, *The Daily Democrat*, and joins with many analysts in predicting the Browns will be no factor in the 1888 AA race.

April 18—The AA opens its seventh season with Silver King, Tony Mullane, Matt Kilroy and Bob Caruthers, arguably the best four pitchers in AA history, all gaining victories on Opening Day.

June 27—Shortstop Ed Herr vaults the Browns into the lead for the first time in the 1888 AA season when he homers off Darby O'Brien of Cleveland to give Nat Hudson a 7–5 win. Herr's blow is only the third since 1882 to clear the distant leftfield wall at St. Louis's Sportsman's Park in a championship game.

July 15—The AA abolishes 25¢ ball and adopts a 50¢ minimum admission price everywhere but in Philadelphia—a short-lived experiment that will be truncated just three weeks later.

July 22—Cleveland thwarts local Sabbatarians by playing the first of several Sunday home games at Geauga Lake Amusement Park.

August 5—The Philadelphia A's circumvent the Pennsylvania laws against Sunday ball by scheduling Sunday home games in Gloucester City, New Jersey, a practice that continues until late in the 1890 season.

October 16—The A's ring down the curtain on the AA season by beating Cleveland 14–4; on that same afternoon St. Louis opens World's Series action against the New York Giants after winning a 19th century-record fourth straight pennant.

October—Cleveland deserts the AA by buying the collapsing Detroit franchise and defecting to the NL.

December—Columbus is admitted in place of Cleveland; AA moguls take a huge backward step when they vote to cut umpires' salaries and to dispense with the double umpire system.

1889

March—Preseason games feature two monumental rule changes—for the first time in major league history a batter is granted a walk after receiving only four called balls and a manager is permitted to substitute for a player for a reason other than injury.

April 17—A record Opening Day crowd of over 10,000 is on hand in Cincinnati to watch Tony Mullane of the Reds lose 5-1 to the Browns' Silver King.

June 22—St. Louis sweeps a doubleheader at Louisville to extend Louisville's losing streak to an all-time record 26 games.

September 7—The infamous "Candlelight Game" at Brooklyn's Washington Park ends in hysteria when Charlie Comiskey pulls his St. Louis team off the field while ahead 4–2 in the bottom of the ninth and umpire Fred Goldsmith forfeits the game to Brooklyn—a decision that AA officials will later overturn.

October 15—St. Louis's four-year reign as AA champion ends on the final day of the season when the Browns lose the opening game of a doubleheader to Cincinnati, giving the pennant to Brooklyn.

November 4—Members of Monte Ward's Brotherhood of Professional Base Ball Players sever all ties with the NL and form the Players League, a rebel loop that at first is endorsed by several AA moguls but will eventually help sink the AA.

November 13—Brooklyn and Cincinnati bolt the AA, followed shortly thereafter by Baltimore and Kansas City; the mass defection leaves the AA with just four teams, a dire situation that persists for nearly two months.

1890

January 6—Rochester, Syracuse and Toledo officially made members of the AA; two weeks later the Brooklyn Gladiators beat out teams in Washington and Newark for the final spot, once again giving the AA eight clubs.

March—Though about to undergo a season that could spell financial ruin, Chris Von der Ahe goes ahead with architect August Beinke's plan to refurbish Sportsman's Park to the tune of $50,000.

March 14—At a meeting to adopt the 1890 schedule, the AA elects to tackle the Sabbatarians head on by scheduling Sunday games in every member city but Philadelphia; the A's later make it unanimous by transferring several home dates to Sunday at Gloucester City, New Jersey.

March 29—Von der Ahe refuses to panic when his Player's League-decimated Browns are beaten in their exhibition opener, 11-8, by a minor league team from Evansville.

May 16—Toledo unsuccessfully demands a forfeit win when Brooklyn, faced with a sparse crowd, avails itself of its right as home team and refuses to play a game, claiming the grounds are too wet even though the Toledo players finish pregame practice with their uniforms covered with dust.

May 25—At the close of a Sunday game at Three Rivers near Syracuse, the grandstand collapses and many are injured to the glee of local Sabbatarians, who contend that God is punishing the Stars for playing on the Sabbath.

June 1—For the final time in AA history, all eight member teams play on Sunday without incident.

August 27—Baltimore returns to the AA, replacing financially strapped Brooklyn.

August 28—Philadelphia third baseman Denny Lyons, the AA's slugging average leader in 1890, plays his last game of the season; Lyons claims he is injured, but the A's suspend him and then sell him to St. Louis, which cannot get him to report until the following season.

September 2—A secret meeting in Philadelphia between the AA and the Players League leads to nothing when PL leaders learn that Philadelphia A's players are poised to strike because the club can't pay their salaries; several key A's players eventually quit the club and others are suspended, forcing the team to fill its lineup by hiring amateur and semi-pro players in whatever town it is currently playing.

October 28—Louisville ties the heavily favored Brooklyn Bridegrooms at three games apiece to give the AA a draw in the last AA–NL World's Series.

November 22—Allan Thurman, a heretofore unknown official of the Columbus club, is made AA president when Zach Phelps resigns the office.

1891

January—Syracuse, Toledo and Rochester are bought off to surrender their AA franchises and are replaced for the 1891 season by the Players League champion Boston Reds, a new team in Washington and a new team in Cincinnati, managed by King Kelly.

February—Thurman casts the decisive vote that awards former Philadelphia A's stars Harry Stovey and Lou Bierbauer to NL teams.

February 18—AA owners angrily vote to unseat Thurman as loop president and to become a rebel federation by withdrawing from the National Agreement.

April 8—The AA begins its tenth and final season on the earliest opening date in major league history to that point.

May 11—Baltimore debuts its new Oriole Park, the AA's largest stadium.

August 17—King Kelly's Cincinnati team disbands and is replaced by a minor league team from Milwaukee.

August 25—Hope for a new National Agreement is killed when Kelly bolts the AA to sign with the NL Boston Beaneaters.

October 6—The AA plays its final championship games, a doubleheader at Washington between the Nationals and the Baltimore Orioles.

October 9—NL president Nick Young formally refuses acting AA president Zach Phelps's challenge to an 1891 World's Series.

October 22—A new Chicago franchise is formally admitted to the AA for the 1892 season, causing the NL to step up its efforts to make the AA give up the fight.

December 18—At a joint meeting in Indianapolis the AA and the NL consolidate and form a single 12-team major league called the National League and the American Association of Professional Base Ball Clubs.

19TH CENTURY MAJOR LEAGUE TEAM GENEALOGY

NATIONAL LEAGUE: 1876–99

CHICAGO (1876–99)

BOSTON (1876–99)

*HARTFORD (1876–77) ✖
- **PROVIDENCE** (1878–85) ✖
  - **WASHINGTON** (1886–89) ✖
    - **BROOKLYN** (1890–99) from AA

ST. LOUIS (1876–77) ✖
- **MILWAUKEE** (1878) ✖
  - **SYRACUSE** (1879) ✖
    - **WORCESTER** (1880–82) ✖
      - **PHILADELPHIA** (1883–99)

PHILADELPHIA (1876) ☆
- **BUFFALO** (1879–85) ☆
  - **KANSAS CITY** (1886) ✖
    - **PITTSBURGH** (1887–99) from AA

NEW YORK (1876) ☆
- **TROY** (1879–82) ▶
  - **NEW YORK** (1883–99)

LOUISVILLE (1876–77) ✖
- **INDIANAPOLIS** (1878)
- **CLEVELAND** (1879–84) ✖
  - **ST. LOUIS** (1885–86) ▶
    - **INDIANAPOLIS** (1887–89) ✖
      - **CINCINNATI** (1890–99) from AA

CINCINNATI (1876–80) ✖
- **DETROIT** (1881–88) ✖
  - **CLEVELAND** (1889–99) from AA

ST. LOUIS (1892–99) from AA

BALTIMORE (1892–99) from AA

LOUISVILLE (1892–99) from AA

WASHINGTON (1892–99) from AA

Legend

▶ direct link between franchises, including player transfers

✖ filled vacancy though not always created by above team

☆ time gap during which vacancy existed

* based in Brooklyn in 1877

AMERICAN ASSOCIATION: 1882–91

ST. LOUIS (1882–91)

LOUISVILLE (1882–91)

CINCINNATI (1882–89)
✖
SYRACUSE (1890)
✖
BOSTON (1891)

PITTSBURGH (1882–86)
✖
CLEVELAND (1887–88)
✖
COLUMBUS (1889–91)

PHILADELPHIA (1882–90)
▶
PHILADELPHIA (1891)

BALTIMORE (1882–89)
✖
BROOKLYN (1890)
✖
BALTIMORE (1890–91)

NEW YORK (1883–87)
✖
KANSAS CITY (1888–89)
✖
TOLEDO (1890)
✖
CINCINNATI (1891)
✖
MILWAUKEE (1891)

BROOKLYN (1884–89)
✖
ROCHESTER (1890)
✖
WASHINGTON (1891)

ALSO:

COLUMBUS (1883–84)

TOLEDO (1884)

INDIANAPOLIS (1884)

WASHINGTON (1884)
✖
VIRGINIA (1884)

UNION ASSOCIATION: 1884

ST. LOUIS	**CINCINNATI**	**CHICAGO**	**BALTIMORE**	**WASHINGTON**	**ALTOONA**	**PHILADELPHIA**	**BOSTON**
*(National League)	(Defunct)		(Defunct)	(Eastern League)			(Defunct)

PITTSBURGH ▼

MILWAUKEE ✖
(Western League)

KANSAS CITY ✖
(Defunct)

WILMINGTON ✖

ST. PAUL ✖
(Western League)

* 1885 location in parenthesis

PLAYERS LEAGUE: 1890

BOSTON	**BROOKLYN**	**BUFFALO**	**CHICAGO**	**CLEVELAND**	**NEW YORK**	**PHILADELPHIA**	**PITTSBURGH**
*(American Association)	(Defunct)	(Defunct)	(Defunct)	(Defunct)	(Defunct)	(American Association)	(Defunct)

* 1891 location in parenthesis

PRELUDE

IN THE FALL OF 1881 THE NATIONAL LEAGUE, having just completed its sixth consecutive season as the only baseball alliance to claim major league status, at long last was able to drop anchor and relax over the winter. For the first time all eight of its member clubs were committed to compete again under its banner the following year.

National League founder and current president William Hulbert drew a hard-earned breath of relief. In 1876, when Hulbert had first hammered together his vessel as an alternative to the National Association of Professional Base Ball Players, he had been careful to avoid his predecessor's mistakes. The National Association had been little more than a loose federation of player-controlled teams that cared next to nothing about winning public favor or about the business end of the sport, and were interested only in playing enough games among themselves to determine a national champion. At the close of each season to date, however, Hulbert had been confronted with at least one monstrous new problem that sidetracked him from his goal of presenting his new league as a bastion of Victorian propriety and so gaining the undying confidence and patronage of every right-minded and well-heeled baseball enthusiast. Indeed, Hulbert's venture was so unstable during its infancy that of the eight teams in his fleet at the start, only two, the Chicago White Stockings—in which Hulbert himself had a substantial investment—and the Boston Red Caps, were still afloat six years later. The 1881 season had been typical. That year Detroit had enlisted in place of Cincinnati, which was expelled for rebelling against Hulbert's stern monitions that to cater to the proper element his clubs must not play on the Sabbath, must refuse to permit the sale or consumption of intoxicating spirits in their parks and must charge a minimum admission price of 50¢.

Cincinnati's ouster prior to the 1881 season for running a beer concession at its Bank Street Grounds park and for permitting semi-pro teams to stage games there on Sunday meant that the National League had yet to field the same crew of teams two years in a row. At the conclusion of his inaugural venture into major league waters in 1876, Hulbert had reluctantly ejected the New York and Philadelphia franchises for trying to cut expenses by refusing to make their final western road trips of the season. His decision helped to establish his authority and the integrity of his new league, but robbed it of the nation's two largest population centers. Almost as devastating to Hulbert's vision, the punitive action shrank his circuit from eight to six teams. Another three sprang a leak after a stormy 1877 season that ended in shame when four players on the Louisville Grays, which had occupied first place most of the summer, conspired to throw enough games down the stretch to steer the pennant to Boston. Hulbert properly banished the culprits, but their ejection stripped the Louisville team of nearly half its crew, compelling it to put its ship in dry dock. When the St. Louis and Hartford franchises also quit the voyage, Hulbert replaced the three mutineers with teams in Providence, Indianapolis and Milwaukee for the 1878 season. The later two barely survived the year, and their departure caused another realignment. On the upside, in 1879 four new recruits—Cleveland, Buffalo, Syracuse and Troy—coughed up the fare to join Hulbert's crumbling fleet and enabled the "League," as it was now called by the working press, to sail forth once again with eight teams.

After failing to finish the 1879 season, Syracuse ceded its berth to Worcester, but the other seven teams held fast, fostering hope that stablility had finally been created. The Cincinnati club's disobedience in 1880 was therefore a serious setback for Hulbert. By the beginning of the 1880s, the stubborn post-Civil

War business depression that gripped the nation throughout the previous decade had finally begun to slacken, and baseball, along with every other enterprise, could now expect to enter a period of growth. With economic prosperity finally on the horizon, Hulbert and the other National League owners redoubled their efforts to paint the game as upright and godly by ridding themselves of Cincinnati despite its potential to be an enormous moneymaker. Known as the "Queen City" because of its prime location on the Ohio River, where it served as the gateway to the West, Cincinnati was nonetheless deemed unacceptable because the franchise could not survive without the economic support of the city's huge German population, which fancied the Continental Sabbath, liked their entertainment to come cheap and craved a schooner or two of beer on a hot summer afternoon at the ballyard.

Thus it happened that the city that just twelve years earlier had been the cradle of professional baseball, when its fabled Cincinnati Red Stockings rolled through an entire season without a defeat and first brought nationwide recognition to the game, found itself excluded from the one and only major league in 1881. Much as he still regretted the loss of Cincinnati, Hulbert entered the winter of 1881–82 secure in the knowledge that come next season his fleet, for the first time, would have an all-veteran flavor.

But Hulbert's euphoria was short-lived. By the spring of 1882, he lay dying of heart failure, and Cincinnati had joined forces with five other cities that, for a variety of reasons, were unrepresented by major league teams. The six clubs formed a rebel organization that christened itself the American Association but almost immediately came to be known by cavilers as the "Beer and Whisky League" for brazenly permitting the sale and consumption of intoxicating beverages at its games. Less publicized, but equally distressing to Hulbert's adherents, was the interloper's sworn intention to flaunt Victorian standards of propriety by playing games on Sunday and carving its admission price to only a quarter to make its product accessible to workingmen and ethnics whose trade, thus far, had been eschewed by the National League.

The American Association at first would challenge its elder's monopoly on major league status and then for a full decade would achieve a coexistence that was always fraught with an undercurrent of distrust and hostility, even as it gave the appearance of being amicable. That ten-year period between 1882 and 1891 would prove to be one of violent tumult for professional baseball that permanently altered its structure and sculpted its future. In the end, the American Association would leave an irrevocable stamp on the game. It would also forever place itself outside the baseball establishment.

In *The Great American Novel*, Philip Roth creates a fictional major league called the Patriot League that collapses in so frightening a way that all record of its existence is obliterated by organized baseball and few are even willing to acknowledge they remember it. The American Association has not quite suffered the same fate, yet there is about it an aura of unreality, more so now that over a century has passed since it sank forever from view beneath an economic tidal wave. Judging by some reports of the time when the American Association flourished, its teams were havens for alcoholics and its owners were all flaming anti-Sabbatarians. Other historians have built a case that the American Association was not really worthy of being called a major league. Part of their evidence rests on the fact that not a single one of its stars has ever been deemed outstanding enough to be voted into baseball's pantheon, the Hall of Fame at Cooperstown, New York.

Each of these myths about the American Association has existed for so long that it is all but accepted now as truth. And there are truths about the American Association that some members of the baseball community, now long dead, prayed would always be looked upon as myths.

ONE
1882

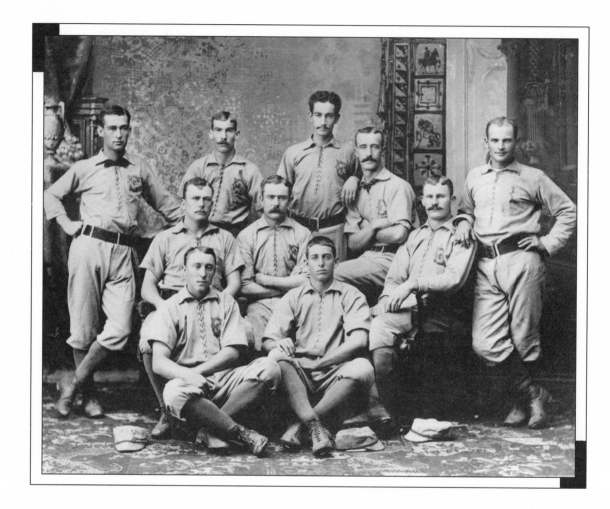

• • •

This elegant photo of the 1882 Eclipse shows the painstaking care that often went into composing team pictures then. More's the mystery that so few survive. Standing (left to right): Leech Maskrey, Pete Browning, Tony Mullane and John Strick. Seated (left to right): Dan Sullivan, Denny Mack, Bill Schenk and Guy Hecker. Front (left to right): John Reccius and Chicken Wolf.

THE QUEEN CITY'S REDUX

O NE SEPTEMBER NIGHT IN 1881 TWO MEN conspired into the small hours in a Philadelphia hotel room. The one who did most of the talking was "Hustling" Horace Phillips, twenty-eight years old and the manager of the Philadelphias baseball club. Phillips was galled that the City of Brotherly Love was without a major league team, as were Cincinnati, St. Louis and New York, and he had a plan for changing that.

His listener was Oliver Perry "Opie" Caylor, a thirty-one-year-old newspaperman with legal training who had quit his job with the *Cincinnati Enquirer* to practice law and write the baseball column for the *Cincinnati Commercial*. The move had been impelled by a growing enmity between Caylor and *Enquirer* publisher John McLean that would eventually have a deleterious impact on Cincinnati's baseball fortunes, but for the moment Caylor was riding high. Along with Justus Thorner, a former owner of the Cincinnati National League team, and several other Queen City businessmen, he had pledged to return professional baseball to

Cincinnati. As yet, however, he had only a dim notion how his goal might be accomplished.

Caylor was in Philadelphia on this late-summer night after a postcard from Phillips had fallen into his hands, inviting baseball-minded men in cities that were currently unrepresented by a major league team to attend a meeting. He was disappointed but not overly surprised to discover that only Cincinnati had responded to Phillips's invitation. For all his energy and exuberance, Phillips lacked the vision and the creative spark to bring off his scheme. Caylor sat silent, still and ready to provide both.

The following morning, telegrams were sent to many of the same men who had ignored Phillips's initial summons, informing them that their city was the only one that had not been at the historic first meeting of the new major league, which was to be called the American Association under the slogan "Liberty for All," and offering them a chance to rectify their blunder. The ruse worked.

• • •

The 1870 Cleveland Forest City club, including many of the participants in the first major league game in 1871, a National Association fray between Forest City and the Kekionga club of Fort Wayne. Eleven years later, two of the Forest City players, Al Pratt (top, center) and Chick Fulmer (seated, far right), were also on hand for the AA's inaugural game in Pittsburgh. Pratt managed the Allegheny club in 1882, and Fulmer was at short for Cincinnati.

Forest City Base-ball Club
Photo taken by Decker
Secured by Harvey L. Brown
from Geo. H. Edmondson
— 1870 —

On October 10, 1881, more than a dozen men took the bait and journeyed to Pittsburgh, where Denny McKnight, a thirty-four-year-old local businessman, had been persuaded to act as host. When Caylor saw that among the attendants were tobacco merchant John Day, the president of the New York Metropolitans,* and Chris Von der Ahe, who had helped revive the Brown Stockings club in St. Louis, he left the stage to them and McKnight and withdrew to the wings, pulling Phillips with him.

At the meeting, as Caylor had hoped, Day was elected temporary chairman and Von der Ahe was named vice president. On November 2, however, when the American Association held its first formal meeting at Cincinnati's Gibson House hotel, Day failed to show. Representing the Metropolitans in his stead were team manager Jim Mutrie and New York publisher W. S. Appleton. Among the other concerned parties in the assembly were Von der Ahe and David Reid from St. Louis, J. H. Pank and Bill Reccius from Louisville, Thorner and Victor Long from Cincinnati, McKnight from Pittsburgh, Billy Barnie representing the Brooklyn Atlantics, Boston sporting goods manufacturer Louis Mahn, and, to Phillips's consternation, a rival faction from Philadelphia headed by Chick Fulmer, shortstop and manager of the Athletics club.

In Day's absence, McKnight suggested that Von der Ahe take the chair, but he demurred and nominated McKnight to serve as temporary chairman. Jimmy Williams, a baseball enthusiast from Columbus, was made temporary secretary. The group then got down to business. First on the agenda was to settle the territorial disputes between the two Philadelphia teams and between Brooklyn and New York. Barnie avowed that he had the old Union Grounds sewed up to serve as home park for his Atlantics, plus the backing of Bob Ferguson, a renowned National League player and manager. Fulmer guaranteed that the Athletics could put up $5,000 that very day, and Phillips also claimed his outfit had plenty of financial backing. McKnight then gave the floor to Mutrie and Appleton, who up to that point had only poked holes in the proposals the others put forward. When the pair still refused to commit the Mets to the new league, they were asked to leave the meeting on the condition that they were welcome to return if and when the Mets were ready to join. Caylor and Phillips watched this contretemps with deep misgivings. Establishing franchises in both New York and Philadelphia was the

---

* The club was originally called the Metropolitan. Likewise, the Athletics were the Athletic, and the Alleghenys were the Allegheny. I've pluralized these nicknames from the outset because by 1884 the teams themselves had begun to pluralize them.

cornerstone of their program to end the National League's monopoly on major league baseball. When they realized that Mahn also was not there to enroll a Boston entry but to further his business interests, Caylor coaxed Phillips to abridge his own ambitions and consolidate, for the sake of unity, with Fulmer's Athletics, so that the two Philadelphia groups would enter the American Association as a single franchise.

With teams seemingly now ensconced in six sizable metropolises—Philadelphia, Pittsburgh, St. Louis, Cincinnati, Louisville and Brooklyn—McKnight swung the meeting to operational matters. The Association delegates copied the National League's playing rules and constitution for the most part but made several major innovations. Since the money backing several of the Association teams—most notably St. Louis, Louisville and Cincinnati—came from brewers, the vote carried to play games on Sundays in cities where the law permitted and to sell spirits to spectators. Member clubs were granted a third important concession the National League denied its constituents: the right to set their own admission prices, which for most teams was put as low as a quarter in order to cater to "the common man." On learning of the main planks in the Association's platform, the *Cincinnati Commercial* crowed, "It is the home-rule policy, instead of the picayunish, mean, centralized power of the League."

Several other radical departures from the National League's method of doing business were incorporated in the Association constitution. One stipulated that a player would be given a half month's salary beyond his date of release if he were not released at his own request in contrast to the League, which cut off a player's pay just ten days after he was history. Secondly, the Association broke with a time-honored tradition that had governed every professional league to that point and opted to determine its champion each year by the percentage of games won rather than by the number of wins. Another important deviation was that Association delegates decided to remain noncommittal as yet on the National League's reserve rule, a contrivance whereby a team could designate a certain number of players as being under its control, even in the absence of a formal contract between the two parties. When the meeting then adjourned owing to the hour, the *Commercial* summed up: "Thus ended the first day's work of the new and powerful rival of the old League."

The following morning, November 3, McKnight was formally elected Association president, Pank vice president and Williams secretary-treasurer, with Thorner, Von der Ahe, Fulmer, Barnie and McKnight comprising the Board of Directors. As per Caylor's plan, he and Phillips continued to act as if they were there only as

supernumeraries. Sitting in silence, they watched the Board set a compromise fee of $65 per playing date for visiting clubs after the Athletics pushed for $75 and several other teams for only $60. After more discussion, in which Caylor artfully took part, if only to offer his legal expertise, the six member clubs pledged to allow all players who had been blacklisted by the National League for minor offenses to play in the Association. Later in the day the Board voted to let the home team choose the umpire for each game and to be obliged to pay him—another departure from the League, where visitors picked up the tab. The Board then shot down the League rule that each member city must have a minimum population of 75,000 and also waived the rule that a team must bear the name of the city it represented. This provision allowed the Philadelphia entry to call itself the Athletics, Pittsburgh to set out as the Alleghenys, and Louisville to carry the label of the Eclipse club.

Near the end of the meeting, Mahn, who had awaited his moment patiently, got his wish to have his sporting goods firm supply the official Association ball and guidebook. The six clubs then went their separate ways on the promise that each would aggressively begin to sign players for the 1882 season. The Athletics, Von der Ahe's Browns and the Eclipse club were viewed as having a considerable advantage because all had played as semi-pro nines in 1881 and so already had a nucleus of talent. But none of them had anyone quite like Caylor.

Although Thorner was the titular head of the resurrected Cincinnati Red Stockings, it was Caylor who soon emerged as the club's dynamo. Even before the November meeting, he had signed Will White, the bespectacled pitching mainstay on the Cincinnati National League club who had encountered arm trouble after the franchise moved to Detroit. Now mended, White agreed to serve as Caylor's advisory council. On White's recommendation, Caylor snatched lefthanded third baseman Hick Carpenter, another former Cincinnati stalwart who had been left off the Worcester club's reserve list. Assuming the Association would agree to his plea to reinstate blacklisted National League players, Caylor had previously acted on his own to secure Charley Jones, the League's top slugger in 1879. The following year Jones had been banished by Boston owner Arthur Soden, allegedly for drunkenness and insubordination (but really for demanding his June 1st paycheck on June 1st even though the team was on the road), and had since been playing for an outlaw team in Portsmouth, Ohio. In mid-November Jones was sent to the hinterlands of Ohio with three blank contracts to scare up the best players he could find. He settled on three members of the Akron club—Bid McPhee, a fancy-fielding second baseman, catcher-outfielder Rudy Kemmler and Sam Wise, a crack shortstop who could hit a bit too.

Caylor meanwhile worked on arranging the return to the Queen City of Cincinnati native Long John Reilly, another ex-Red Stocking currently playing first base for Day's New York Metropolitans. Though he was unsuccessful with Reilly, he corralled the lone League player of significance who chose to defy the reserve rule and cast his lot with the Association, Boston catcher Pop Snyder. As part of his reward, Snyder was named Cincinnati player-manager.

By early December, between Caylor and Jones, Cincinnati had nine players under contract, one more than St. Louis. The other four clubs lagged far behind, and Brooklyn's behavior was particularly worrisome. Not only did the Atlantics not as yet have a single player under contract, but McKnight was beginning to chafe that the club had not found a home field. After admitting that his boast that he had the Union Grounds locked up was premature, Barnie proposed relocating his team to Columbus, but when the Ohio move also fell through, McKnight awarded the franchise in mid-March to Baltimore. To help the fledgling team

• • •
The 1877 Syracuse Stars, an independent team that was stocked with future AA contributors. In the back (left to right) are Tom Mansell, Hick Carpenter and Pete Hotaling. Jim Clinton sits at middle, center, and Billy Geer and Jack Farrell sprawl (left to right) in the foreground. Mansell was the eldest of the only trio of brothers to play in the AA. The three Mansells—Tom, Mike and John—formed an all-brother outfield for the Albany minor league club in 1881.

get off the ground, McKnight sheared his own Pittsburgh club of shortstop Henry Myers and sent him to Baltimore to act as player-manager. Later in the season, Henry Von der Horst, a local brewer, took over the team and gave it a solid financial base, but the dilatory start put the Maryland franchise at a personnel handicap from which it would never entirely recover.

In early April, Baltimore still had only two players signed, Myers and pitcher Tricky Nichols. The other five clubs, though their rosters were nearly completed, had little more reason to feel optimistic. With the season less than a month away, heavy spring rains had hamstrung both Pittsburgh and Cincinnati in their efforts to ready their home fields. In St. Louis, Von der Ahe, as green about baseball as he was savvy about beer, heard mutterings that he was relying too heavily for guidance on George Seward and Ned Cuthbert, two ex-National League players who were thought to be a bit too long in the tooth. The Eclipse owners, Pank and Reccius, after striving all winter to land some experienced major leaguers to complement their corps of local semi-pros, acquired only Tony Mullane, a bust the previous year with Detroit. And the City of Brotherly Love had split into two factions again with the Athletics the winner, leaving Horace Phillips, one of the prime movers to create a new major league, for the moment aced out of a spot in it. Another casualty of the struggle was Chick Fulmer, who deserted the Athletics and fled to Cincinnati when he sensed the Queen City might be the only Association entry that had its act together.

But even Caylor was having personnel problems. Sam Wise had broken his contract with the Red Stockings to sign with the Boston League team, leading to a court battle that Cincinnati ultimately lost. A second skirmish cost the Red Stockings Charley Jones, when Association magnates, reacting to threats from the National League's war council, recanted on their pledge to hire blacklisted League players. Even the *Commercial*, whose stance up to that point had been one of unremitting defiance, recommended the Association not "run its head against a wall to champion Mr. Jones's wrongs, especially when they cannot bring about a change by it."

When Cincinnati took the field on April 13 for its first practice game against a local Picked Nine, this was the batting order that produced a 6–2 victory: Joe Sommer LF, Bid McPhee 2B, Hick Carpenter 3B, Dan Stearns RF, Rudy Kemmler CF, Pop Snyder C, Chick Fulmer SS, Dave Rowe 1B and Will White P. The win was not without a price, for White's arm went sour again midway through the game, forcing Rowe to the box, and Snyder's head was gashed open when one of the Picked Nine batters took

• • •
Ned Cuthbert, Browns player-manager and Chris Von der Ahe's closest advisor on baseball matters in 1882. Von der Ahe needed no advice on how to please his patrons. Sportsman's Park, the Browns' home, was the AA's benchmark facility, featuring an open bar behind the top row of the grandstand, where patrons could stand with a foot up on the rail and drink beer, wine, or whiskey by the glass while they watched the action down on the field. Meanwhile, vendors in white aprons and Browns caps worked the aisles, maneuvering trays of beer mugs.

Buffington, Pitcher and   Hornung, Left Field.   Sutton, 3d Base.   Wise, Short Stop.   Burdock, 2d Base.
Right Field.   Radford, Right Field.   Whitney, Pitcher and Centre Field.   Morrill, 1st Base.   Hines, Catcher.   Hackett, Catcher.   Smith, Substitute.

THE BOSTON BASE-BALL CLUB.—Photographed by Black.

● ● ●

Sam Wise, seen here in this woodcut of the 1882 Bostons beside his keystone partner Jack Burdock, contracted to be Cincinnati's shortstop in 1882 but reneged on his commitment and signed with the NL Beantown entry. Wise did not find his way back to the AA until its last hurrah in 1891. Burdock also played in the AA eventually, albeit to his and Brooklyn's chagrin.

a wild swing and sent the catcher reeling to his knees where he "began to bleed like a butchered animal." The loss of both pointsmen to injuries caused the *Commercial* to moan that it was yet one more example of the bad luck that "so persistently follows the Cincinnati club at the beginning of every season."

The previous afternoon, April 12, in the first two games played between League and Association rivals, St. Louis had lost to Detroit, 10–7, and Pittsburgh was trounced by the Cleveland Blues, 11–2. These one-sided results struck an ominous chord that grew louder over the next few days as Association clubs were brutally made to face the fact that they were no match as yet for established League teams. On April 15, Pittsburgh fell 16–2 to the Buffalo Bisons; two days later the Alleghenys were thrashed for the fourth straight time when the Bisons rolled, 18–3. Louisville fared no better on April 17, losing 6–0 to Detroit, but Cincinnati for the second endeavor in a row put on a strong showing. After dropping their April 15 exhibition opener to Cleveland, 4–2, with Rowe still in the box for the ailing White, the Red Stockings took the Blues to 11 innings on the 17th, before submitting 7–4 to Fred Dunlap's three-run homer.

But on April 18, during a 20–9 defeat in the finale of the Cleveland series, the roof caved in on Cincinnati when Carpenter went down with a sprained ankle, Sommer hurt his foot and

Pittsburgh's first major league team—the 1882 Alleghenys. The accepted player identifications are, top (left to right): George Strief, Johnny Peters, Joe Battin, Chappy Lane, Charlie Morton. Center (left to right): Ed Swartwood, Denny Driscoll, Rudy Kemmler, manager Al Pratt, Harry Salisbury, Jack Leary, Mike Mansell. Front (left to right): Billy Taylor and Jim Keenan. However, "Mansell" is probably Harry Arundel and "Leary" is really Mansell; Peters and Morton also are almost certainly misidentified. Salisbury, the team's ace, became a pariah after he was crushed 20–6 by Louisville on September 22. Pratt accused him of playing a "double hand" because he'd already secretly signed with Louisville for the 1883 season. Salisbury never pitched again in the majors.

Snyder joined White on the disabled list with a bum arm. Too banged up to travel to Cleveland for a return match with the Blues the following week, the Red Stockings sat idle for a full seven days licking their wounds. Then on April 25 the Detroit Wolverines came to Cincinnati for the first of what were scheduled to be six games between the two clubs. A 15–1 Detroit massacre in the opening contest evoked this crestfallen admission from the *Commercial*: "The home team feel a good deal like a man who caught a bear and then wanted somebody to help him let it go." Unwilling to subject themselves to further humiliation, the Red Stockings begged off from continuing the mismatch with the Wolves, pleading ill health, and then hit the practice field to regroup. With only a few days left to prepare for the official Opening Day of the first Association season, prospects by rights should have seemed bleak in all six of the loop's cities, but hopes nonetheless ran high everywhere. This was the major leagues come to town, after all.

The oldest known photograph of Pete Browning. He's seated second from left at age sixteen with the Louisville Eclipse in 1877, the club's initial season. Standing at far left is John Reccius, Browning's boyhood crony and the only other player still with the Eclipse five years later when it joined the AA. Reccius was also the younger brother of the part-owner of the team and the purported twin of Phil Reccius, who joined the club late in the 1882 season. However, John Reccius's recently discovered death certificate makes it seem doubtful he and Phil were really twins.

In 1882 it was not the same major league game we know. The six charter Association teams could expect to play before crowds that numbered between 400 and 2,000, and on stony, lopsided fields that were soggy in the spring and fall, and baked hard as rock in the summer. None of the parks had facilities for visiting players. They dressed at their hotels and then rode to the game in large horse-drawn conveyances that hauled them through the streets of the alien city whose urchins jeeringly pelted them with rotten fruit and offal as they passed. Few fielders wore gloves and many hitters used bats with one side flattened so they could tap pitches in the strike zone that were not to their liking into foul ground, since foul balls were not yet considered strikes. Batters had a further advantage in that they could order a pitcher to throw them either high or low pitches, but balancing that was the shorter pitching distance, which put hurlers a mere 50 feet from the plate when they released the ball. Seven balls were needed to gain a walk and a batter who was struck by a pitch, rather than being given his base, was granted a moment to rub the spot and then ordered by the lone umpire working the game to get back up to

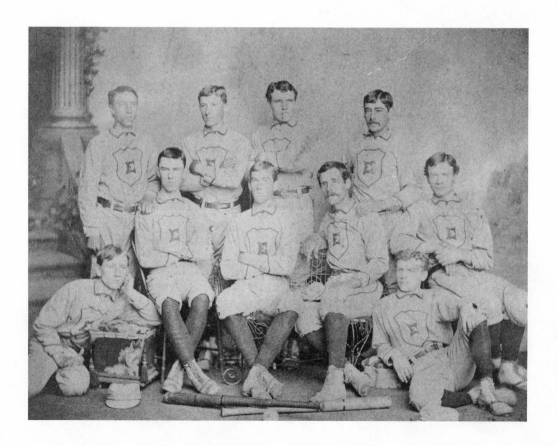

• • •

Jim Keenan caught for the Alleghenys on Opening Day in 1882 but soon lost his spot to Billy Taylor. For years Keenan bounced around the AA as a backup catcher before winning Cincinnati's first-string job in 1888. Keenan's longevity was aided by his light work load early in his career. Robert Smith wrote that a catcher's hands in Keenan's time "often resembled dead cypress roots that had been pulled out of a swamp."

bat. Substitutions were allowed only when a disabling injury occurred, which meant that pitchers had to swap positions with fielders if they were shelled from the box and teams seldom dressed more than 10 or 11 men. There was no infield fly rule, freeing shortstops to drop popups deliberately on the chance of doubling or tripling up baserunners, and base coaches were at liberty to scamper up and down the baselines in foul territory (and even into fair territory), trying to decoy fielders into mistaking them for runners. Catchers were protected only by rudimentary masks and chest protectors and so crouched well back of the batter for safety reasons. Behind them stood the umpire, whose reward for working alone was that he could seek help from the crowd on plays were his vision was obscured or he was positioned too far away to see. But seeking help often embroiled him in a free-for-all dispute between opposing viewpoints that could only end with the game being forfeited to whichever side yelled the loudest.

Consequently, umpiring was not a job with a bright future in 1882, but then being a player was no great bargain either. Except for stars of the first magnitude, a crippling injury like a broken leg or a mashed hand could result in instant release and, as added punishment, the player had to foot his own medical bill. Most players earned around $150 a month and at that only during the season, which ran from mid-April through mid-October. On the road they stayed three or four to a room at hotels where their presence was barely tolerated. While a player might be lionized at the ball park, away from it he was likely to be shunned by the same crowd that had cheered him only hours earlier. Ballplayers were stereotyped, not altogether unfairly, as lushers. Those who did not drink were in such a small minority they were nicknamed "Deacon" and "Grandma" and "Parson." At the other end of the spectrum was Louis Rogers "Pete" Browning.

An outstanding all-around athlete, Browning excelled at virtually every physical endeavor he attempted. As a boy, he was glorified as perhaps the best marble shooter in Louisville, so feared that other youths held out their most precious agates rather than risk them against him in competition. Browning was also an excellent ice skater but, curiously, avoided ponds and creeks when they were not frozen. Only his family and closest friends knew it was because swimming aggravated a painful ear condition that had rendered him nearly deaf by the time he was in his teens.

Browning was a feast for sportswriters of his day looking for an easy story. Always good for a lengthy discourse about his favorite topic—hitting a baseball—or an argument about his drinking habits, he was nicknamed "The Gladiator" owing to his supposedly contentious nature. What most of the baseball scribes missed seeing were his many strange paradoxes. Though linked with various women and reported on numerous occasions to be contemplating marriage, Browning lived with his mother for his entire life. During the winter months he worked out zealously and never touched a drop of alcohol, enabling him to report to spring training in perfect shape, but no sooner had he picked up a bat and faced his first pitch of the new season than he began drinking again. No one ever understood the reason Browning succumbed to his nemesis only when the opening bell rang. Few even noticed the disparity.

Still just twenty years old in the spring of 1882, Browning was already manifesting the behavior that would soon prompt a Louisville newspaper to dub him "Pietro Redlight District Distillery Interests Browning." He had remained a member of the Eclipse club since its inception in 1877 despite numerous offers to play elsewhere. It was not loyalty that bound him but a fear of the unfamiliar. Unbeknownst even to many of his teammates, by 1882 Browning's auditory skills had grown so poor that the handicap put his guard up among strangers lest they think him "touched" in the head and made him sometimes appear to be in another world on the ball field. While many members of the Eclipse lay sleepless on the night of May 1, 1882, hearing the wheels of their St. Louis-bound train loudly clacking away beneath them, if Browning was kept awake, it was solely by his vision of himself at bat the following afternoon in the Mound City against the Browns' vaunted eighteen-year-old pitching phenom, Jumbo McGinnis.

The next day, in his major league debut, Browning went 0-for-4, as the Browns celebrated the formal opening of Von der Ahe's bizarrely designed new ballground with a 9–7 win. Named Sportsman's Park and rebuilt from the hull of Grand Avenue Park, which had housed the St. Louis National League team in 1876-77, the Browns' home field was outfitted with lawn bowling and handball courts, which were sometimes available to spectators. The more sedentary could watch the game from the beer garden in the rightfield corner, where Von der Ahe had chosen to convert the two-story house that sat there into a commercial establishment rather than tear it down. Balls hit into the beer garden were in play, requiring outfielders to wade through patrons to dig them out. In the years to come, this odd groundrule would prove useful to the Browns, but it played no part in their Association inaugural. St. Louis began under the field leadership of Ned Cuthbert, and Denny Mack piloted the Eclipse club. These were their Opening Day batting orders:

• • •

In 1882, Jumbo McGinnis was purported to be just eighteen years old, but the proof of his tender age is less than compelling. It's definite, however, that the young St. Louis hurler inflicted nearly a quarter of champion Cincinnati's 25 losses in 1882, beating the Reds six times in 11 tries.

ST. LOUIS		LOUISVILLE	
3B	Jack Gleason	3B	Pete Browning
SS	Bill Gleason	C	Dan Sullivan
CF	Oscar Walker	P	Tony Mullane
1B	Charlie Comiskey	CF	John Reccius
2B	Bill Smiley	LF	Leach Maskrey
C	Sleeper Sullivan	1B	Guy Hecker
CF	Ned Cuthbert	RF	Chicken Wolf
P	Jumbo McGinnis	2B	Gracie Pierce
RF	George Seward	SS	Denny Mack

Umpire—Charlie Houtz

Though the Sullivans were both catchers, they were not related, but the two Gleasons were brothers—the first in major league history to play beside each other in the same infield. If Browning was disappointing in his debut, Hecker, a late addition to the club at Mullane's urging, was a pleasant surprise, going 4-for-5.

In Philadelphia on Opening Day, the Athletics topped Baltimore, 10–7. A's manager Latham and Baltimore skipper Myers went with these batting orders:

PHILADELPHIA		BALTIMORE	
RF	Jerry Dorgan	SS	Henry Myers
SS	Lew Say	CF	Bill Wise
1B	Juice Latham	2B	Jimmy Shetzline
LF	Jud Birchall	C	Ed Whiting
P	Sam Weaver	1B	Charlie Householder
C	Jack O'Brien	3B	Henry Jacoby
3B	Bob Blakiston	P	Tricky Nichols
2B	Cub Stricker	RF	Charlie Waitt
CF	Doc Landis	LF	Frank Burt

Umpire—Bill McLean

Both centerfielders also doubled as change pitchers, and neither was with his original club for long. Landis was in fact sent to Baltimore soon afterward and became the Orioles' front-line pitcher. Of the Orioles' starting nine in the team's first game, only five—Householder, Shetzline, Myers, Waitt and Whiting—held their jobs for any appreciable length of time. Seven years before, in a National Association game, Waitt reputedly had been the first player in history to use a glove in the field, but by 1882 the sport had grown so much faster that he batted a paltry .156, the lowest average ever by a regular outfielder. In 1882, Whiting played in all 74 of the Orioles' championship games and was behind the plate in 72 of them, at that time an incredible demonstration of pluck and stamina by a catcher.

The third Association opener was played in Pittsburgh and proved the most exciting. Before a crowd of about 1,500, the Alleghenys won a 10–9 cliffhanger when Cincinnati first sacker Bill

• • •

Bill Gleason, the AA's best shortstop in its early years. In 1882 he and his brother, Jack, anchored the left side of the Browns infield. Following the 1891 season, Gleason became a fireman, an occupation he'd previously pursued part-time.

In 1878, Utica of the International Association was studded with future AA performers. Among them are Eddie Kennedy (back, far left), Blondie Purcell (beside Kennedy), John Richmond (center, second from left); Utica native Juice Latham (center, second from right) and Hardy Richardson (front, left). In 1882 the Philadelphia Athletics were managed by Latham, who by then had ballooned to nearly 250 pounds. Soon after that he was gone from baseball and working as a fare collector on a Louisville streetcar line.

Tierney ended matters by flying out in the bottom of the ninth, leaving the potential tying and winning runs stranded. Tierney, who had been hired by the Red Stockings only the day before along with change pitcher Harry McCormick, was released by nightfall. The other Cincinnati starters were solid, however, and Pittsburgh also offered what appeared to be a stable cast under manager Al Pratt.

CINCINNATI		PITTSBURGH	
LF	Joe Sommer	RF	Ed Swartwood
2B	Bid McPhee	3B	Billy Taylor
3B	Hick Carpenter	P	Jack Leary
C	Pop Snyder	LF	Mike Mansell
RF	Dan Stearns	1B	Jake Goodman
1B	Bill Tierney	SS	John Peters
SS	Chick Fulmer	CF	Charlie Morton
CF	Jimmy Macullar	2B	George Strief
P	Will White	C	Jim Keenan

Umpire—Harry Wheeler

After the game, Wheeler was recruited by Caylor to supplant Tierney at first base because he could also serve as a change pitcher. Wheeler's replacement at umpire when the teams met again the following day was Pigtail Billy Riley, a one-time National League outfielder who had since attached himself to the Cincin-

Along with future Hall of Famers Roger Connor and Mickey Welch, the 1879 Holyoke club had Pete Gillespie, an object of dispute between the NL and the AA in 1883, and Jerry Dorgan, Pittsburgh's lead-off hitter early in the 1882 season. Dorgan's obit in 1891 rued that he'd given "early promise of attaining a high rank" as a player before dying in a New Haven drunk tank. By 1891, Gillespie was back living with his father in Carbondale, PA and making a dollar a day as a laborer in a local coal mine.

nati club hoping to catch on as a player but willing to take whatever baseball work he could get in the interim. In the box for the second day in a row—not at all uncommon then—was White, and this time he prevailed 7–3, giving the Red Stockings their first win against an Association foe. When White won again on May 4, as the Athletics were losing for the first time, it brought Cincinnati even with Philadelphia at 2–1, while St. Louis stood alone in first place with a perfect 3–0 record after sweeping Louisville in the pair's opening series.

By early June, however, the Athletics had seized the top spot after bagging three of five games with Cincinnati in the first series between the two clubs that would eventually emerge as the cream of the Association in its initial season. Returning to their Bank Street Grounds home on June 6, the Red Stockings then reeled off 10 straight wins against the three Eastern teams, Baltimore, Philadelphia and Pittsburgh, before succumbing 8–5 on June 23 to Harry Salisbury of the Alleghenys. The skein vaulted Cincinnati into first place at 20–10 on the last day of the month when Association action halted momentarily as the world awaited the execution of Charles Guiteau for assassinating President Garfield the previous autumn.

On July 2 several hundred Cincinnati rooters accompanied the team to Louisville for the price of a $2.00 ticket—which included round-trip train fare plus a reduced rate for dinner and supper at Louisville's Galt House hotel—to witness the Red Stockings' first Sunday game of the year. Harry McCormick edged Tony Mullane 2–1, making for a gleeful return journey, but back in Cincinnati the day had not been a light one for Caylor, who was gathered at the Gibson House with the other Association leaders to thresh out a rapidly festering umpiring problem. All six clubs were agreed that the policy of allowing the home team to pick the umpire for each game was a mistake. To curb the rampant charges of favoritism, three men who had no affiliations with any particular team were selected to serve as full-time salaried umpires for the rest of the year. Of the trio, only Mike Walsh of Louisville would still be at his post when the season ended, but it was at least a step in the right direction and one that the National League would soon copy.

Before the new umpiring system was implemented, though, the Red Stockings had one last chance to name a favorite son to officiate. On Independence Day, after a morning exhibition game with the Athletics that was called a 9–9 draw after 10 innings, both teams were served a sumptuous feast catered by the Vienna Bakery while the Bank Street park was cleared. Then, around 3:00 PM, the turnstiles were opened to the huge throng that had been pressing against the gates outside since mid-morning. Some 5,890 Cincinnatians paid the special 50¢ price for general admis-

• • •

Yet another minor league unit rife with later-day AA performers—the 1879 Indianapolis Hoosiers. The obvious ones are Denny Mack, Fred Warner and Joe Quest. But also here are Edward "the Only" Nolan, a loser in all seven of his starts with Pittsburgh in 1883; the much-traveled Trick McSorley, a 5'4" first baseman with Toledo in 1884; and two early AA umpires, "Pigtail" Billy Riley (Reilly) and Charlie Houtz. Riley came by his nickname because of his "Asiatic aspect."

THE ONLY INDIANAPOLIS TEAM OF 1879—Standing up and reading from left to right: Fred Warner, 3b; Ed Nolan, p.; Denny Mack, s. s.; Frank Flint, c.; W. Reilly, rf. and substitute. Sitting down and reading from left to right: Charles Houtz, 1b; Trick McSorley, p. and f.; Adam Rocap, rf.; Mike Golden, lf. and change p.; Joe Quest, 2b. A story of them is given elsewhere in this book.

John Mansell, the youngest of the three Mansell brothers. The twenty-one-year-old rookie held the Athletics' centerfield job at the beginning of the 1882 season but was released when he was injured.

sion tickets and another 600 anted up an extra quarter to sit in the grandstand for the second half of a morning-afternoon doubleheader. But the crowd got less than its money's worth when the Red Stockings played one of their worst games of the year, committing 12 errors behind Will White. In losing 6–1 to Bill Sweeney of the A's, White scored the lone Cincinnati run and tallied two of the team's five hits, including a leadoff double in the sixth inning that ended Sweeney's no-hit bid. Apart from White, the sole reason spectators were inclined to linger until the dreary end was to watch the pride of Cincinnati, Buck Ewing, officiate. Home for the holiday, Ewing, a catcher with the League Troy Trojans, stayed in town to call balls and strikes, though his own team was playing that afternoon against Chicago.

Despite the Independence Day fiasco the Red Stockings completed their long homestand with 12 wins in 14 decisions. Heading east again, they continued their victorious ways and returned to Bank Street on the 28th three full games ahead of the A's and eight games up on the fourth-place Browns. Von der Ahe's men could be forgiven if they were unconvinced of Cincinnati's superiority, for the two Western clubs had yet to meet even though the season was more than half over. This sort of scheduling solecism was only one example of the many ways in which the Association was still a novice. It meant that in the final 36 games Cincinnati would meet the Browns 16 times. In the first contest, White topped Jumbo McGinnis 5–3 in front of over 2,400 Queen City devotees. Two days later, in a Sunday exhibition game at St. Louis on July 30, White beat Ed Doyle when umpire Tom Carey helped kill an eighth-inning Browns rally by ruling Sleeper Sullivan out for delaying the game after Sully ran all the way home from second base on a foul ball hit by Jack Gleason. Sullivan argued that he hadn't heard the ball called foul, and when Carey stood by his peculiar ruling, the Browns successfully lobbied to fire him. Hired in his stead was none other than Horace Phillips, who in turn was replaced as manager of the Philadelphias club by Billy Barnie. Before Phillips could head west, though, he got a second job offer, this one from Pittsburgh, where Denny McKnight had begun to find his league administrative duties so burdensome he needed help in running the Alleghenys.

While the Browns and Red Stockings played each other exclusively during the next fortnight, with Cincinnati winning six of the nine contests, the A's slowly lost ground and St. Louis slid down to fifth. On August 20, after the A's staged a 6-run rally in their last at bat to pull out a 10–6 win at St. Louis, the standings were: Cincinnati 38–17, Philadelphia 34–22, Louisville 28–24, Pittsburgh 25–30, St. Louis 27–34 and Baltimore, a tailender ever

since mid-May, at 14–39. Though the season was not yet two-thirds over, the clubs already were in the exact order they would finish when the last pitch was thrown six weeks later.

The Red Stockings still had one last hurdle to conquer, though, before the pennant could be claimed. On September 11, at Cincinnati, Tony Mullane notched the first no-hitter in Association history when he held the home side without a safety en route to a 2–0 shutout. After the Eclipse ace triumphed again the following day, 10–4, it provoked Caylor to print in the *Commercial*'s baseball column that Cincinnati had "played like whipped school children and walked on and off the field with the manner of a dog caught stealing meat." His withering commentary on the morning of the 13th embarrassed the Red Stockings into nipping the Eclipse 3–1 that afternoon and then clinching the flag three days later with a 6–1 victory over Guy Hecker, while the A's were losing to Pittsburgh.

Brimming with confidence, Cincinnati invited the Cleveland Blues to the Queen City after the season closed to play for the championship of the State of Ohio, but McKnight, on learning of the challenge, forbade it as well as any other contests with League teams while the two circuits were still at loggerheads. To dodge McKnight's fiat, Caylor released all the Red Stockings from their contracts, which were not due to expire until October 15, and then invented an anonymous "wealthy admirer" of the team who volunteered to pay them the two weeks of salary they would lose if they played three games against Cleveland, two against the League champion Chicago White Stockings, and four against the League runner-up Providence Grays.

Not having forgotten how convincingly they had won the spring matches with the Red Stockings, the Blues felt they could afford to hold back their pitching ace Jim McCormick until Cincinnati had evened the Ohio series at one-all with a 5–2 win on October 4. The next afternoon, in a rubber-game battle between two McCormicks, Jim drubbed Cincinnati's Harry 8–0 to give Cleveland the Buckeye crown.

Undaunted, Caylor apprised Chicago owner Al Spalding of his intention to go through with the two games against the White Stockings, even though McKnight was again pressuring him to desist. The White Stockings had to cope with pressure of a different sort from League officials, who had cornered them into playing a nine-game postseason series with Providence because of the controversial way in which the regular season had ended. The Grays contended that Chicago had grabbed the League flag largely by dint of winning three games against the Buffalo Bisons that had been transferred illegally to the Windy City from Buffalo. Rightly

CINCINNATIS.

A black-and-white rendition of the cover photo of the first American Association champion—the 1882 Cincinnati Red Stockings. Front (left to right): CF Jimmy Macullar and RF Harry Wheeler. Middle (left to right): 3B Hick Carpenter, C Pop Snyder, P Will White, SS Chick Fulmer and LF Joe Sommer. Top (left to right): 1st sub Harry McCormick, 2nd sub Grandmother Powers, 1B Dan Stearns and 2B Bid McPhee. As the new kid on the block in 1882, the AA adorned its teams in gaudy, multihued silk uniforms, with each player's shirt color corresponding to his position. Though it derided the AA's flamboyancy, the National League hurriedly followed suit. The experiment was dropped when fans and players alike were confused who was friend and who was foe.

or wrongly, Spalding and his star first baseman-manager Cap Anson had their minds more heavily on the series due to begin on the 10th in Providence than on the two clashes with Cincinnati.

Because Snyder was still nursing a finger injury he had sustained in the second Cleveland game, he had to replace himself behind the bat with Grandmother Powers, but otherwise he was able to field the Red Stockings' entire first-string lineup when Chicago appeared at Bank Street Grounds on October 6 for the first postseason game in history between two major league champions. Anson, in contrast, had left one of his brightest stars, Mike "King" Kelly, behind in New York and was using pitcher Larry Corcoran at shortstop. The game began a couple of minutes past two with some 2,700 spectators on hand and Pop Smith, a substitute infielder for two Association teams during the season, serving as umpire. Expecting to win in a rout, Anson stood by disdainfully while Smith went over the park rules and then prepared to flip the Red Stockings' special $20 gold coin with CBBC (Cincinnati Base Ball Club) on one side and the head of a fox on the other. Snyder, accorded the honor of making the call as captain of the home side, correctly predicted the fox would land face up and so had his choice to take the field first.

To Anson's horror, his powerful White Stockings, after averaging nearly seven runs a game during the regular season, were held scoreless by White through 6 innings. When Cincinnati pushed across four markers in the bottom of the sixth, with McPhee's two-run triple to deep right-center the key blow, Chicago suddenly found itself in an unfamiliar position, forced to come from far behind. White continued to be all but invincible, however, until the ninth inning. Chicago then got Ned Williamson to second and Abner Dalrymple to third with but one out and the great Anson himself at the plate. Calling for high pitches, Anson skied the first good one he saw to Macullar in center field for the second out, but Dalrymple, determined to avert a mortifying shutout, tagged at third and tried to score. When Macullar's throw to Powers cut down the impatient Dalrymple, the *Cincinnati Enquirer* chortled that "Will White and his Lilliputian crew" had "astonished the Chicagos, the champions of the League, the great, high-toned and only moral base ball show."

The following afternoon Chicago got a dollop of revenge and evened the series at one–all, when Corcoran, given a pair of unearned first-inning runs, spun a tidy 2–0 shutout. But contrary to the popular tale that McKnight then brought the affair to a screeching halt by firing off a telegram to Caylor and Thorner threatening the Red Stockings with expulsion if they continued to flaunt his authority, the likelihood is that there had never been any plan to play more than two games. The strongest evidence of this is newspaper accounts bewailing the impossibility of a rubber game because both teams had commitments elsewhere the following day. Chicago headed for New York to tune up for its match with Providence three days hence, and on the evening of October 7, the Red Stockings boarded a train for St. Louis, where the following afternoon they played their final contest of the season as a team, a 5–4 exhibition win over the Browns.

Cincinnati was nevertheless fined $100 by McKnight for disobeying him. Though not a large penalty even by 1882 standards, it helped to convince Thorner when Caylor and the other owners made their case that the team had lost money. Appalled that he could not make a profit even with a pennant-winner, Thorner ceded to George Herancourt his one-eighth share of the club that the two had held in joint ownership, only to learn later that he ought to have demanded to examine the books before allowing himself to be finessed out of his piece of the team. For the Red Stockings, even after paying the $100 fine, ended the season in the black, as did the Association as a whole.

Indeed, the fledgling loop's financial picture was so rosy that Day and Mutrie swallowed their reservations and enlisted the Metropolitans for the 1883 campaign at an Association meeting in Columbus on October 23. The host Ohio city, nearly an entry in 1882, was also awarded a franchise to balance the Association at eight teams, and Horace Phillips, an Ohio native, moved to the state's capital from Pittsburgh and took on the unenviable task of assembling a team that had at the start only himself as manager.

After the loop's composition for 1883 was established, Caylor moved to admit every blacklisted League player except the infamous "Louisville Four" to the Association. McKnight and the Board of Directors, hectored by a legal suit Charley Jones had instigated when his 1882 contract was breached, belatedly voted to endorse Caylor's motion. The action not only finally freed the Red Stockings to put Jones in uniform, but also brought several other talented outlaw performers into the Association, including Joe Gerhardt, Buttercup Dickerson and Herman Doscher, destined to become arguably the loop's most polemical umpire. Hectoring from several club owners, who thought the balls made by Mahn "varied too greatly in weight and texture," also induced McKnight to deem Mahn's product "unsatisfactory" and to adopt a ball made by Al Reach, a notable early-day player, for the 1883 season.

The Reach ball would be used by the Association for the remainder of its tenure as a major league, but the rebel loop in almost every other area was still in an experimental mode. For the 1883 season, the schedule was increased to 98 games, calling for a team to meet each of its seven opponents 14 times. In 1884, when the Association swelled to 12 clubs, the schedule grew to 110 games but reduced the number of meetings between clubs to ten. After cutting back to eight teams in 1885, McKnight returned to his 1882 format, when rivals had met one another 16 times, and multiplied 16 by seven to create a 112-game schedule. The following year, the schedule was lengthened to 140 games, where it stayed for the duration.

So too were many issues surrounding the playing rules, umpires and players' salaries yet to be settled, but in one very important respect the Beer and Whisky League had proven itself to be uniquely resolute. Caylor and Horace Phillips, if they shook hands at the close of the October loop meeting, as they properly should have, to congratulate one another on a venture neatly achieved, could also have glowed in the knowledge that the Association was the first professional league, major or minor, to finish its schedule in its initial season without any franchise transfers or casualties.

1882 FINAL STANDINGS

	W	L	PCT	HOME	ROAD	GB
1. Cincinnati Red Stockings	55	25	.668	31–11	24–14	
2. Philadelphia Athletics	41	34	.547	21–18	20–16	11.5
3. Louisville Eclipse	42	38	.525	26–13	16–25	13
4. Pittsburgh Alleghenys	39	39	.500	17–18	22–21	15
5. St. Louis Browns	37	43	.463	24–20	13–23	18
6. Baltimore Orioles	19	54	.260	9–25	10–29	32.5

1882 SEASON LEADERS*

BATTING

BATTING AVERAGE (225 ABs)

1. Browning, Louis	.378
2. Carpenter, Cinci	.342
3. Swartwood, Pitts	.329
4. O'Brien, Phila	.303
5. Wolf, Louis	.299
6. Snyder, Cinci	.291
7. Sommer, Cinci	.288
B. Gleason, StL	.288
Peters, Pitts	.288
10. Leary, Pitts-Balt	.287

SLUGGING AVERAGE

1. Browning, Louis	.510
2. Swartwood, Pitts	.498
3. Taylor, Pitts	.455
4. M. Mansell, Pitts	.438
5. Carpenter, Cinci	.422
6. O'Brien, Phila	.419
7. Walker, StL	.396
8. Wolf, Louis	.384
9. Hecker, Louis	.368
10. Sommer, Cinci	.364

ON-BASE PERCENTAGE

1. Browning, Louis	.430
2. Swartwood, Pitts	.370
3. Carpenter, Cinci	.360
4. O'Brien, Phila	.339
5. Sommer, Cinci	.333
6. Wolf, Louis	.318
7. Snyder, Cinci	.311
8. J. Gleason, StL	.310
9. J. Latham, Phila	.306
10. Fulmer, Cinci	.302

TOTAL BASES

1. Swartwood, Pitts	162
2. M. Mansell, Pitts	152
3. Carpenter, Cinci	148
4. Browning, Louis	147
5. Taylor, Pitts	136
6. Sommer, Cinci	129
7. B. Gleason, StL	126
Walker, StL	126
9. Hecker, Louis	125
10. Wolf, Louis	122
Wheeler, Cinci	122

*Stolen Base and RBI leaders unavailable.

HOME RUNS	
1. Walker, StL	7
2. Browning, Louis	5
Swartwood, Pitts	5
4. Taylor, Pitts	4
5. Lane, Pitts	3
O'Brien, Phila	3
Hecker, Louis	3
8. Leary, Pitts-Balt	2
Strief, Pitts	2
J. Gleason, StL	2
M. Mansell, Pitts	2

RUNS	
1. Swartwood, Pitts	86
2. Sommer, Cinci	82
3. Carpenter, Cinci	78
4. Browning, Louis	67
5. Birchall, Phila	65
6. B. Gleason, StL	63
7. Hecker, Louis	62
8. M. Mansell, Pitts	59
Wheeler, Cinci	59
10. Comiskey, StL	58

HITS	
1. Carpenter, Cinci	120
2. Browning, Louis	109
3. Swartwood, Pitts	107
4. Sommer, Cinci	102
5. B. Gleason, StL	100
6. M. Mansell, Pitts	96
Peters, Pitts	96
8. Wolf, Louis	95
9. Hecker, Louis	94
10. J. Latham, Phila	92

PITCHING

....

WINS	
1. White, Cinci	40
2. Mullane, Louis	30
3. Weaver, Phila	26
4. McGinnis, StL	25
5. Salisbury, Pitts	20
6. McCormick, Cinci	14
7. Driscoll, Pitts	13
8. Landis, Phila-Balt	12
9. B. Sweeney, Phila	9
10. Schappert, StL	8

LOSSES	
1. Landis, Phila-Balt	28
2. Mullane, Louis	24
3. Salisbury, Pitts	18
4. McGinnis, StL	17
5. Weaver, Phila	15
6. Nichols, Balt	12
White, Cinci	12
8. B. Sweeney, Phila	11
McCormick, Cinci	11
10. Arundel, Pitts	10

INNINGS	
1. White, Cinci	480
2. Mullane, Louis	460.1
3. McGinnis, StL	379.1
4. Weaver, Phila	371
5. Landis, Phila-Balt	358
6. Salisbury, Pitts	315
7. McCormick, Cinci	220
8. Driscoll, Pitts	201
9. B. Sweeney, Phila	170
10. Schappert, StL	128

COMPLETE GAMES	
1. White, Cinci	52
2. Mullane, Louis	51
3. McGinnis, StL	42
4. Weaver, Phila	41
5. Salisbury, Pitts	38
6. Landis, Phila-Balt	37
7. McCormick, Cinci	24
8. Driscoll, Pitts	23
9. B. Sweeney, Phila	18
10. Schappert, StL	13
Arundel, Pitts	13

STRIKEOUTS	
1. Mullane, Louis	170
2. Salisbury, Pitts	135
3. McGinnis, StL	134
4. White, Cinci	122
5. Weaver, Phila	104
6. McCormick, Cinci	96
7. Landis, Phila-Balt	75
8. Driscoll, Pitts	59
9. B. Sweeney, Phila	48
10. Arundel, Pitts	47

WINNING PCT. (10 DECISIONS)	
1. White, Cinci	.769
2. Weaver, Phila	.634
3. McGinnis, StL	.595
4. Driscoll, Pitts	.591
5. McCormick, Cinci	.560
6. Mullane, Louis	.556
7. Schappert, StL	.533
8. Salisbury, Pitts	.526
9. Hecker, Louis	.500
10. B. Sweeney, Phila	.474

ERA (80 INNINGS)	
1. Driscoll, Pitts	1.21
2. Hecker, Louis	1.30
3. McCormick, Cinci	1.52
4. White, Cinci	1.54
5. Mullane, Louis	1.88
6. McGinnis, StL	2.47
7. Salisbury, Pitts	2.63
8. Weaver, Phila	2.74
9. B. Sweeney, Phila	2.91
10. J. Reccius, Louis	3.03

LOWEST ON-BASE PCT.	
1. Hecker, Louis	.199
2. Driscoll, Pitts	.218
3. McCormick, Cinci	.243
4. White, Cinci	.244
5. Salisbury, Pitts	.253
6. Mullane, Louis	.257
7. Weaver, Phila	.262
8. Geis, Balt	.263
9. McGinnis, StL	.267
10. Schappert, StL	.291

TWO

1883

• • •
Captured here at Sportsman's Park in perhaps the most intriguing AA team picture yet to be discovered are the 1883 St. Louis Browns before a game with Louisville. Behind the team is an early scoreboard, then called a "bulletin board." The upcoming game, hidden behind the unidentified gent in civvies, was between Pittsburgh and Baltimore. Among the others in the picture are: Charlie Comiskey, standing far left; Arlie Latham, seated third from left; Jumbo McGinnis, seated to the gent's right; Hugh Nicol, sprawled far left; Pat Deasley, standing far right; and Tony Mullane, seated second from the gent's left.

PEACE COMES IN PARLOR 9

❝_While away from home every player must report at the hotel to the Manager before 11:30 PM and retire to his room for the night. No player shall lie abed after eight o'clock in the morning while on a trip unless he is sick or disabled._**❞**

—Philadelphia Athletics club rule no. 6 in 1883

EVEN THOUGH CINCINNATI WON THE FIRST Association pennant handily, Caylor knew his team had flaws. The largest was at first base, where Dan Stearns had finally won the job by default after Dave Rowe, Harry Wheeler and Harry Luff had all been tried and found wanting. In the fall of 1882, Caylor went to New York in a fresh bid to draw Long John Reilly away from the Metropolitans. After watching the Mets lose an exhibition game to Cleveland at the Polo Grounds, Caylor invited Reilly to supper. Later they repaired to Caylor's hotel room at the Hoffman House, where Reilly was at last persuaded to come home to Cincinnati.

Caylor had more work to do. That fall he also beat Baltimore to the punch and landed Pop Corkhill to replace the weak-hitting Jimmy Macullar in center field, but his grandest coup came when he collared another popular Cincinnatian, Buck Ewing of the collapsing Troy team. Ewing promised to bring with him his favorite batterymate, Mickey Welch, and Troy outfielder Pete Gillespie. If

43

the three had reported to Cincinnati in the spring, the Red Stockings would have been loaded, for Ewing was soon to gain respect as the best catcher in the last century, and Welch collected over 300 victories. The deal fell through, however, when the Metropolitans joined the Association in October of 1882. Had William Hulbert still been alive, the National League might have continued its embargo on both New York and Philadelphia, but Boston owner Arthur Soden, who had temporarily assumed the League's mantle after Hulbert's death the previous spring, was not about to cede the nation's two largest cities to the Association without a fight. Already unhappy with the fact that in 1882 the six Association clubs had a greater population base than the League's eight members, he hastily arranged for the Troy franchise to be moved to New York and prevailed upon Ewing, Welch and Gillespie to accompany it. Whether the three had broken their contracts with Cincinnati to play in the Gotham, as Caylor contended, was almost beside the point, as both circuits were now fervidly raiding each other's ranks. Of necessity the Athletics were among the most active teams in the free-for-all players' market. While the Association still vacillated over whether to adopt the reserve rule, the A's entire 1882 pitching staff of Sam Weaver, Bill Sweeney and Frank Mountain all drifted to other teams over the winter, and the Philadelphia club scrambled to replace them with a trio of ex-National Leaguers—Bobby Mathews, George Bradley and Fred Corey. But it was the acquisition of Harry Stovey, another League veteran, that gave the team its spine.

Born Harry Duffield Stowe in 1856, Stovey adopted a new name as a teenager to keep his mother from learning that he was pursuing a career as a ballplayer. As Stovey, he made his play-for-pay debut in 1877 with the Philadelphia Athletics, reborn as a semi-pro team after the original Philadelphia Athletics were expelled from the League after the 1876 season. Originally a pitcher, Stovey was converted to a first baseman-outfielder in 1878 by Frank Bancroft, his first professional manager at New Bedford of the International Association. Like many early-day players, Stovey later resided permanently in the town where he had first known acclaim, but before returning to New Bedford he grew to become the game's leading slugger. At the time of his retirement in 1893, he led all major league hitters, past or present, with 122 career home runs. Stovey was also a daring and intelligent baserunner who, at one time, was credited (erroneously) with the single-season record for stolen bases and who is believed by many authorities to have pioneered the use of sliding pads.

By 1882, Stovey was in his third major league season, all spent with the Worcester League Club. Rather than stay with the

Massachusetts franchise when it was transferred to Philadelphia to compete with the Athletics as part of Soden's plan to take the battle for the two key cities to the Association, Stovey bolted to the Beer and Whisky League. A Philadelphia native, Stovey could have come back home by casting his oar with either team. That he chose the Athletics would have everlasting repercussions on both the Association and his own career.

To further bolster themselves, the Athletics picked up Mike Moynahan from the Philadelphias club to replace Lew Say at shortstop. A spotty fielder who grew even more erratic when a finger on his throwing hand was so badly broken in May 1882 that he had to have part of it amputated, Moynahan had flunked an earlier National League test and, at first, seemed no improvement on Say. *Sporting Life* saw enough, though, in Moynahan and the other newcomers to venture this spring forecast: "The Athletic team for 1883 is considered by competent critics to be the strongest in the American Association and one which, barring accident, will almost certainly bring the championship [to Philadelphia]. Certainly no pains nor expenses have been spared by the management to secure this much desired prize." The A's management in 1883 consisted of field captain and right fielder Lon Knight and three co-owners, Bill Sharsig, Lew Simmons and Charlie Mason. Sharsig would eventually show himself to be the most enduring and the best baseball man, but initially the most prominent of the trio was Mason, a former player who still worked out with the team and even got into a game in 1883. Simmons, a minstrel by trade, specialized in making clubhouse pep talks and "soldering" other club executives.

So valued a palaverer was Simmons that he was chosen by his fellow moguls as one of the Association's three delegates when it had its first official tete-a-tete with the League. After months of jockeying between the two loops, the long-awaited meeting finally came to pass on Saturday, February 17, 1883, at the Fifth Avenue Hotel in New York. Representing the League were Soden, John Day* and its former secretary and new president-elect Abraham G. Mills. Attending on the Association's behalf were Simmons, Baltimore's recently appointed new manager Billy Barnie and Caylor, the chairman of its three-man committee. Overriding a protest from the Association, Mills also invited Northwestern League president, Elias Mather, to act as a kind of informal refer-

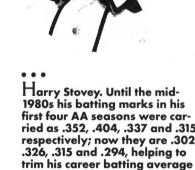

• • •
Harry Stovey. Until the mid-1980s his batting marks in his first four AA seasons were carried as .352, .404, .337 and .315, respectively; now they are .302, .326, .315 and .294, helping to trim his career batting average from .301 to .288. Billed as the AA's greatest player in its formative years, Stovey may have had his averages deliberately padded by AA officials to inflate his stature and make the NL eat its heart out over having lost him.

* The Metropolitan Exhibition Company owned both the Association Mets and the League Gothams. As president of the MEC, Day could probably have served on either loop's committee at the New York Conference. That he chose to work for the League should have been a tipoff that the Association could have a major problem ahead, but only David Reid, the baseball editor of the Missouri Republican and one of Von der Ahe's underlings, saw it coming as early as the spring of 1883.

Let go by Chicago, Hugh Nicol joined the Browns in 1883. Nicknamed "Little Nick," the Scottish-born Nicol was the darling of the media and was always handy for an interview. Many of his teammates were not overly fond of him, though, and few liked to be on base in front of him. The fleet Nicol often would make a fellow player look foolish by passing him on the basepaths.

Pat ("Give me six schooners for a quarter") Deasley had oodles of talent, but a small drinking problem kept him from realizing most of it. The Browns' highest-paid player in 1883, Deasley had become a temperance orator by 1887, only to backslide. He flipped out completely for a time at his Philadelphia home and started reporting to work every day as if he were a groundskeeper at the Phillies park.

ee. But Mather's role at the conference proved to be only that of a neutral observer, for the two warriors were surprisingly irenic, each agreeing to almost everything the other proposed. In only a single five-and-a-half-hour session, a temporary peace agreement was drafted that so pleased Caylor he wired the news to Cincinnati in time for his *Commercial* subscribers to read the next morning over their coffee that "these two heretofore antipathetical parties adjust all differences, join hands and principals upon the question of contracts, expulsions and the black list and will play games among each other whenever they desire."

The largest concession made by the Association at the "New York Conference" was to agree to the League's reserve rule, which, for the 1883 season, allowed each team to lock in up to 11 players. In turn the League agreed to grant the Association major league status, pending its ratification of the agreement. Foreseeing that Von der Ahe, who adamantly opposed pow-wowing with the League, would continue to be a stumbling block, Caylor left it to Simmons to softsoap the Browns owner. Within two weeks Simmons had done his job so well that when the Association held its spring meeting on March 12 at St. Louis's Lindell Hotel, Von der Ahe, though still wary of the League's armistice overture, grudgingly became the eighth and final club president to sign the agreement.

His mission accomplished, Simmons was freed to return to Philadelphia and help Sharsig and Mason rally the construction crew to finish refurbishing the A's new home in time for the season. At the close of the 1882 campaign, Sharsig, after holding the lease on Oakdale Park for three years, lost it when the grounds were sold to a company that thought the property too valuable for a mere ballpark. Fortunately he was able to scour up Jefferson Street Grounds, the old homesite of the original Philadelphia Athletics team before it was stripped of its League franchise.

On April 7, 1883, the A's debuted their newly renovated Jefferson Street park by skunking Yale 12–0 in their opening exhibition game. In quick order, they then demolished the Hartsville, Auburn and Trenton clubs, only to dampen momentarily the enthusiasm of their followers by dropping three straight practice games to the Philadelphia Phillies (then called the Quakers), the new National League entry. The A's subsequently turned on the Phillies and evened the preseason series at 3–3, but the other three Association teams based in the East struggled pitifully against League teams. Pittsburgh was 0–3, Baltimore was 0–8 and the Mets won just one of 14 contests, that against their rival New York entry, to bring the Association's overall preseason record to a dismal 4–27 versus its elder. Meanwhile the Association's four

western clubs—St. Louis, Cincinnati, Louisville and Columbus—steered clear of the League. Columbus's avoidance of confrontation was so obvious *Sporting Life* remarked sarcastically, "Sly Phillips! He isn't letting the League teams have a picnic with his team. He tackles the [minor] Northwestern League; wins cheap victories and gives Columbians something to shout about. He knows better than to let home audiences sour on the club before the season opens."

Cincinnati initially went a step farther, refusing to play any preseason games at all. Still reeling from the memory of last year's catastrophic rash of injuries during spring play, the Red Stockings confined themselves at first to intrasquad games, but by the middle of April this routine began to feel too hermetic, and Caylor scheduled several last-minute contests with neighboring semi-pro teams. Columbus also got a late start and did not play its first match until April 14, when the Kenyon College team journeyed from Gambier to the state capital for a 21–0 spanking.

Notwithstanding several other one-sided outings, Horace Phillips's Columbus Buckeyes were expected to bring up the rear in their first season. They were the "baby" in the Association, after all. The Metropolitans, though also new to the Association, were not viewed as babies because they had been in existence since 1880 and the previous year, as an independent club, had more than held their own even against League teams. Baltimore, technically a returning veteran, was in reality a much more callow entry than the Mets, and in some ways made even Columbus seem mature. The 1882 Orioles had only one player worth keeping, catcher Ed Whiting, and after being outbid for his services by Louisville, Henry Von der Horst cleaned house entirely, starting at the top. Billy Barnie was brought in from Philadelphia to run the club on the field, and with so many holes to fill he stocked his larder with as many experienced players as he could find and then began weeding them out. Some, alas, weeded themselves out. Terry Larkin, a former League pitcher who was trying to mount a comeback as a second baseman, shot his wife on April 24 and then cut his own throat, forcing Barnie to look elsewhere for a keystone operative. Among those who stuck with the Orioles and got to wear the club's new black and yellow uniforms were Jim Clinton, a thirty-two-year-old outfielder who had not put in a full season in the majors since 1872; former Cincinnati first baseman Dan Stearns, made expendable when the Red Stockings garnered Long John Reilly; Dave Rowe, another ex-Red Stocking; and Lew Say, the talented but profligate shortstop whose habit of showing up at games too drunk to play had cost him his spot with the Athletics.

It was perhaps their frustration with Say that prodded the

• • •

Ted Sullivan. While managing the Browns in 1883 he coined the word "fan"—short for fanatic, Chris Von der Ahe's appellation for a crank, the term then for a rabid rooter. Sullivan had a colossal reputation as a baseball scout, but the results didn't always bear it out. Following the 1889 season, Cincinnati gave him a $3,000 check to land Kid Nichols, but he handed over the check to the Omaha club for Nichols's release without first making sure Nichols would sign with Cincinnati. The Reds panicked and stopped payment on the check. Nichols then signed with Boston, where he was a 30-game winner a record seven years in a row.

three A's owners to draft a set of ten club rules prior to the 1883 campaign that included prohibitions against players smoking after eating their pregame dinners, consorting with members of the opposite sex while in uniform or staying out past 11:30 PM on road trips. The rules appeared to work, as Mathews utilized perfect support from his teammates to blank the Alleghenys 4–0 on May 1 in the A's season opener at Pittsburgh. In the other lidlifters, Cincinnati edged St. Louis 6–5, the Eclipse topped Columbus by the same score and Baltimore's John Fox squeezed by Tim Keefe of the Mets, 4–3, when Stearns tripled home the winning run in the 11th inning. The A's won again the following day and eight games into the season held first place with a 7–1 mark, their only loss coming on May 9 when Baltimore rookie Jim Devine, given 15 runs, held on to notch his lone major league triumph. Two games back of Philadelphia at 5–3 was Cincinnati, while St. Louis brought up the rear at 2–6.

The Browns' slow start was discouraging to Von der Ahe, who thought he had molded a winner by outbidding Louisville for the multitalented Tony Mullane and ordaining Ted Sullivan the field leader of his club. A railroad news agent by trade, and the organizer of the first Northwestern League in 1879, Sullivan possessed Caylor's shrewdness and Horace Phillips's verve but was eventually worn down by the combination of Von der Ahe's meddling and the feud between the team's two catchers, Tom Dolan and Pat Deasley, that divided the rest of the players into enemy camps. Pittsburgh also had dissension problems, compounded by rampant alcoholism. Misled by Buttercup Dickerson, Bollicky Billy Taylor and Frank McLaughlin, the Alleghenys lushed their way to a 12–20 start, earning manager Al Pratt a pink slip in late June. His replacement was Ormond Butler, an umpire who worked on the side as a booking agent for Buffalo Bill Cody. Under Butler, Pittsburgh came apart completely and finished seventh, saved from the cellar only by Baltimore. The dismal performance of his supporting cast made Ed Swartwood's loop-leading .356 batting average all the more impressive.

Even though Will White was once again the top pitcher in the Association, and Charley Jones and Long John Reilly contributed considerable added punch, the Red Stockings trailed the Athletics by five and a half games in early June. The gap was swiftly narrowed when both the Browns and the Red Stockings caught fire and Philadelphia led off a Western swing in the middle of the month with three straight losses at Cincinnati, all of them to White. After the third, an 11–1 blowout on June 20, St. Louis temporarily took over first place by beating the Mets. The hot pennant race had pulled a record Sunday crowd of 15,000 to

• • •
An early-season picture of the 1883 Alleghenys, reputed to be the hardest drinking team of all-time. Front (left to right): Denny Driscoll, Johnny Peters and Frank McLaughlin. Middle (left to right): Jack Hayes, Buttercup Dickerson, manager Al Pratt (seen here just days before he was fired), Mike Mansell and Edward "The Only" Nolan. Top (left to right): Henry Oberbeck, Ed Swartwood, Bollicky Billy Taylor, Joe Battin and George Creamer. In 1883, Mansell's older brother Tom, who was also known to tip a few, was awarded the AA bat title by super-chauvinists in the loop, until someone was crass enough to point out that while his .402 average was terrific all right, he only appeared in 28 games.

Sportsman's Park three days earlier to watch Jumbo McGinnis down Tim Keefe, 7–5. Philadelphia regained the lead, however, by salvaging the last game at Cincinnati when White could not pitch a fourth day in a row and the A's teed off on Harry Mc-Cormick for 14 runs.

Moving to St. Louis on June 28, the A's took the opener of a crucial four-game set, 3–1. *Sporting Life* deemed both the game and the umpiring of Honest John Kelly "very fine," but the Browns disagreed, castigating him for too many close calls that went the visitors' way. Refusing to play if Kelly umped again as scheduled, Von der Ahe hired a special O&M train just for Charlie Daniels so he could reach St. Louis in time to officiate the remaining contests of the series. But even with Daniels making the calls, the A's won three of four in St. Louis, losing only a Sunday game on July 1, when the Browns scored a run in the bottom of the ninth to give Tony Mullane an expensive 9–8 win as Deasley broke his right thumb. The injury left Dolan, who had been playing the outfield, the team's only able catcher, and brought ancient Ned Cuthbert out of mothballs to man left field.

Heading eastward to Louisville after leaving St. Louis, the A's dropped the opener of a morning-afternoon July 4th doubleheader to Guy Hecker but then won a 14–9 endurance test in which pitcher Sam Weaver and first baseman Juice Latham, two former A's who had taken advantage of the Association's lack of a reserve rule to join the Eclipse club, both collapsed from heat stroke. Weaver and Latham recovered by the following day, but a week later, while sitting in front of the St. James Hotel in St. Louis, second baseman Joe Gerhardt suffered a paralyzing stroke in his left side that hit the Louisville club where it was already perilously thin. Losing Gerhardt, although only temporarily as it developed, saddled the Eclipse with no one better than the 240-pound Latham at the keystone sack and left the pitching to Weaver, since Hecker was needed to replace Latham at first base.

Even less deep in reserve strength was Columbus. To spell Frank Mountain in the box, Horace Phillips had only sore-armed John Valentine and Ed "Dummy" Dundon, a deaf mute who three years later was nearly stabbed to death outside a Columbus army barracks when a soldier mistook his stone silence for an insult. The other positions were handled all season by the same eight regulars, most of them rejects Phillips had picked up cheaply. In 1883 the best of the lot was John Richmond, an erstwhile National League outfielder turned shortstop, but in the years ahead four other Buckeyes—second baseman Pop Smith, third sacker Willie Kuehne, rightfielder Tom Brown and center gardener Fred Mann—would show that Phillips, when put on his own to form a team, had an eye for talent.

Jim Mutrie's Mets were another nine that rarely substituted, but for Mutrie it was a matter of philosophy. Mutrie believed in finding nine players who meshed well together, establishing a workable batting order and then never deviating from his lineup, barring injury. In 1883 the Mets used just two pitchers all year, Keefe and Jack Lynch. Bill Holbert and Charlie Reipschlager shared the catching, with Reipschlager (whose name was often shortened to "Rip" in box scores) filling in elsewhere when needed. The only other Met to get into a game that year was Dave Orr, a first-base hopeful whom Mutrie pressed to shed some suet. At 250 pounds, Orr was the only player in the Association more elephantine than Juice Latham.

In contrast, Barnie needed 31 players to get through the season in Baltimore. His catching situation was especially desperate. It got so bad that Barnie himself went back of the bat in 13 games. The club's lone stroke of good luck was netting Rooney Sweeney, Gid Gardner and Bob Emslie of the minor league Merritt team after it disbanded in July. Sweeney, a catcher who was also coveted by the A's, was seemingly the jewel of the three, but Emslie won nine of 22 decisions in the season's final two months, no small feat for a team that otherwise had a 19–55 won-lost record.

By the end of July, the Athletics, Browns and Red Stockings had begun to pull away from the pack. The A's entered August by crushing Pittsburgh 19–2 in the last meeting of the season between the two clubs. Three days later the Browns, still right on the A's heels, were dealt a heavy blow when one of the two new outfielders Von der Ahe and Sullivan had snagged recently from League clubs, Tom Mansell, fell through an open elevator shaft at Cincinnati's Grand Hotel on returning from an evening tour of the Ohio city's Vine Street haunts. The mishap shelved Mansell for several weeks, leaving Fred Lewis, late of the Philadelphia Phillies, and Hugh Nicol, a Chicago White Stockings castoff who had been acquired prior to the season, as the team's only reliable outfielders. Even so, the Browns hung close to the A's, and Cincinnati also stayed in hot pursuit. On August 21, the Red Stockings came to Philadelphia for a make-or-break series, with Caylor

• • •
Joe Gerhardt, here a member of the 1886 Giants, was a graceful fielder with great range whose bat sprang a huge hole when pitchers won the right to throw overhand. He revived his career in 1883 by joining Louisville after being blacklisted by the NL. That year Gerhardt hit .263, but he never again topped .220.

A woodcut of the 1882 New York Mets, the year before they joined the AA. Standing (left to right): Jack Lynch, Charlie Reipschlager, Tip O'Neill, Eddie Kennedy, John Clapp, John Doyle, Frank Hankinson and Steve Brady. Seated (left to right): Tom Mansell, Terry Larkin, Candy Nelson and Long John Reilly. Destined to be the team's greatest AA stars—though not with the Mets—were O'Neill and Reilly. Destined to have the most tormented life was Larkin, who shot his wife in 1883 and then tried to end it all by slitting his throat. Eleven years later, in a second suicide attempt, he succeeded.

still confidently predicting another Cincinnati pennant. The Red Stockings took three of four to tighten the race further, but it was Cincinnati's last charge at the top rung. In September, while Cincinnati continued to pitch White day after day, the A's picked up Jumping Jack Jones from Detroit to help the tiring Bobby Mathews. In his Association debut on September 4, Jones beat Tony Mullane 11–1 at Philadelphia and then squeaked by the Browns again the following day, 5–4, when St. Louis shortstop Bill Gleason lined out crisply to third base with two on and two out in the bottom of the ninth. Jones followed by beating Columbus twice in a five-day span to swell the A's lead to three games, their largest margin since mid-June.

As the A's swung through Ohio on their last western trip, matters came to a head in St. Louis, where Ted Sullivan resigned as the Browns manager and first baseman Charlie Comiskey was named his interim replacement. In the A's final game at Columbus on September 13, newcomer Al West played short in place of Moynahan. After Philadelphia won 11–5, West revealed that his real name was Hubbard. Two days later, as Hubbard, he worked behind the bat in his second and last major league game and the

A's worst outing of the year, an ugly 11–0 shellacking at Cincinnati that tagged Jones with his first defeat as an Athletic.

Despite losing two of three to Cincinnati, the A's sat a comfortable two and a half games ahead of St. Louis on the next to last Sunday morning of the season, September 23. A 9–2 win that afternoon at Sportsman's Park by George Bradley seemingly spoiled the last hopes of the 16,800 payees, though it gave the Browns another new Association attendance record. However, the race was not over. Moving to Louisville for a season-ending series, the A's lost two straight games to the Eclipse while St. Louis was pummeling Pittsburgh. Philadelphia got the one additional win it needed to clinch on Friday, September 28, when Jack Jones beat Guy Hecker 7–6 in 10 innings. The pennant-winning run was scored fittingly by club sparkplug Harry Stovey, who reached first on a walk, scooted to second on a wild pitch, was moved to third when Lon Knight singled and then raced home on Moynahan's single. Two afternoons later, on the closing day of the season, the A's lost to Louisville, while St. Louis was beating Pittsburgh again, but the reversal was meaningless, for Philadelphia had begun the day with an insurmountable two-game lead.

On their return home, the A's were met at the train station by a jubilant Philadelphia mob. The heroes who got the most lavish welcome were Jack Jones, victor in the pennant-clinching game, Stovey, who had scored the winning run, and Moynahan, whose hit had sent Harry home. It was to be the one and only moment in the limelight for Jones and Moynahan. The Eli alum

• • •

A baroque cartoon of the 1883 AA champs "marching" home behind their troika of owners. Some of these A's were indeed among the lame, the halt, and the just plain quirky. Bob Blakiston claimed his real name was Blackstone and he was a descendent of the English legal luminary. Jud Birchall was a physical wreck in 1884, purportedly after overdoing it in 1883. Later he was found to be dying of consumption. Mike Moynahan's descent from stardom was incredibly swift; the AA's top shortstop in 1883, he could not even hold a job in the minors by the end of the following year.

"SEE THE CONQUERING HEROES COME.

• • •

Bobby Mathews (above) and Will White were the last two pitching greats to utilize an underhand delivery. In 1883, Mathews enjoyed the first of three consecutive 30-win seasons with the A's and was the toast of Philadelphia. The celebration for the champions culminated in a gargantuan banquet at which Mathews, not known to demur when spirits were present, led toast after toast. By 1897 he was working as a greeter at Joe Start's Providence roadhouse, his last job before his death of paresis.

never played again, preferring to use his baseball earnings to set up a dental practice, and Moynahan participated in just one more game with the Athletics the following spring before being cut loose to make room for Sadie Houck, another veteran the A's plucked from the penny-pinching Detroit franchise.

Two days after their triumphant homecoming, the A's opened the fall leg of their city series with the Phillies. After concluding the spring round knotted 2–all, the Philadelphia rivals had then gone very separate paths. While the A's were streaking to the Association pennant, the Phillies floundered to 81 losses in 98 games for an agonizingly awful .173 winning percentage. Matters grew so odious for the Phillies that the other seven National League teams in mid-season threw one of the loop's founding principals to the winds and granted them permission to carve their general admission price from half a dollar to a quarter. Still, the Phillies continued to draw poorly and play like puddings. When the A's pounded them 13–3 on October 3, the poolsellers were willing to wager the Phillies would not win a single game in the fall series. But it was the A's who then went into the tank, suffering a string of defeats not only to the Phillies, but also to two other League teams, Providence and Buffalo. The exhibition games had been touted as a tune-up for a possible postseason series with League champion Boston, but by the middle of the month that notion, which had never gotten beyond the talking stage, was scrapped by mutual consent. It almost seemed that the League, for all the ease with which its teams had dispatched Association rivals in exhibition contests, remained leery of trying to press its claim of superiority in games that meant something.

Near the end of the month two meetings were held that would have an enormous bearing on the Association's future. On October 26, with principal owner and Association president Denny McKnight chairing the proceeding, Allegheny club officials scrimped to unearth the financial resources to pay their players and keep afloat. Needing $10,000 to put the club back on its feet, the board decided to transfer stock from small shareholders to larger ones, to be held in trust while they made good on all debts and paid the salaries for which the club was in arrears, amounting to some $2,500. It was then debated which players to retain. All were in accord that Denny Driscoll, Buttercup Dickerson and Billy Taylor had to go. The first two were irredeemable lushers and Taylor was a thief to boot. Earlier in the month he had been arrested and charged with stealing a $1,000 diamond pin from millionaire Pittsburgh coal king Charles Brown. Taylor's defense was that Brown had befriended him and given him the pin as a gift. Eventually, Brown dropped the charge, but Taylor was nonetheless viewed as a bad apple. It was also not a healthy sign that the team belonging to the president of the Association was in such precarious shape.

If Abraham Mills had known the state of affairs in Pittsburgh, he might have pushed for a different objective at the meeting he conducted the following day. Mills was under the impression, however, that 1883 had been baseball's most profitable season to date. Between them both major leagues had topped 1,000,000 in attendance. Though profits in the Association were smaller because of its 25¢ tariff, each of its clubs except the Mets boasted that it had made money. Von der Ahe bragged he had cleared a sumptuous $70,000 on "mein poys" as the Browns stayed in the race until the final weekend of the season. These claims, though probably exaggerated in every case and certainly false in Pittsburgh's, steered Mills to push for a permanent peace settlement. On October 27, 1883, in Parlor 9 at the Fifth Avenue Hotel, the League president put his legs under the table with the same seven potentates who had sat down with him at the New York Conference the previous February. Once Mills had been elected chairman of the joint proceeding, Caylor secretary and Northwestern League president Mather treasurer, the group set itself to the task of crafting the first constitution that would govern all of baseball. Their efforts resulted in the formation of the National Agreement of Professional Base Ball Clubs, known thereafter as "The National Agreement." Before the afternoon was out, the seven-member committee drafted 10 amendments that included allowing each team to reserve up to 14 players in October for the following season and a pledge from all three leagues to refrain from encroaching on one another's territory. Later events would suggest that Mills probably led the move for an addendum to the encroachment rule, permitting a club to transfer from one league to another. But when the discussion swung to the problem of spiraling player salaries, all present united to pass a rule that a player could not be signed for a minimum of 10 days after he was released to give all clubs a fair crack at him and prevent a "huge signing bonus" like the one Fred Lewis had wangled from the Browns a few months earlier after the Phillies let him loose.

It was not lost on Mills that Caylor continued to be the leading spokesman for the Association when there was delicate work to be done. The meeting might have gone very differently if McKnight had been the main opponent to be curried, but McKnight, once again, was not even there. In any case, it was a strange and not-easy-to-target group that would bank its future on a man who did not even have any official standing within it rather than on its duly elected president.

• • •
Abraham G. Mills, the orchestrator of the game's first "National Agreement." Upon becoming NL president, Mills made it his mission to kill other aspirant major leagues. Because of his militant stance, particularly toward the Union Association threat, Mills was deposed after the 1884 season in favor of the more conciliatory Nick Young, whose style was much closer to the NL's subtler methods of slaying competitors.

1883 FINAL STANDINGS

	W	L	PCT	HOME	ROAD	GB
1. Philadelphia Athletics	66	32	.673	37–13	29–19	
2. St. Louis Browns	65	33	.663	35–14	30–19	1
3. Cincinnati Red Stockings	61	37	.622	37–13	24–24	5
4. New York Metropolitans	54	42	.563	30–17	24–25	11
5. Louisville Eclipse	52	45	.536	29–19	23–26	13.5
6. Columbus Buckeyes	32	65	.330	18–29	14–36	33.5
7. Pittsburgh Alleghenys	31	67	.316	18–31	13–36	35
8. Baltimore Orioles	28	68	.292	18–31	10–37	37

• • •

Bob Barr, a rookie latecomer to the Pittsburgh club in 1883 who nevertheless managed to lose 18 games while winning just six. The following year, split between Washington and Indianapolis, he dropped 34 of 46 decisions. In his only other AA season—1890 with Rochester—the luckless Barr topped the loop in losses.

• • •

Ed Swartwood, the only left-handed hitter prior to 1891 to win an AA batting crown. The 1883 season was his best and one of the AA's worst, owing to the huge disparity between the haves and the have-nots. The bottom three teams—Columbus, Baltimore, and Swartwood's Pittsburgh club—lost 200 games combined and won just 91, and that included wins in games among themselves.

1883 SEASON LEADERS*

BATTING

BATTING AVERAGE (275 ABs)

1. Swartwood, Pitts	.356
2. Browning, Louis	.338
3. Clinton, Balt	.313
4. Reilly, Cinci	.311
5. Moynahan, Phila	.308
6. Nelson, NY	.305
7. Stovey, Phila	.302
8. Carpenter, Cinci	.296
9. Comiskey, StL	.294
C. Jones, Cinci	.294

SLUGGING AVERAGE

1. Stovey, Phila	.504
2. Reilly, Cinci	.485
3. Swartwood, Pitts	.475
4. C. Jones, Cinci	.473
5. Browning, Louis	.458
6. P. Smith, Colum	.410
Moynahan, Phila	.410
8. Comiskey, StL	.397
9. B. Gleason, StL	.393
Clinton, Balt	.393

ON-BASE PERCENTAGE

1. Swartwood, Pitts	.391
2. Browning, Louis	.370
3. Clinton, Balt	.357
4. Moynahan, Phila	.356
5. Nelson, NY	.353
6. Stovey, Phila	.342
7. J. Gleason, StL-Louis	.340
8. Sommer, Cinci	.333
O'Brien, Phila	.333
10. C. Jones, Cinci	.328

TOTAL BASES

1. Stovey, Phila	212
Reilly, Cinci	212
3. Swartwood, Pitts	196
4. C. Jones, Cinci	185
5. B. Gleason, StL	167
6. Browning, Louis	166
P. Smith, Colum	166
8. Moynahan, Phila	164
Carpenter, Cinci	164
10. Comiskey, StL	159

*Stolen Base and RBI leaders unavailable.

HOME RUNS		RUNS		HITS	
1. Stovey, Phila	14	1. Stovey, Phila	110	1. Swartwood, Pitts	147
2. C. Jones, Cinci	11	2. Reilly, Cinci	103	2. Reilly, Cinci	136
3. Reilly, Cinci	9	3. Carpenter, Cinci	99	3. Carpenter, Cinci	129
4. Fulmer, Cinci	5	4. Knight, Phila	98	4. Stovey, Phila	127
T. Brown, Colum	5	5. Birchall, Phila	95	Nelson, NY	127
6. P. Smith, Colum	4	Browning, Louis	95	6. Clinton, Balt	125
7. Hayes, Pitts	3	7. Moynahan, Phila	90	7. Moynahan, Phila	123
Mountain, Colum	3	M. Mansell, Pitts	90	8. B. Gleason, StL	122
Sommer, Cinci	3	9. Swartwood, Pitts	86	9. Browning, Louis	121
Carpenter, Cinci	3	A. Latham, StL	86	10. Comiskey, StL	118
M. Mansell, Pitts	3				
Swartwood, Pitts	3				
Leary, Louis-Balt	3				

PITTING

PITCHING

WINS		LOSSES		INNINGS	
1. White, Cinci	43	1. Mountain, Colum	33	1. Keefe, NY	619
2. Keefe, NY	41	2. Henderson, Balt	32	2. White, Cinci	577
3. Mullane, StL	35	3. Keefe, NY	27	3. Mountain, Colum	503
4. Mathews, Phila	30	4. Hecker, Louis	25	4. Mullane, StL	460.2
5. McGinnis, StL	28	5. White, Cinci	22	5. Hecker, Louis	451
Hecker, Louis	28	6. Driscoll, Pitts	21	6. Weaver, Louis	418.2
7. Mountain, Colum	26	7. Weaver, Louis	20	7. McGinnis, StL	382.2
8. Weaver, Louis	24	8. Barr, Pitts	18	8. Mathews, Phila	381
9. Driscoll, Pitts	18	9. Dundon, Colum	16	9. Henderson, Balt	358.1
10. Bradley, Phila	16	McGinnis, StL	16	10. Driscoll, Pitts	336.1

COMPLETE GAMES		STRIKEOUTS		WINNING PCT. (15 DECISIONS)	
1. Keefe, NY	68	1. Keefe, NY	361	1. Mullane, StL	.700
2. White, Cinci	64	2. Mathews, Phila	203	2. Mathews, Phila	.698
3. Mountain, Colum	57	3. Mullane, StL	191	3. Bradley, Phila	.696
4. Hecker, Louis	53	4. Mountain, Colum	159	4. White, Cinci	.662
5. Mullane, StL	49	5. Hecker, Louis	153	5. McGinnis, StL	.636
6. Weaver, Louis	47	6. Henderson, Balt	145	6. Keefe, NY	.603
7. Mathews, Phila	41	7. McGinnis, StL	128	7. Corey, Phila	.588
McGinnis, StL	41	8. Lynch, NY	119	8. Deagle, Cinci	.556
9. Henderson, Balt	38	9. Weaver, Louis	116	9. Weaver, Louis	.542
10. Driscoll, Pitts	35	10. Barr, Pitts	81	10. Hecker, Louis	.531

ERA (98 INNINGS)		LOWEST ON-BASE PCT.	
1. White, Cinci	2.09	1. Keefe, NY	.233
2. Mullane, StL	2.19	2. Mullane, StL	.238
3. Deagle, Cinci	2.31	3. White, Cinci	.244
4. McGinnis, StL	2.33	4. McGinnis, StL	.249
5. Keefe, NY	2.41	5. Bradley, Phila	.263
6. Mathews, Phila	2.46	6. Mathews, Phila	.265
7. McCormick, Cinci	2.87	7. Lynch, NY	.267
8. Bradley, Phila	3.15	8. Emslie, Balt	.268
9. Emslie, Balt	3.17	9. Deagle, Cinci	.270
10. Corey, Phila	3.40	10. Weaver, Louis	.280

THREE

1884

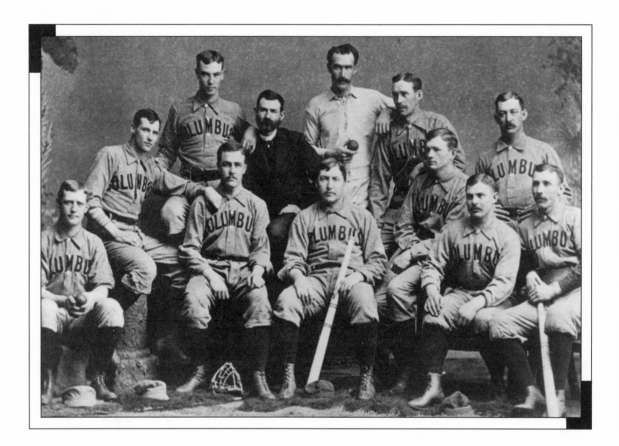

• • •

The 1884 Columbus Buckeyes, which narrowly missed becoming the second Ohio-based team to capture an AA pennant. Jim Field and Frank Mountain stand (left to right); Field has his hand on manager Gus Schmelz's shoulder and Mountain leans on Pop Smith. Seated (left to right) are Ed Morris, Tom Brown, Fred Carroll, Rudy Kemmler, Ed "Dummy" Dundon, Willie Kuehne, and Fred Mann. John Richmond stands between Kuehne and Mann. In 1884, Morris and Kuehne first became road roommates and fast friends. Kuehne married a Columbus woman who would invite Morris and other Buckeyes to visit her when her husband was out, though according to *Sporting Life* none ever would because she was "very homely."

THE ORIGINAL AMAZING METS

“ *There never was a team who lushed more beer, won a champi- onship and had fewer properties to do it with than the Mets. Why, we started the season with two bats—a long stick and a short stick—and every duffer could take his choice.* ”

—Jack Lynch

I N DECEMBER 1881, AFTER DETROIT FILCHED a player who was already under contract to the Philadel- phia Athletics, Washington baseball promoter Mike Scanlon warned the Association that to survive against the National League, it would have to assume an aggres- sive posture from the outset. One of the tactical moves that Scanlon strongly urged was that Association teams sign play- ers who had been blacklisted for minor offenses like overimbibing and contract-jumping, regardless of the League's threat to ostra- cize its junior if it did so. When the Association waffled, first vowing to take on blackballed stars like Charley Jones, and then deferring the decision until the close of the 1882 season, Scanlon changed his mind about bringing a Washington team into the As- sociation in 1883. He allowed himself to be courted instead by Henry Lucas, the young scion of a Midwestern railroad baron who talked confidently of creating yet a third major league. After the National Agreement was adopted, imposing the reserve rule across the board in every professional league, Lucas had his polit- ical hook and in Scanlon he found one of his first converts.

Over the winter of 1883-84, Lucas, Scanlon and baseball figures from six other cities organized the Union Association on the premise that a player should be free to sell his services to the highest bidder and to change teams whenever his contract expired. Handed this brazen challenge to the National Agreement he had so painstakingly just fashioned, League president Abraham Mills angrily vowed to crush the upstart alliance before it could even get off the ground, but other League chieftains reacted more sagaciously. Though the League was menaced as much as the American Association by Lucas, Association owners were cleverly persuaded that they had more to lose to the Unioneers. To protect against a possible Lucas invasion into territories he regarded as the Association's domain, in November 1883 president Denny McKnight accepted bids for membership from teams representing Brooklyn, Indianapolis and Washington. The Brooklyn and Indianapolis teams were already intact. Brooklyn had even won the Inter-State League championship in 1883 and was backed by Charlie Byrne and Ferd Abell, two casino owners with plenty of capital. The Washington club had to be formed from scratch, however, which was never a good omen.

While the League stood pat with eight teams, McKnight found himself stuck for the moment with a bloated and unworkable 11-club circuit. To make it an even dozen, he entreated Felix Moses's club from Richmond, Virginia, but had to settle for Toledo. The 1883 Northwestern League champ, Toledo would prove to be the best of the four expansion teams on the field and the weakest at the gate, substantiating McKnight's fear that the city was too small to support major league ball. Of the eight National League teams in 1884, only Providence, with around 104,000, had fewer than 150,000 people. The Association, in dire contrast, now had two clubs, Toledo (50,000) and Columbus (51,000), that were under the League's population barrier of 75,000 and a third, Indianapolis, that barely attained the League's minimum figure.

The Association teams blessed with the largest population base were, of course, the Metropolitans and the Brooklyn Grays. In 1884 New York had some 1,206,000 and Brooklyn, then a separate city, had 566,000, swelling the total for the New York area to around a million and three-quarters, roughly double the size of Philadelphia and more than triple the population of Boston and Chicago, the next two largest cities. Still the Grays had to get special dispensation from the Mets to join the Association since they played at Washington Park, within five miles of the Mets' home ground and a violation of the new National Agreement, which required that two cities in the same league be at least 10 miles apart. *Sporting Life* approved of the new Brooklyn entry and

Richmond native Billy Nash went unnoticed when he made his major league debut with his hometown team on August 5, 1884, in Virginia's first game in the AA—a 14–0 blasting at the hands of the Athletics. Everyone was agog over Virginia's brother battery of Ed and Pete Dugan, the first sibling battery in AA history. Nash, however, proved to be by far the best player the Richmond-based club developed. Some rate him the top third baseman in the last century.

advised the Association to take on only Indianapolis to balance its geographical composition and form, at the largest, a 10-team loop. Twelve teams, the Philadelphia paper said, would be "a mistake, and the number will entail largely increasing travel expenses and give fewer games at home, where all the money must be made under the guarantee system. . . . As the clubs now stand they are pretty evenly matched. With increased membership would come a larger proportion of weaker clubs with no drawing power."

By July 1884, McKnight had long since begun wishing he had heeded *Sporting Life's* prophecy. No major league season was ever more lopsided than the 1884 Association campaign. But the chief beneficiary, rather than being Cincinnati or Philadelphia, the two Association flag winners to date—or even St. Louis or Louisville, contenders in both 1882 and 1883—turned out to be the New York Mets. Under the aegis of the Metropolitan Exhibition Company, which also owned the League New York Gothams, the Mets were treated by club president John Day as a kind of afterthought. Convinced the League would outlive the Association, Day persuaded the dual ownership to run the Mets on a shoestring. So bereft of equipment was the team that its players took to swiping bats from rival clubs when they emptied their bat bags on the playing field. Cincinnati, a particularly well-endowed team, was the Mets' pet victim. Known pejoratively in New York as the "Porkapolitans," and by this time called simply the Reds in the Queen City, Cincinnati had first earned the Mets' enmity by outbidding the New York club for Long John Reilly. The envy and loathing of the Reds was quickly manifested when play began. In 1883 the Mets won 10 of the 14 meetings between the two teams,

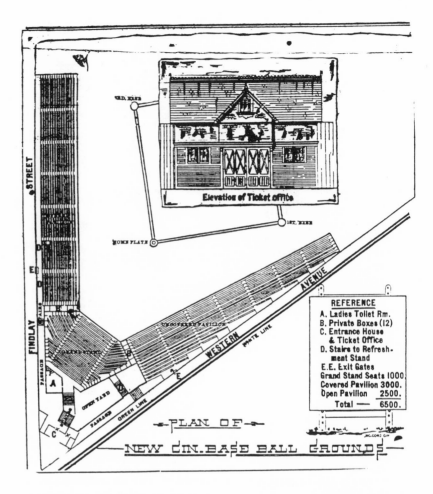

... A drawing of the Cincinnati Reds' new park in 1884. After making Bank Street Grounds their home in 1882–83, the Reds experienced a rude jolt when Justus Thorner and John McLean of the Cincinnati Unions snatched their park, hoping to drive them out of the AA by leaving them with no place to play. A mad scramble turned up an alternate site at the junction of Western Avenue and Findlay Street, and there was then a furious rush to build the new "American Park" before the season started. On Opening Day in 1884, a section of the hastily assembled rightfield bleachers collapsed as fans were filing out after the game, injuring scores and resulting in a spate of lawsuits. The Reds nevertheless remained at the site until 1970.

contributing more than any other single factor to Cincinnati's failure to repeat as Association champion.

For the 1884 season, Day consigned the Mets to play at Metropolitan Park, a small and windy facility on the East River that was known by New Yorkers as "The Dump" because it resided on the site of an old city dump on 108th Street. Team wag Jack Lynch, after playing a couple of games there, deemed it a place where you could "go down for a grounder and come up with six months of malaria." Moreover, the site was so near a wall of factories on the other side of the river that the winds constantly wafted noxious fumes into the park and made it all but lethal for fans, of which there were precious few. In late May, *Sporting Life* noticed that "the New Yorkers are drawing much better to 50 cents than the Metropolitans are at 25 cents when both teams are playing in the city at the same time. It is a characteristic of New Yorkers that they must have the best even if it comes high."

Two months later, however, Day moved the Mets to the Polo

The 19th-century counterpart to Earl Weaver was Jim Mutrie, a banjo-hitting middle infielder who never made the majors but became a top-notch big-league manager. A great PR man, Mutrie was instrumental in arranging the 1884 World's Series. The following year he nicknamed his New York NL team the "Giants."

Tim Keefe, one of only two Hall of Famers who were selected solely for their playing accomplishments after spending as many as two full seasons in the AA (Tommy McCarthy is the other). In 1883, "Sir Timothy" destroyed Cincinnati, bagging nine wins in 11 tries, and he was only slightly less spectacular the following year.

Grounds Southeast Diamond and used The Dump only when there was a schedule conflict with the League team, for whom the Polo Grounds had been built. By then Day had fathomed that the Mets were a serious contender, whereas his Gothams had the smell of also-rans. Back in the spring, though, not even Mutrie, the most upbeat manager in the Association, thought much of his team. His spirits ebbed still more when the Mets dropped their season opener on May 1 to perennial cellar-dweller Baltimore, 5–3, and then lost again the following day. After rescuing the last game of the Baltimore series, the Mets then reeled off five quick wins to rank second to St. Louis, which had roared to a 6–0 start. The sharp turnaround followed a lineup adjustment Mutrie made on May 5 when he replaced Gracie Pierce at second base with Dasher Troy, a member of the New York League club Day had shifted to the Mets when he hit a docile .215 in 1883. Troy was no world-beater, but he was an improvement on the ubiquitous Pierce, who was playing for his fifth team in three seasons. Furthermore, Troy's annexation was the last lineup change the Mets would make all season. As in 1883, until the final game of the year Keefe and Lynch pitched every single inning, and except for four games centerfielder Chief Roseman missed in late July, the Mets lineup card from May 5 to the close of the season almost unvaryingly read, in order batted: Candy Nelson SS, Steve Brady RF, Dude Esterbrook 3B, Roseman CF, Dave Orr 1B, Bill Holbert or Charlie Reipschlager C, Ed Kennedy LF, Keefe or Lynch P.

It should not, by all the laws of probability, have been a formidable team. In 1884, Kennedy hit .190 and collected just 85 total bases in 103 games. Holbert finished his major league career in 1888 as the only player to come to the plate more than 2,000 times without ever hitting a home run. The dapper and suave Esterbrook was the Mets' most revered player in 1884, but the remaining seventeen years of his life were a downward spiral to the moment when he jumped to his death from a moving train that was carting him off to a mental hospital. At one time Reipschlager was thought to have been born in 1855 under the nearly as cumbrous surname of Strothkamp, but today not a single morsel of biographical information is known about him. Nelson, although he began playing major league ball in 1872, never had much success at it until he joined the Association with the Mets in 1883. The record books list him as having been born in 1854, but like many of the Mets, he was coy about providing genuine biographical data. In 1890, when he was arrested in Rochester for playing on Sunday as a member of the Brooklyn Gladiators, Nelson gave his age as forty-one, which would move his year of birth back to 1849. About first baseman Dave Orr much is known, but little is under-

Dave Orr, anointed the 1884 AA bat king in 1969. Although he probably never beat out an infield hit in his life, Orr posted a mammoth .342 career batting average. By today's scoring rules, it would have been even higher because many of Orr's rockets that handcuffed infielders were deemed errors as per the custom of his day that charged a fielder with a bobble almost every time he got a hand on the ball.

Luckily for us, in 1883 the *New York Clipper* ran this drawing of Charlie Reipschlager. It's just about all we have now of the Mets backup catcher in 1884. Though a popular player in his day, Reipschlager left nary a trace of his past nor any hint of his future when he packed away his mitt and bat in 1890 for the last time as a major leaguer, after he was cut by the Brooklyn Gladiators.

stood. At the close of the 1884 season, he was ranked third in the Association in batting, behind Harry Stovey and Esterbrook, and there is no indication that he ever disputed his show-position rating. But a century later it emerged that he was the real batting leader that year. Orr was a maze of paradoxical achievements. He set a single-season Association record for triples when he collected 31 three-baggers in 1886, not because he was fast at traveling the bases but because he was so impossibly *slow*. Almost all of Orr's triples would have been inside-the-park home runs if he had not been toting far too much weight.

Roseman was another who did not attach much importance to looking like a ballplayer. In 1890 the portly outfielder was released by the Browns late in the season even though he was hitting .341. Mutrie himself was something of a paradox. Articulate, genteel and jaw-droppingly handsome, he was universally thought to be one of the most astute and best-liked managers of his time but was fired mysteriously by the New York Giants in 1891, never to work in the major leagues again and doomed to spend the rest of his life fending off poverty. For that matter, even John Day's life was shadowed by ironical twists. Finessed out of the Giants' ownership in 1891, he was hired eight years later, partly out of pity, for a short stint as the team's field manager and ended his days in a bleak Bowery tenement so weak and inchoate that he was unable to attend to his wife, who lay dying in an adjoining bed.

Only Tim Keefe was without an unlit corner. One of the very few players who were selected for the Hall of Fame after spending a significant portion of their careers in the Association, Keefe joined with Lynch in 1884 to make the Mets the first team to have two 30-game winners. Between them, the pair logged 74 victories, just 22 more than Guy Hecker collected all by himself for Louisville, but the Eclipse searched without success all season for a reliable second pitcher, and this failure probably cost the Falls City club the pennant.

Following the action on July 3, Louisville held first place with a 28–13 record, followed closely by St. Louis, the Mets, Cincinnati, Columbus and a vastly refurbished Baltimore team, in that order. The top half of the Association standings was so densely packed that the sixth place Orioles were only two games out of first and even the Athletics, languishing for the moment in seventh place, were still in contention. Below the A's, however, lay a disaster area. Toledo and Brooklyn were sporadically competitive, but the three bottom clubs—Indianapolis, Pittsburgh and Washington—were simply awful. With its .200 team batting average, Washington eventually just gave up, surrendering its spot in the Association to Moses's Virginia club on the first Sunday in

August, and the situation in Pittsburgh turned so foul that, to save money at the start of the season, McKnight tried his hand at managing the club himself rather than pay someone else to lose virtually every day. For a couple of weeks the Alleghenys actually played half decently for McKnight before he was coaxed into handing the reins to Bob Ferguson and then, when the players hated the tactless Ferguson, to third sacker Joe Battin. Eventually, Horace Phillips was summoned back to the Smoke City to run the club on the field after a stopover in Peoria, where he had fled after being fired by Columbus for fiddling the Buckeyes' books and for skipping out on the team's hotel bills in several other Association cities.

Phillips's replacement at the Columbus helm was Gustavus Heinrich Schmelz, a resident of the Ohio capital whose only other ostensible credential for the job was his flaming red beard, which gave him a rather fierce look. Since Schmelz had to suffer along with almost the same team that had finished a weak sixth in 1883, all the sharps expected the Buckeyes to crumble by the 4th of July. But Schmelz's one new addition of consequence was rookie Ed "Cannonball" Morris, the first truly outstanding southpaw pitcher in major league history. In 1884, while another rookie hurler, Larry McKeon of Indianapolis, was setting an Association frosh record for losses with 41, Morris combined with Frank Mountain to win two out of every three games the duo pitched. On July 22, the Morris-Mountain tandem propelled the Buckeyes all the way to first place, percentage points ahead of the Mets, which had grabbed the top rung earlier in the month.

If the Mets were looked upon as unfashionable by New Yorkers, the Buckeyes were all the go in central Ohio. The club played in Recreation Park on Parsons Avenue on the far east end of town, at the end of a trolley line run by the company that also owned a chunk of the team. Some thirteen minutes from the Statehouse, the park was reached by special cars that flew "Game Today" banners. Action in Recreation Park commenced at 4:15, prefaced by a first gong at 4:10; a second announced the opening pitch. In their spiffy pearl and blue uniforms, the Buckeyes first served notice that they might be more than a sartorial attraction when Morris and Mountain both hurled no-hitters a week apart, scarcely a month into the season. A few days later the team had to cancel its Sunday playing dates, by far the most lucrative, when the local police burst into the ball ground one Sabbath to break up a game with Brooklyn and then delayed hauling all the players on both teams off to the courthouse until they had stayed and watch the Buckeyes beat the Grays. After a week of legal wrangling, Columbus agreed to cease playing on Sunday. Indianapolis faced a similar impasse as Sabbatarians throughout the Midwest wielded their saintly cudgels. In the Ohio capital the war against Sunday ball was spearheaded by Raymond Burr, the assistant postmaster of Columbus. Burr's influence eventually worked to kill the Ohio team financially, but for the moment the hassle curiously seemed to trigger Schmelz's men to go on a tear. Over the next seven weeks the Buckeyes won 31 of 36 games, causing swarms of locals to ring the front window of the *Columbus Dispatch* office, where the paper posted inning-by-inning scores of away games.

With telegraph systems now operating in all major cities, running scores of other games of interest could be followed by spectators on "bulletin boards" in every Association park where telephone connections had been made to telegraph headquarters. The 1884 season was probably the first in which scoreboard-watching became a vital part of the national pastime, as the six-team fight for the Association flag seemed likely to go down to the wire. But for a tinge of complacency, and the gaping void George Bradley left in their pitching corps when he ran off to the Union Association after a nasty salary dispute, the A's would have made it a seven-team dog-fight. In an effort to bring discipline to the clubhouse, Bill Sharsig grabbed the reins halfway into the season. Sharsig abducted ex-Pittsburgh problem child Billy Taylor from the St. Louis Maroons to bolster his pitching, but the move was undercut when another Union team, the Chicago Browns, swiped rookie A's hurler Al Atkinson. The A's ended the season seventh in the 12-team loop but with a .570 winning percentage that fell just a single point short of the 1890 Boston Beaneaters' record high for a second-division team.

One step above the A's when the curtain fell was Baltimore. The Orioles' surprisingly strong showing entrenched Billy Barnie. For the rest of the decade, though his teams never again would match the .594 winning percentage of his 1884 club, he was canonized in Baltimore. As responsible as Barnie for the Orioles' sudden renascence was the acquisition of Joe Sommer and Jimmy Macullar from Cincinnati. The pair, after leading an unsuccessful cabal to drive Chick Fulmer and Pop Corkhill off the Reds, were encouraged to look elsewhere for jobs when Cincinnati reorganized after a disheartening third-place finish in 1883. Even though Caylor was still the principal decision-maker, a cadre composed of Aaron Stern, George Herancourt and Louis Kramer now owned most of the club's stock, and the field general's role passed from Pop Snyder to Will White. A new rule that gave a batter his base if he was hit by a pitch, other rule changes that paved the way for overhand pitching and age all hampered White the player in 1884, and the loss of Sommer and Macullar limited

· · ·

Bob Emslie had a full head of hair when he won 32 games for Baltimore in 1884, but he began to go bald after he slipped to just three wins in 1885. His sudden hair loss was laid to fragile nerves, but one might question that diagnosis. The Canadian-born Emslie later donned a rug and umpired in the NL for some 34 years, most of them during an era that Tim Murnane claimed would have tested even the nerves of a hangman.

THE BEER AND WHISKY LEAGUE

his mobility as a manager. In Sommer's stead the Reds landed Tom Mansell by offering $400 more than Von der Ahe cared to pay him to stay with the Browns, and Macullar, a lefty whose best position was shortstop, seemed superfluous with Chick Fulmer on hand. But the 1884 season was scarcely a month old when Cincinnati began shopping Mansell to other Association teams, ideally in exchange for a shortstop, for Fulmer, who had considered retiring anyway, was shot as a hitter and had slowed badly in the field. In July the Reds resolved the dilemma by releasing Fulmer and then, later in the month, purchasing rookie star Frank Fennelly when the Washington club held a fire sale of its players before it sank.

Mansell's release by Cincinnati soon thereafter vindicated Von der Ahe in his judgment to use the money that Mansell had tried to wheedle out of him to buy new talent. Prior to the season, the Browns acquired Tip O'Neill, a gifted but wildly inconsistent pitcher the New York Gothams had despaired of making into a winner. Though O'Neill continued to show flashes of brilliance in the box, Jimmy Williams, who had left his secretarial post with the Association to become the Browns new manager, liked him better as a hitter and converted him into an outfielder. To shore up their pitching, the Browns then purchased Dave Foutz and Bob Caruthers from Bay City and Minneapolis, respectively, in the Northwestern League. The pair teamed for 22 wins and just eight losses in the closing weeks of the season but could not save Williams from the same obstacles that had finally stymied Ted Sullivan. In May, during the Browns' first visit to Toledo, Pat Deasley was given a working over by Tom Dolan and Joe Quest outside the Boody House hotel one night. Deasley contended the two were trying to run him off the team because they were jealous of his club-high $2,500 salary. Wherever the truth lay in the Deasley situation, Williams was certain of his reasons when he resigned as manager in early September after his top hitter, centerfielder Fred Lewis, went on a toot. Before leaving town, Williams let it be known that he "would rather tackle a hundred angry water works customers than a solitary St. Louis base baller—especially when the slugger is drunk and in possession of the idea that it is his solemn duty to slug the manager of the nine." Once again, Von der Ahe called on first baseman Charlie Comiskey to finish out the year at the helm, and then decided to give him the job permanently when the Browns rallied to edge out Cincinnati for fourth place.

In the third spot, just a game out of second, came Louisville under new ownership as Will Jackson succeeded Pank as club president. Below Jackson, though, the chain of command grew

In June, 1884, Guy Hecker's wife won a domino tournament in Oil City, PA. That month Hecker was in Louisville, embarked on winning an AA record 52 games despite taking almost no spring training. "The Big Blond" contended that a few days in the gym and a couple of tune-up games just before the season started were all he needed. His success as a pitcher pretty well ended in 1887, when a new rule limited hurlers to one forward step and thereby eliminated his patented running start. Another rule that year—ending a batter's right to call for either a high or a low pitch—similarly impaired Hecker's prowess at the plate.

cloudy, a problem that would plague the franchise until 1899 when Louisville finally left the major league scene. Current record books maintain that Mike Walsh, previously an Association umpire, ran the club on the field, but in 1884 the players all looked on second baseman Joe Gerhardt as their general. Gerhardt had the Association's best fielding club, its top pitcher in Hecker and the redoubtable Pete Browning. In 1884, Browning added several new chapters to his swiftly growing legend when, in early May, he saved a young Louisville boy from being crushed to death by yanking him from beneath the wheels of a streetcar where he had been knocked by a team of pulling horses. A few days later Browning, who lived to hit, asked Bud Hillerich, the twenty-one-year-old son of a local craftsman whose business was making wooden farm implements, to sculpt two more bats for his collection, which already numbered several dozen. From that casual request sprang a permanent business arrangement between Browning and young Hillerich that fathered Hillerich & Bradsby, manufacturers for over a century now of Louisville Slugger bats. On the field, though, Browning had something of an off year, as he hit just .330 and lost his third-base niche because of his peculiar habits of deferring all pop flies to his teammates whether or not he heard himself called off the ball, and of standing at third base, whenever a runner was on second, like a stork on one leg with the other pointed warily toward the runner. The move from the infield to the outfield, where Browning could be kept more easily out of harm's way, was mandated when surgery on May 12 failed to stem an ever-increasing hearing loss that left him totally deaf in one ear and with only partial function in the other. Not until years later would it emerge that many of Browning's eccentricities were a defense against his impaired hearing, which was a result of chronic mastoiditis, an inflammation that in his time was often fatal because of the proximity of the mastoid bone to the brain.

A late-season slump, which included three costly losses to lowly Virginia, sentenced the Columbus Buckeyes to second place —still a commendable achievement. Another team that had trouble with the Richmond-based team, though of a different nature, was Toledo. The Blue Stockings retained many of the members of their 1883 Northwestern League club in 1884, among them catcher Moses Walker, the first African-American performer in major league history. Walker was a fine defensive receiver and worked well with all of Toledo's pitchers, even Tony Mullane, much as Mullane hated having his pitches called by a black man, but he was missing when the club played a late-season series in Richmond. Toledo manager Charlie Morton claimed to reporters that Walker was still troubled by a rib injury that had idled him earlier, and though Walker went along with the story, he later revealed that in truth he had avoided the Virginia park because of a written threat to kill him if he appeared on the field. Good enough to beat out fellow rookie Deacon McGuire for the Toledo catching job, Walker would never again perform in the majors, a victim of the unwritten color barrier that was first imposed by moguls in 1885 and lasted sixty-two years. Though he played second fiddle to Walker, McGuire would not play his last major league game until twenty-eight years later, in 1912.

After wrapping up the pennant with a 4–1 win against Columbus on October 1, the Mets cruised through the final two weeks of the season while Mutrie and Ned Allen, managing director of the Providence Grays, haggled over the terms under which the first "World's Series" that was sanctioned by both leagues would be played.* Mutrie had originally challenged the Grays back in August to play an exhibition game, but the Grays had declined. When fans and sportswriters in both cities began

* *Throughout their duration the NL vs. AA postseason matches in the last century were called a World's Series with an "s."*

• • •

The J.F. Hillerich Company's staff in the late 1880s. Founder J.F. Hillerich is second from left. His son John A. "Bud" Hillerich stands, bat in hand, in the doorway. In the spring of 1884, Bud brought his pal, Pete Browning, into the shop for a look around, and soon the place was making bats rather than wagon tongues and butter churns.

The 1884 Toledo Blue Stockings pose at Tri-State Fair-
grounds. Standing (left to right):
Frank Olin, Chappy Lane, Curt
Welch, Sam Barkley, Tony
Mullane, Hank O'Day, George
Meister (whose 1884 stats for
years were erroneously credit-
ed to John Meister) and Tom
Poorman. Seated (left to right):
Joe Miller, manager Charlie
Morton, Deacon McGuire and
Tug Arundel. Conspicuously
absent are the Walker brothers.
The Blue Stockings used the
fairground park—where the
ball field was in the center of
a horse racetrack—for only
one championship game, on
September 13.

clamoring for the two champions to meet, however, Allen finally
relented, but not before the wrangling had set a pattern for all future postseason encounters between the Association and the
League. For the next six years, although a World's Series was held
at the end of every season, it was never a fixture on the sporting
scene and no rules or systems governed its presentation. Rather, it
was arranged each autumn by the owners of the two pennant-winning teams, and all details such as the number of games, where
they would be played and how the gate receipts would be divided
were subject entirely to their whims and financial considerations.
In mid-October 1884, Providence and the Mets each finally
agreed to put up a $1,000 purse, which was held by the *New York
Clipper*. Even though the best two-of-three affair was played by
Association rules and was scheduled to take place in New York on
the supposition that more money would be made there than in
Providence, the Grays were heavily favored to capture the prize.
On this occasion the oddsmakers were right.

With Honest John Kelly serving as the umpire, Providence,
behind 60-game winner Hoss Radbourn, took the opening game
on October 23 by tallying two runs in the first inning and then
coasting to a 6–0 win. The following afternoon, Radbourn, sup-

The 1881 Oberlin College team, featuring the Walker brothers, Moses (6) and Welday (10). Sons of an Ohio doctor who was born into slavery, the Walkers were the only confirmed African Americans to play in the majors prior to 1947. In 1884, Welday appeared in just a handful of games for Toledo, but Moses was the genuine article. An excellent defensive catcher who belonged in top company, he knew what had been denied him when both major leagues imposed an unwritten color ban in 1885.

ported by Jerry Denny's two-run homer, again prevailed 3–1 in cold dank conditions that helped to halt the battle after the Grays had pushed across two runs in the top of the eighth inning, seemingly cinching the win. Because umpire Jack Remsen called the game, though, before the inning was done, the score reverted to 3–1, the tally at the end of the seventh and last completed inning.

Though Providence had already clinched the Series, the third game was played anyway on October 25. In front of less than 300 witnesses at the Polo Grounds, Radbourn tossed his third straight complete-game victory. The contest meant so little that Mutrie put Buck Becannon in the box and Tom Forster at second base. Forster was playing his first game ever for the Mets after finishing the season with Pittsburgh, and Becannon had worked in only one previous game, a 13–2 win over Indianapolis in the season finale on October 15. Still, the meager crowd expected a run for its money and came away disgruntled when the Mets "played like children" in one reporter's eyes and action was halted after just six innings with Providence up, 11–2.

So thoroughly dominant had the League been in the first meaningful on-the-field rendezvous between the two rivals that the Association's claim of parity now seemed laughable. Away from the field, the League had all the more reason to gloat. In October, even as the Association's best team was being blasted in the World's Series, Columbus, its second-best team, declared bankruptcy and was absorbed by Pittsburgh. The ease with which the Ohio franchise turned over all its players to the Alleghenys deepened the suspicion that the two clubs may have been under a common ownership all along. But even if true, there was no policy against it at the time. In the years ahead, both the League and the Association would look the other way more and more as executives with deep pockets purchased stock in several different clubs. Brooklyn owner Charlie Byrne took advantage of this sort of loophole prior to the 1885 season, when the Cleveland League club prepared to fold after Union Association raiders left its ranks too depleted to continue. Byrne snaffled up Cleveland's few remaining assets so he could bring seven of its players to Brooklyn, after hiding them in a hotel for the requisite ten-day waiting period before an inter-team transfer could occur. It was the sort of quasi-legal move he would repeat again and again in a frantic effort to build a winning club.

At the Association winter meeting in December 1884, Byrne took an unexpectedly prominent role, leading the fight for a new division of gate receipts. The Brooklyn owner argued that the current system was unfair because the schedule was drawn up so that western clubs could play at home on Sunday, while eastern clubs, for the most part based in sectors where Sunday ball was illegal, often had to sit idle for days at a time in western cities, piling up road expenses in wait for a Sunday date. When Byrne proposed giving visiting teams 25 percent of the gate, he was voted down, however, as the other owners preferred to stay with a guarantee of $65 per game. Byrne also lost a motion to have the guarantee doubled for Sunday games and, finally, he was defeated in a bid to unseat McKnight as Association president. But Byrne's voice registered nonetheless. The meeting ended with only Brooklyn retained for the 1885 season of the four new clubs that had been added in 1884. Toledo, a big financial loser, meekly gave up its slot, but both Virginia and Indianapolis fought hard against being ousted. In an angry letter to *Sporting Life*, the Indianapolis directors asserted, with some justification, that the Association was secretly run by "the big three" of Caylor, Von der Ahe and Lew Simmons of Philadelphia, who cared only about their own selfish interests.

With Indianapolis, Toledo and Virginia gone, most of their players became, in effect, free agents. Cincinnati eventually gar-

• • •
Hank O'Day. He and Tony Mullane combined for all of Toledo's 46 victories in 1884 (albeit he won only nine of them). Though O'Day was caught by both Moses Walker and Connie Mack, he is best remembered not as a pitcher, but as the umpire in the famous 1908 Cubs-Giants game who called Fred Merkle out for failing to touch second base.

John "Patsy" Cahill, the California League star who was believed by some students of the period to have been Ernest Thayer's model when he wrote "Casey at the Bat" for a San Francisco newspaper. Cahill's major league slugging credentials are slim. A broken ankle in 1884 cut short his rookie season with Columbus. The following year he led the Southern League in homers but then was a dud with the St. Louis Maroons in 1886. Perhaps the strongest evidence that he might have been Casey is a long piece in the December 26, 1891, issue of *The Sporting News*, written as if the speaker were Cahill's bat.

nered the Hoosiers' luckless rookie hurler, Larry McKeon, along with Tony Mullane, who had registered 36 of Toledo's 46 wins in 1884. Before the Reds could utilize Mullane, though, they had to wait a full year after the Association voted to suspend him for the entire 1885 season as punishment for his whirlwind contract jumping that landed him with his fourth different Association team in four seasons. The decision enraged Caylor and set off a chain of events that would eventually turn him against his own brainchild. Mullane's absence in 1885 meanwhile helped Von der Ahe, another member of the so-called big three who heretofore had been a disappointment both to himself and the city his team represented, to seize the Association throne when he plucked two of Mullane's Toledo teammates, Sam Barkley, a nimble second baseman, and centerfielder Curt Welch.

1884 FINAL STANDINGS

	W	L	PCT	HOME	ROAD	GB
1. New York Metropolitans	75	32	.701	42–9	33–23	
2. Columbus Buckeyes	69	39	.639	36–16	31–23	6.5
3. Louisville Eclipse	68	40	.630	41–14	27–26	7.5
4. St. Louis Browns	67	40	.626	38–15	29–25	8
5. Cincinnati Reds	68	41	.624	40–16	28–25	8
6. Baltimore Orioles	63	43	.594	42–13	21–30	11.5
7. Philadelphia Athletics	61	46	.570	38–16	23–30	14
8. Toledo Blue Stockings	46	58	.442	28–25	18–33	27.5
9. Brooklyn Grays	40	64	.385	23–26	17–38	33.5
10. Virginia	12	30	.286	5–15	7–15	30
11. Pittsburgh Alleghenys	30	78	.278	18–37	12–41	45.5
12. Indianapolis Hoosiers	29	78	.271	16–39	13–39	46
13. Washington Statesmen	12	51	.190	10–20	2–31	41

In this dazzling card of the 1892 Brooklyn Bridegrooms, only Adonis Terry remains from the Brooklyn club that joined the AA in 1884. Though never a great pitcher, Terry outlasted many changes in pitching rules to forge a solid 14-year career. He is the only hurler to win 20 games in a major league that still outlawed overhand pitching (the AA in 1884) and again at the 60'6" distance (in 1895 with Chicago).

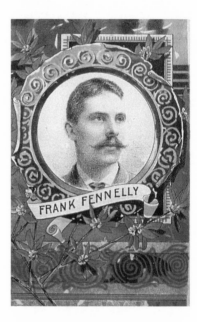

FRANK FENNELLY

• • •

The 1884 Washington Statesmen had only two regulars who hit above .217—shortstop Frank Fennelly (seen here on a Cincinnati scorecard) and second baseman Thorny Hawkes. A latecomer to the team, Frank Olin, hit .386 in a handful of games before the franchise folded and he went to Toledo. Olin later became a wealthy industrialist, and Fennelly a noted New England politician. Without them, the Statesmen would have had a munificent .179 team batting average.

1884 SEASON LEADERS*

BATTING

BATTING AVERAGE (300 ABs)

1. Orr, NY	.354
2. Reilly, Cinci	.339
3. Browning, Louis	.336
4. Stovey, Phila	.326
5. Lewis, StL	.323
6. Esterbrook, NY	.314
C. Jones, Cinci	.314
8. Fennelly, Wash-Cinci	.311
9. Barkley, Tol	.306
10. Wolf, Louis	.300

SLUGGING AVERAGE

1. Reilly, Cinci	.551
2. Stovey, Phila	.545
3. Orr, NY	.539
4. Fennelly, Wash-Cinci	.480
5. Browning, Louis	.472
6. C. Jones, Cinci	.470
7. Mann, Colum	.464
8. Barkley, Tol	.444
9. Hecker, Louis	.430
10. Esterbrook, NY	.428

ON-BASE PERCENTAGE

1. C. Jones, Cinci	.376
2. Nelson, NY	.375
3. Stovey, Phila	.368
4. Fennelly, Wash-Cinci	.367
5. Reilly, Cinci	.366
Lewis, StL	.366
7. Swartwood, Pitts	.365
8. Orr, NY	.362
9. Browning, Louis	.357
10. Esterbrook, NY	.345

TOTAL BASES

1. Reilly, Cinci	247
Orr, NY	247
3. Stovey, Phila	244
4. C. Jones, Cinci	222
5. Browning, Louis	211
6. Esterbrook, NY	204
7. Wolf, Louis	201
8. Barkley, Tol	193
9. Houck, Phila	187
10. Corey, Phila	185

*Stolen Base and RBI leaders unavailable.

HOME RUNS		RUNS		HITS	
1. Reilly, Cinci	11	1. Stovey, Phila	124	1. Orr, NY	162
2. Stovey, Phila	10	2. C. Jones, Cinci	117	2. Reilly, Cinci	152
3. Orr, NY	9	3. A. Latham, StL	115	3. Browning, Louis	150
4. Mann, Colum	7	4. Nelson, NY	114	Esterbrook, NY	150
C. Jones, Cinci	7	Reilly, Cinci	114	5. Jones, Cinci	148
6. Kerins, Ind	6	6. Esterbrook, NY	110	6. Wolf, Louis	146
F. Carroll, Colum	6	7. McPhee, Cinci	107	7. Houck, Phila	140
P. Smith, Colum	6	8. Brady, NY	102	8. Barkley, Tol	133
O. Burns, Balt	6	9. Browning, Louis	101	9. A. Latham, StL	130
10. Four with five		10. B. Gleason, StL	97	Roseman, NY	130
		Roseman, NY	97		

PITCHING

WINS		LOSSES		INNINGS	
1. Hecker, Louis	52	1. McKeon, Ind	41	1. Hecker, Louis	670.2
2. Lynch, NY	37	2. Sullivan, Pitts	35	2. Mullane, Tol	576
Keefe, NY	37	Terry, Brook	35	3. McKeon, Ind	512
Mullane, Tol	37	4. Barr, Wash-Ind	34	4. Keefe, NY	491.2
5. Morris, Colum	34	5. O'Day, Tol	28	5. Lynch, NY	487
White, Cinci	34	6. Mullane, Tol	26	6. Terry, Brook	485
7. Emslie, Balt	32	Neagle, Pitts	26	7. White, Cinci	456
8. Mathews, Phila	30	8. Henderson, Balt	23	8. Emslie, Balt	455
9. Henderson, Balt	27	9. Hecker, Louis	20	9. Sullivan, Pitts	441
10. McGinnis, StL	24	Kimber, Brook	20	10. Henderson, Balt	439

COMPLETE GAMES		STRIKEOUTS		WINNING PCT. (20 DECISIONS)	
1. Hecker, Louis	72	1. Hecker, Louis	385	1. Morris, Colum	.723
2. Mullane, Tol	65	2. Henderson, Balt	346	2. Hecker, Louis	.722
3. McKeon, Ind	59	3. Mullane, Tol	334	3. Foutz, StL	.714
4. Keefe, NY	57	4. Keefe, NY	323	4. Lynch, NY	.712
5. Terry, Brook	55	5. McKeon, Ind	308	5. Keefe, NY	.685
6. Lynch, NY	53	6. Morris, Colum	302	6. White, Cinci	.654
7. White, Cinci	52	7. Mathews, Phila	286	7. Emslie, Balt	.653
8. Sullivan, Pitts	51	Lynch, NY	286	8. Mathews, Phila	.625
9. Emslie, Balt	50	9. Emslie, Balt	264	9. Mountjoy, Cinci	.613
Henderson, Balt	50	10. Terry, Brook	233	10. Taylor, Phila	.600

ERA (110 INNINGS)		LOWEST ON-BASE PCT.	
1. Hecker, Louis	1.80	1. Hecker, Louis	.221
2. Foutz, StL	2.18	2. Morris, Colum	.227
Morris, Colum	2.18	3. Lynch, NY	.233
4. Keefe, NY	2.29	4. Keefe, NY	.236
5. Mountain, Colum	2.45	5. Foutz, StL	.243
6. Mullane, Tol	2.48	6. Mullane, Tol	.249
7. Taylor, Phila	2.53	7. Mountain, Colum	.250
8. Henderson, Balt	2.62	8. McGinnis, StL	.252
9. Lynch, NY	2.64	9. Mathews, Phila	.255
10. O'Neill, StL	2.68	10. P. Reccius, Louis	.257

FOUR

• • •

Here again is Gus Schmelz, at the helm of the 1886 St. Louis Maroons (a.k.a. "Black Diamonds"). Still around from the 1884 Union Association juggernaut are Fred Dunlap (8), Charlie Sweeney (5), Henry Boyle (1) and Joe Quinn (3), plus Jack Glasscock (13) of the Outlaw Reds and Emmett Seery (9) of the Baltimore Unions. In 1885, Sweeney and Seery had a vicious fight, with everyone siding with Seery, against the man *Sporting Life* called "the whisky-guzzling cowardly nincompoop." By 1886 the nincompoop, a 41-game winner just two years earlier, could buy just five wins.

THE UNION ASSOCIATION: SAINT LUCAS

IN 1876, THE YEAR THAT WILLIAM HULBERT ORganized the National League, his Chicago White Stockings won the first pennant. Likewise, when Opie Caylor orchestrated the birth of the American Association in 1882, his Cincinnati Red Stockings claimed the first Association title. In neither case was it coincidence. Both Hulbert and Caylor already had many of the components of a successful team in place and needed only a league in which to operate. But Hulbert wisely resisted a movement to make him the first president of his creation, preferring to let the honor fall to Morgan Bulkeley, president of the Hartford club, and Caylor initially stayed in the background altogether. It was as if each man understood that sometimes the best way to achieve power is to let others think they have foisted it upon you almost against your will. Henry Lucas never learned that lesson. When Lucas launched the Union Association as a third major league in 1884, he ran the whole show, hungry to get all the credit. Even more damaging to his invention, he stacked the deck so much in favor of his own team, the St. Louis Maroons, that the Union Association barely survived one season.

Yet, for that one year, Lucas's name eclipsed every other in baseball. Week upon week even his most trivial proclamations were headlined on the front pages of all leading sporting papers as the nation closely followed the progress of his bold challenge to the established order. Though publicly sneered at and derisively called "Saint Lucas" by baseball's inner circle, Lucas struck terror within it. The National League was in a panic that his vision of a player-controlled market would unravel its artfully woven reserve rule, and the American Association not only hastened to expand to 12 teams but created a satellite league of reserve squads to guard as many cities and players from Lucas as possible.

It was all in vain. By 1884, although the notion of making baseball a full-time profession was only some fifteen years old, a career as a player already held such an irresistible allure that thousands of young males throughout the country were eager to test their mettle with one of the 28 franchises that claimed major league stature. Not many of these men had apprenticed at any great length in the minor leagues, if only because there were few minor leagues in the early 1880s. There were also few scouts and a dearth of accurate statistical information. If a shortstop said he was twenty-two when he was really twenty-six, it was unlikely his lie would ever be uncovered. Pitchers who boasted they had invented reverse inshoots that won them 50 games one year in Nebraska could only be revealed as frauds by a team in Pennsylvania if they were tried out in a game or two. The Union Association was a fertile preserve for players with a talent for self-promotion and little else, but so, for that matter, were the National League and the American Association in 1884. A year later, when the market once again shrank to only 16 major league teams, most of the hucksters and mountebanks and sideshow performers were gone from the scene, but for that one season they were all on baseball's midway.

The Union Association was actually an amalgamation of an eastern bloc and a western bloc of baseball mavericks. The eastern bloc, which called itself the Union League and consisted of clubs from Richmond, Washington, Baltimore, Philadelphia, Reading, Boston and Brooklyn, was coaxed by Lucas to combine forces with his western alliance in November 1883. The twenty-six-year-old son of a wealthy St. Louis lawyer and banker who was one of the founders of the Missouri Pacific Railroad, Lucas had previously assuaged his baseball ambitions by spending his leisure hours managing and playing third base for a local amateur team of his own creation while serving as president of the Mound City Transportation Company. Lucas had been bitten by the baseball

· BOSTON UNIONS OF 1884 ·
STANDING — JIM McKEEVER, MIKE SLATTERY, TIM MURNANE, TOM O'BRIEN, JOHN IRWIN.
SITTING — WALTER HACKETT, CHAS. DANIELS, LEW BROWN, JACK DOYLE.
INSERT — FRANK BUTLER.

• • •
Alas, only two UA team pics survive, and both are in poor condition. To the right are the Boston Reds. Though patsies for the Cincinnati Outlaw Reds, the Bostons were the only nine to put up a decent fight against the mighty St. Louis Maroons, playing them dead even in 16 games. Frank Butler (inset) unsurprisingly was nicknamed "Kid." He was actually twenty-two, but also here is seventeen-year-old Mike Slattery, the youngest regular in major league history.

bug nearly a decade earlier when his older brother, John, helped organize the Brown Stockings, St. Louis's first major league team, and headed the club during its two seasons as a member of the National League in 1876-77. Though he was only an average player, Lucas fancied himself a masterful baseball organizer, and events bore out his opinion of himself. Despite having no experience in the professional baseball arena and the emotional support of only his wife's brother, Frederick Espenscheid, he was able to seize the Union Association throne with almost no opposition.

When Lucas's amalgam first met as one unit on December 18, 1883, at the Bingham House in Philadelphia, present were representatives from five clubs that were already firmly committed to the Union Association: the Chicago Browns; the Philadelphia Keystones; Baltimore; Mike Scanlon's Washington Nationals, a veteran semi-pro team that Scanlon sponsored with the profits from his pool hall, a popular hangout for senators and even, at times, presidents; and the St. Louis Maroons, headed by Lucas and Espenscheid. The most significant absentee was George Wright, who had retired as a player two years earlier to head the Wright & Ditson sporting goods company. Though he had told Lucas he would bankroll a Boston club in the Union Association, the famous shortstop was unwilling to stand revealed as a partner in the rebel league until he was certain it would fly. The five Union teams in the room voted to admit a Cincinnati group captained by

Justus Thorner and John McLean, publisher of the *Cincinnati Enquirer*, two former owners of the Red Stockings who were only awaiting the chance to avenge the manner in which they had been squeezed out of their stock in the Association club. Lucas was voted president, Thomas Pratt of Philadelphia vice president and Warren White of Washington was made secretary-treasurer. Wright's real reason for affiliating himself with Lucas was then bared when Lucas persuaded the others to designate the ball made by Wright & Ditson as the official Union ball and also to authorize Wright to do the loop's guidebook.

The addition of Cincinnati left Lucas still one team short of the eight needed to open the season. He tried to cajole Hartford into joining so the league would have an even balance of eastern and western teams, but the winter fled without any response from Connecticut. In desperation Lucas admitted the Mountain City team from Altoona as the eighth member on February 20, 1884, after turning down a bid from the Pennsylvania city earlier in the month. Lucas must have known that tiny Altoona would struggle to survive. He nevertheless dealt the Mountain Citys' owner and manager, Ed Curtis, a killer hand. When the Union Association season opened on April 17, Curtis's club was in Cincinnati for its first three games. From the Queen City, Altoona then journeyed to St. Louis to play four games against Lucas's powerful Maroons. Off to an 0–7 start and fading fast, the Mountain Citys returned to Altoona on April 30 for their home opener, only to find that their opponent again would be the Maroons. After playing eight of its first 11 games against Lucas's juggernaut, Altoona stood at 0–11. A 9–4 win against Boston on May 10 was too little too late. Six weeks into the season, after Altoona could win just six of its first 25 games, Lucas pulled the rug out from under the Pennsylvania franchise and shifted it to Kansas City.

History certainly makes it seem that Lucas cared more about his Maroons than he did about the fate of his league. There can be little doubt that he rigged the schedule so the Maroons would be virtually guaranteed to get off to a flying start by fattening up on Altoona. Helped by his shenanigans, the Maroons won their first 20 games to set a record for the most consecutive victories at the start of a season before finally bowing 8–1 on May 24 to Boston's Tommy Bond. The streak dispensed with all pretense of a pennant race in the Union Association by the end of May.

Lucas was not content, though, merely to build a winning team. He was out to create a monster. When the League and the Association made the mistake of looting his Maroons of two players in the early summer, he retaliated by shanghaiing Providence pitcher Charlie Sweeney, just days after Sweeney fanned a record

Former Outlaw Reds secretary Frank Wright belatedly admitted in 1887 that it had been a mistake in 1884 for his club to pilfer the AA ballpark in an attempt to freeze out the Cincinnati AA team. A wiser plan would have been to spend the money pilfering players. "But they didn't do it," lamented *Sporting Life*, "and it is only in this reminiscent way that the grave of the Union Association is kept green." Jack Glasscock (seated second from left, with the 1888 Indianapolis Hoosiers) was one player the Outlaw Reds sprang for. Part of Wright's "Cleveland coup," he became the club's shortstop in August after it had run through Frank McLaughlin and Angel Sleeves Jones. In 38 late-season UA games, Glasscock batted a classy .419.

19 Boston batters in a League game. Branded a felon in Rhode Island, Lucas defended himself by saying, "I don't take any pride in contract-breaking as a regular business, but it is a good thing to succeed when self-preservation forces you to engage in it. There is also great pleasure in going into the enemy's camp, capturing their guns and using them on your own side."

Once he felt secure that his Maroons had the pennant safely tucked away, Lucas encouraged Thorner and McLean to follow his lead. In early August, the pair raided the Cleveland League team of pitcher Jim McCormick, shortstop Jack Glasscock and catcher Fatty Briody. The threesome instantly cannonballed the Cincinnati Outlaw Reds—heretofore barely a .500 club—to the forefront of the seven Union teams chasing the Maroons. A fair case can even be made that by the end of the season the Outlaw Reds were the cream of the Union Association, especially after second baseman Sam Crane replaced centerfielder "Hustling" Dan O'Leary as manager. O'Leary was just an average player and no master strategist, yet he kept people wondering. Is the man ahead of his time or just a charlatan? But while they were decid-

1. Esterbrook.
2. Glasscock.
3. Buckley.
4. Myers.
5. Bassett.
6. Healy.
7. Daily.
8. Spence, Mgr.
9. Shreve.
10. Burdick.
11. McGeachy.
12. Hines.
13. Denny.
14. Boyle.
15. Seery.

JOSEPH HALL, Photo., Brooklyn, N. Y.

INDIANAPOLIS BALL CLUB, 1888.

• • •

Fred Dunlap couldn't read or write, but he was the game's highest paid player in 1884. Of his performance that year it was written: "The Maroons without Dunlap are like the play of Hamlet without the melancholy Dane." The next autumn, after the Maroons finished last in the NL, owner Henry Lucas snapped, "Dunlap is the most ungrateful man I have ever seen." So bereft was Dunlap when he died in 1902 in a seedy Philadelphia rooming house that his body lay unidentified in the city morgue until a former teammate finally came to look at it.

ing, O'Leary would introduce another new twist that would have to be taken into account. He'd get behind the most outrageous schemes, like playing baseball on roller skates in indoor arenas during the winter months, but then he would upset everyone's opinion of him by doing something quite shrewd. Still, O'Leary was not really among the more memorable figures of his time, even in Cincinnati, though he worked hard at becoming one by living at the Gibson House hotel in a room with a private bath and by making certain he always had a fresh carnation in his coat lapel. The carnation was O'Leary's trademark. As was his intention, baseball writers in every city where the Outlaw Reds played observed that he was never without one and made mention of the adornment in their papers. Late one night in July 1884, O'Leary was seen wearing a coat without a carnation in its lapel. It turned out he had on the wrong coat. Earlier in the evening, he and Henry Lucas had shed their coats to duke it out over a matter that neither man would ever divulge, and each had somehow wound up with the other's coat. In the inside breast pocket of O'Leary's were train tickets to Kansas City for the entire Cincinnati team. Lucas returned the tickets to Thorner when he found them, but O'Leary didn't learn that until after he'd gone to Thorner with a tale that he'd lost the tickets when his pocket was picked. He was fired on the spot. In 1886 *The Sporting News* reminisced: "Dan O'Leary, the well-known ball player, said two years ago that the day would come when 20,000 spectators would see a game at one time. Dan thinks that base ball is still in its infancy and that, if it grows in the next two years as it has in the past ten, nothing will be thought of a crowd of 50,000 spectators watching a game." A few weeks later the same journal was obliged to report that the prescient O'Leary had been jailed in New York City for masterminding an alleged swindling operation.

Sam Crane was looked upon by his Outlaw Reds teammates as a welcome change from the unpredictable O'Leary, and the club played accordingly, winning 36 of its last 43 games under his command. Later, Crane would become a respected New York sportswriter, but first he took a page from O'Leary's dossier. In the summer of 1889, Crane ran off with Hattie Fraunfelter, who worked as the head cashier for her husband, a Scranton merchant, and was later arrested in New York City on a larceny charge when Fraunfelter swore out a warrant, saying that his wife had made off with $1,500 at Crane's urging. Crane maintained that the money was Hattie's and that Fraunfelter was bankrupt, yet he never quite explained why, if all that were true, he and Hattie lived in New York prior to his arrest under the name of Morrison.

Before the Union Association's sole campaign as a major

league was concluded, teams in 14 different cities would play under its umbrella, and only the Maroons would be at the same station and under the same leadership all season. But while Lucas naturally listed himself as the team's manager, the club was actually handled on the field by Fred Dunlap. The best second baseman anywhere in 1884, and perhaps the best in the entire last century, Dunlap had been Lucas's first and most daring acquisition, plundered from Cleveland on the promise that he would be made the richest player in the game. In 1884 Dunlap was paid a reported $5,000, an unheard of sum at the time, and he was cheap at the price. No hitter ever again would dominate a league as Dunlap did the Union Association, and his batting was only part of his worth. Along with leading the Unions in every major hitting department, Dunlap also won all the fielding crowns for second basemen, pacing his peers by a wide margin in putouts, assists, doubleplays and fielding average. Dunlap batted leadoff for the Maroons, followed in the order by Orator Shaffer, Buttercup Dickerson, Jack Gleason and Dave Rowe. Dickerson deserted the team in midstream to return to the American Association. When he left, he was hitting .365, second only to Dunlap. At the end of the season, among players with over 250 at bats, Shaffer ranked third at .360 and Gleason stood fifth with a .324 mark.

Shaffer, Dunlap, Gleason and Rowe all had considerable prior major league experience, as did most of the leading players in the Union Association. Two who did not were 40-game winner Bill Sweeney of Baltimore and Washington's Henry Moore. Sweeney had at least appeared in a handful of games with the Philadelphia Athletics in 1882, but Moore was an utter rookie. He nevertheless hit .336 and finished among the Union leaders in almost every bat-

Jack Clements was a twenty-year-old rookie with the Philadelphia Keystones. One of the few UA graduates to go on to a long major league career, Clements stayed in Philadelphia with the Phillies when the Keystones folded. He was one of the first catchers to use a chest protector (originally called a "sheepskin") but is best known for being the top lefty receiver in big league history.

ting department. Yet Moore lapsed thereafter into obscurity. After a couple of years in the minors, he completely disappeared. As well as the record for the highest batting average of any player who appeared in the major leagues only one full season, Moore left behind another unique legacy: He is the only .300 hitter about whom not a single biographical fact is known—where he was born, when he died, which way he batted and threw, none of it.

Deepening the mystery enshrouding Moore is that he performed in the nation's capital and for one of the five Union teams that played out the schedule without at least one franchise shift. Two months after Altoona quit Lucas's one-ring circus, the Philadelphia Keystones packed their trunks. Lucas induced the Wilmington Quicksteps, the top club in the Eastern League, to take Philadelphia's spot, but not until he had personally screened the candidacy of Quincy, Illinois, a recent dropout from the Northwestern League. To prove their might, the Quincys challenged Lucas's Maroons to a game on August 14 and then were dismissed after they were beaten 5–1. The Quincys "Boy" battery of Bob Black and Kid Baldwin showed enough, however, that Kansas City manager Ted Sullivan signed them for his Cowboys.

Sullivan also tried some 40 other players including himself, but to little avail. The Cowboys hit .199, the worst batting average ever for a team that competed in more than 50 games, and were victorious just 16 times in 79 efforts. Still, they finished out the season in Kansas City and drew phenomenally well for a last-place team, which seemed to affirm that major league baseball could flourish west of the Mississippi. The Chicago Browns meanwhile decamped for Pittsburgh when they were demolished at the gate by Cap Anson's White Stockings and then folded entirely in September, compelling Lucas to install a new team in Milwaukee to play out the Union schedule. No sooner had Lucas solved that problem than the Quicksteps quit on the eve of their last western road trip. After Omaha declined, the St. Paul White Caps volunteered to fill the breach for the final two weeks of the season and so become the 14th and last city to enlist in the Union cause and the only major league entry never to play a home game.

But even the clubs that had been in the race from start to finish were in disarray. Scanlon pulled his Nationals out of the Union Association because they were poorly treated on their final road trips to St. Louis and Cincinnati and were given far less for their share of the gate receipts in those two cities than the Maroons and Outlaw Reds had received in Washington. The Boston club, after running second most of the season, slipped to fourth during a calamitous season-ending road trip before salvaging a crumb of pride by blanking the Maroons 5–0 on October 19, at

St. Louis, in the regular-season finale for both teams. Commended early in the season for being gentlemen and a class act all the way, especially while on the road, Baltimore's players were released en masse after their final game of the season in Cincinnati and had to borrow train fare from members of the Outlaw Reds just so they could get out of town.

As the only two franchises that still had a degree of solvency and stability, Lucas's Maroons and Thorner's Outlaw Reds played a final contest on October 20 in Cincinnati that was ballyhooed as being for the Union championship. After the Maroons won 2–1 by scoring two quick tallies in their first at bat against Jim McCormick and then playing crisp defense behind Charlie Sweeney, Lucas and Thorner held a strategy meeting. For public consumption, the two averred that they were determined to reconstruct the Union Association, but it gradually grew apparent that privately they had hatched a plan to sneak their clubs into the National League in place of Cleveland and Detroit. On December 17, 1884, *Sporting Life* flaunted a letter, purported to be from one A. Bird, asserting that Lucas was poised to desert the Union Association for the League after meeting certain considerations demanded by Von der Ahe for putting a second major league team in St. Louis. A month later, Bird's allegation was confirmed as the League formally admitted the Maroons to replace Cleveland. Thorner and his Outlaw Reds were left out in the snow, however, when Detroit regrouped and refused at the last moment to give up its League berth.

A home in the League may have been Lucas's secret goal all along, but the cost was unbearably high. In return for being allowed to compete with the Browns for the St. Louis market, Lucas's Maroons had to pay Von der Ahe $2,500 in damages and then were made to adopt the League's 50¢ minimum admission price and were forbidden from scheduling Sunday games at Palace Park. As added punishment, all of the League players who had jumped to the Union Association were permanently blacklisted. Since League jumpers like Dunlap, Shaffer and Sweeney were the heart of his team, Lucas fought this last penalty and eventually won. In April 1885, on the eve of the opening of the season, the League capitulated and reinstated all the reserve rule violators on the condition that they first pay hefty fines ranging from $500 to $1,000. Lucas reportedly paid the fines for his own men and advanced the trio of Cleveland jumpers—Glasscock, Briody and McCormick—the funds to pay theirs. He then grabbed Glasscock and Briody for the Maroons to round out a starting nine that was rated a preseason favorite for the League pennant.

When Briody reported woefully out of shape, Sweeney hurt

• • •
Bill **Barnes, a St. Paul outfielder in 1884. Three years later he was lolling in a rowboat on the Mississippi one May afternoon with two Duluth teammates, John Ake, a former Baltimore second baseman, and nineteen-year-old Billy Earle, already known as something of a weirdo. Suddenly the boat was capsized by a wave from a passing steamer. Barnes and Earle swam to shore and then turned and saw Ake, a non-swimmer, sitting on the overturned boat. Barnes wanted to go to the rescue with a skiff, but Earle just stood and gazed at Ake until Ake left the boat and tried to swim. After a few strokes, Ake raised his arms, shouted for help, and then went under and drowned. Barnes never forgot the way Earle's eyes had stared at Ake.**

his elbow and Dunlap and Lucas wound up despising each other, the Maroons instead came in last. Whether out of pity or recognition that Lucas was a dead duck regardless, the League permitted the Maroons to shave their minimum admission charge to a quarter in 1886.

Notwithstanding this important concession, Lucas could not resuscitate his Maroons. Near the close of the 1886 season, his fortune gone and his ego shattered, he left baseball broke and embittered. From time to time during the next few years he turned up at a ballpark or otherwise hinted that he might like to return to the game, but in 1889, when there had been no invitations, he took a job as a railway clerk. Recouping somewhat, Lucas later tried to stage indoor bike races, but this sporting venture only led to another financial bath. The last years of his life were cloudy and disheartening. Sometime around 1907 he began living with his niece and working as an inspector with the St. Louis Street Department. When he died in 1910 of heart disease, his obituary in *The Sporting News* opined that "he possessed many fine traits and deserved more consideration and better care than was afforded him in his declining days by relatives and former friends."

At the time of his death, a mere quarter-century after his name had been heard more often and his doings dissected more intensely than those of any other baseball figure, Lucas had already come to be regarded as no more that a sidebar in the game's history. As but one indication of the depth to which his eminence so swiftly descended, not a single photograph of him or of his great Union Association team in 1884 has survived.

	W	L	PCT	HOME	ROAD	GB
1. St. Louis Maroons	94	19	.832	50–6	44–13	
2. Milwaukee Brewers	8	4	.667	8–4	0–0	35.5
3. Cincinnati Outlaw Reds	69	36	.657	35–17	34–19	21
4. Baltimore	58	47	.552	29–21	29–26	32
5. Boston Reds	58	51	.532	34–23	24–28	34
6. Chicago-Pittsburgh	41	50	.451	21–18	20–32	42
7. Washington Nationals	47	65	.420	36–27	11–38	46.5
8. Philadelphia Keystones	21	46	.313	13–21	8–25	50
9. St. Paul White Caps	2	6	.250	0–0	2–6	39.5
10. Altoona Mountain Citys	6	19	.240	6–12	0–7	44
11. Kansas City Cowboys	16	63	.203	11–23	5–40	61
12. Wilmington Quicksteps	2	16	.111	1–6	1–10	44.5

• • •

Cannonball Crane winds up. On October 12, 1884, before a UA game at Cincinnati, Crane threw a baseball 406 feet and half an inch to set a record that stood until 1910. When he wasn't raising holy hell, Crane could do it all—hit, throw, run and play any position. In 1890, six years after he nearly paced the UA in home runs, he led the AA in ERA. Off the field, however, Crane's life was usually in shambles. He committed suicide at thirty-four by drinking chloric acid.

BATTING

BATTING AVERAGE (250ABs)

1. Dunlap, StL	.412
2. Hoover, Phila	.364
3. Shaffer, StL	.360
4. Moore, Wash	.336
5. J. Gleason, StL	.324
6. Seery, Balt-KC	.313
7. Schoeneck, CP	.308
8. D. Burns, Cinci	.306
9. D. Rowe, StL	.293
10. P. Baker, Wash	.288

SLUGGING AVERAGE

1. Dunlap, StL	.621
2. Shaffer, StL	.501
3. Hoover, Phila	.495
4. D. Burns, Cinci	.457
5. C. Crane, Boston	.451
6. J. Gleason, StL	.433
7. D. Rowe, StL	.429
8. Moore, Wash	.414
9. Seery, Balt-KC	.411
10. O'Brien, Boston	.404

ON-BASE PERCENTAGE

1. Dunlap, StL	.448
2. Shaffer, StL	.398
3. Hoover, Phila	.390
4. Moore, Wash	.363
5. J. Gleason, StL	.361
6. Seery, Balt-KC	.342
7. Harbridge, Cinci	.328
8. Robinson, Balt	.327
9. Schoeneck, CP	.320
10. D. Burns, Cinci	.315

TOTAL BASES

1. Dunlap, StL	279
2. Shaffer, StL	234
3. D. Rowe, StL	208
4. C. Crane, Boston	193
5. Seery, Balt-KC	192
6. Moore, Wash	191
7. O'Brien, Boston	177
8. J. Gleason, StL	174
9. Schoeneck, CP	165
10. D. Burns, Cinci	162

HOME RUNS

1. Dunlap, StL	13
2. C. Crane, Boston	12
3. Levis, Balt-Wash	6
4. Flynn, Phila-Boston	4
Boyle, StL	4
O'Brien, Boston	4
Hawes, Cinci	4
D. Burns, Cinci	4
9. Five with three	

RUNS

1. Dunlap, StL	160
2. Shaffer, StL	130
3. Seery, Balt-KC	115
4. Robinson, Balt	101
5. D. Rowe, StL	95
6. J. Gleason, StL	90
7. D. Burns, Cinci	84
8. C. Crane, Boston	83
9. Hawes, Cinci	80
O'Brien, Boston	80

HITS

1. Dunlap, StL	185
2. Shaffer, StL	168
3. Moore, Wash	155
Seery, Balt-KC	146
5. D. Rowe, StL	142
6. Schoeneck, CP	131
7. J. Gleason, StL	128
8. C. Crane, Boston	122
9. O'Brien, Boston	118
J. McCormick, Phila-Wash	118

*Stolen Base and RBI leaders unavailable.

PITCHING

● ● ●

This fuzzy photo is our only remaining link to Hugh "One Arm" Daily. There are several stories of how Daily lost his left forearm as a teenager, but all agree the accident didn't improve his prickly disposition. In 1884, Daily hurled well over 600 innings, including the many exhibition games that were then part of being a big leaguer. He was never again completely sound. Like Henry Moore, he vanished after leaving the game.

WINS

1. B. Sweeney, Balt	40
2. Daily, CP-Wash	28
3. Taylor, StL	25
Bradley, Cinci	25
5. C. Sweeney, StL	24
6. Wise, Wash	23
D. Burns, Cinci	23
8. McCormick, Cinci	21
Shaw, Boston	21
10. Burke, Boston	19

LOSSES

1. Bakely, Phila-Wm-KC	30
2. Daily, CP-Wash	28
3. B. Sweeney, Balt	21
4. Voss, Wash-KC	20
5. Wise, Wash	18
6. Atkinson, CP-Balt	15
Burke, Boston	15
Shaw, Boston	15
D. Burns, Cinci	15
Bradley, Cinci	15

INNINGS

1. B. Sweeney, Balt	538
2. Daily, CP-Wash	500.2
3. Bakely, Phila-Wm-KC	394.2
4. Wise, Wash	364.1
5. Bradley, Cinci	342
6. D. Burns, Cinci	329.2
7. Burke, Boston	322
8. Shaw, Boston	315.2
9. C. Sweeney, StL	271
10. Taylor, StL	263

COMPLETE GAMES

1. B. Sweeney, Balt	58
2. Daily, CP-Wash	56
3. Bakely, Phila-Wm-KC	43
4. Bradley, Cinci	36
5. Shaw, Boston	35
6. D. Burns, Cinci	34
Burke, Boston	34
Wise, Wash	34
9. C. Sweeney, StL	31
10. Taylor, StL	29

STRIKEOUTS

1. Daily, CP-Wash	483
2. B. Sweeney, Balt	374
3. Shaw, Boston	309
4. Wise, Wash	268
5. Burke, Boston	255
6. Bakely, Phila-Wm-KC	226
7. C. Sweeney, StL	192
8. Bradley, Cinci	168
9. D. Burns, Cinci	167
10. McCormick, Cinci	161

WINNING PCT. (20 DECISIONS)

1. McCormick, Cinci	.875
2. Taylor, StL	.862
3. C. Sweeney, StL	.774
4. B. Sweeney, Balt	.656
5. Bradley, Cinci	.625
6. D. Burns, Cinci	.605
7. Bond, Boston	.591
8. Shaw, Boston	.583
9. Wise, Wash	.561
10. Burke, Boston	.559

ERA (100 INNINGS)

1. McCormick, Cinci	1.54
2. Taylor, StL	1.68
3. Boyle, StL	1.74
4. Shaw, Boston	1.77
5. C. Sweeney, StL	1.83
6. Werden, StL	1.97
7. Hodnett, StL	2.01
8. Veach, KC	2.42
9. Daily, CP-Wash	2.43
10. D. Burns, Cinci	2.46

LOWEST ON-BASE PCT.

1. McCormick, Cinci	.202
2. C. Sweeney, StL	.207
3. Shaw, Boston	.212
4. Boyle, StL	.215
5. Werden, StL	.235
6. Taylor, StL	.243
7. Veach, KC	.245
8. Geggus, Wash	.247
9. Daily, CP-Wash	.250
10. D. Burns, Cinci	.252
Atkinson, CP-Balt	.252

FIVE

1885

• • •

1885 Cincinnati Reds. Top (left to right): **Billy Mountjoy, Hick Carpenter, Pop Corkhill, Gus Shallix, Will White, Grandmother Powers** and **Frank Fennelly.** Bottom (left to right): **Kid Baldwin, Jimmy Peoples, Bid McPhee, Pop Snyder, Charley Jones, Jim Clinton** and **Long John Reilly.** Gus Schmelz deemed Baldwin a great catcher, "wiry and very rhetorical," but he was despised by Opie Caylor, who labeled him foul-mouthed and ungrateful. Baldwin denied that he was foul-mouthed, claiming he was just excitable. He wore a bright pink uniform shirt with "Our Pet" knitted on it in glaring letters by a lady friend. Learning that Baldwin planned to marry a rich heiress in the fall of 1886, *Sporting Life* predicted, "He will just about go through her wealth like a bullet through cheese."

THE CHRIS AND CHARLIE SHOW

"_The National League is still the leading base ball organization, but solely by reason of prestige and seniority. In all other respects it now has a formidable rival in the American Association, which body has been steadily growing in power, influence and playing strength, and has time and again compelled the League to recognize it as a rival worth conciliating._**"**

—**Sporting Life**, November 4, 1885

EVEN THOUGH THE NEW YORK METS WERE routed by Providence in the 1884 World's Series, their successful pennant bid induced John Day, the president of the Metropolitan Exhibition Company, which owned both the Mets and the League New York Gothams, to take fresh stock of their assets. Rather than attempt to beef up the Mets, however, so that they might repeat as Association champion, Day continued to believe that even a winning Association team in New York at 25¢ per customer could never be as profitable as a winning League club that charged 50¢.

Acting on that conviction, Day fired Jim Price as manager of the Gothams in November 1884 and shifted Jim Mutrie from the Mets to his League club's driver's seat. Day also wanted to bolster the Gothams' playing strength by shuttling the Mets pitching star, Tim Keefe, and the club's top hitter, third baseman Dude Esterbrook, from the Association to the League, but he had to be more delicate about it. The rules of the National Agreement forbad him from transferring the two even though his Metropolitan Exhi-

Horace Phillips was sure Pud Galvin (above) would team with Ed Morris to bring a pennant to Pittsburgh in 1886 after Galvin was acquired from Buffalo. But the future Hall of Famer was only a mediocre 32–28 in the AA before returning to the NL in 1887, when Pittsburgh jumped ship. Galvin is the lone 300-game winner who never pitched on a pennant winner or from a 60'6" mound in the majors.

bition Company owned both teams. Instead, he first had to release them from the Mets and then he had to wait ten days before signing them to League contracts. Because Keefe and Esterbrook were also highly coveted by other clubs, Day had a further problem. During the ten-day hiatus, he needed to safeguard the duo from being heisted by a rival owner who made them a better offer.

Day's solution was to have Mutrie invite Keefe and Esterbrook to spend the ten days after their release in April 1885 cloistered at his onion farm in Bermuda. The trio all got seasick on the return voyage to New York, but the ploy worked. No sooner had the boat docked than Keefe and Esterbrook signed with the Gothams, and the club became an instant contender, vying for the League pennant all season with the Chicago White Stockings before finishing with the best record in history by a second-place team. Minus Keefe, Esterbrook and Mutrie, and appalled at the cavalier manner in which Day had skimmed them, the remaining members of the Mets lost heart. When the franchise seemed about to disband, Mike Scanlon was hopeful that his Washington Nationals team would be offered a spot in the Association. In March 1885, while the League and Henry Lucas were still warring over how to treat the players who had jumped to the Union Association, a rumor gathered steam that Lucas was negotiating to buy the Mets and combine them with his Maroons. Meanwhile, Brooklyn owner Charlie Byrne laid low, refusing to sign many of his players for the 1885 season on the chance the Mets would collapse and he would fall heir to their few lingering stars like Dave Orr and Jack Lynch. When Byrne gave up waiting and bagged seven players from the defunct Cleveland League club, eliminating the probability that Brooklyn and the Mets would merge, the other Association moguls were stirred to action. At a loop meeting on April 29, 1885, the Association's Board of Directors voted to expel the Mets. Since the season at that point was already underway, the ballot was only done to save face. No one really wanted the Mets to exit because it would require a hectic search for a team to fill their spot. The threat succeeded, however, in bullying acting Mets president Frank Rhoner into paying a $500 fine for releasing Keefe and Esterbrook, plus posting a bond to assure the Mets would stay in the Association through the 1885 season. As a final gesture of their indignation, the Board banned Mutrie from the Association for his skullduggery.

Eleven days before they staved off expulsion, the Mets had been thrashed 13–2 in their season opener with the Athletics, and on the same afternoon Pittsburgh blanked the Browns, 7–0. The one-sided results buttressed observers who felt the two Pennsylvania clubs were the most improved teams in the Association. Pitts-

The best thing about the 1885 Baltimore Orioles was their "tony" candy-striped uniforms. Though the O's had three members of the 1882 AA champion Cincinnati club—Joe Sommer (standing, far right), Dan Stearns (standing, third from left) and Jimmy Macullar (seated on Sommer's right)—they finished in the cellar for the third time in the AA's first four years of existence. Also on the team was Sandy Nava (seated, far left), the first San Franciscan to make the majors. Nava contended that he was the son of an English father and a Mexican mother, but some thought he was a mulatto. Whatever the case, Nava was out of the majors by 1886.

burgh's new vigor came from the merger that brought many of the key players from Columbus's 1884 contender to the Allegheny club, most importantly pitcher Ed Morris, second baseman Pop Smith and rightfielder Tom Brown. Where the Athletics had improved, the sharps felt, was in the front office. In early December 1884, Philadelphia co-owner Lew Simmons announced that he would take over as the field manager, claiming that in 1884 the A's had lost "$20,000 on the season by poor management and worse playing" and crediting himself with the club's championship run in 1883. Simmons laid most of the blame for the slump in 1884 on Harry Stovey, citing an incident when Stovey was too drunk to play but tried to cover up his inebriation by averring he had fallen off a scaffold and injured himself. Simmons's blast rallied the A's other two owners, Bill Sharsig and Charlie Mason, to praise Stovey and decry their cohort in a public statement that "Mr Simmons' claim that his management won the championship in 1883 was simply one of his midnight dreams." When Stovey wrote an amazingly long and eloquent letter to *Sporting Life* defending himself, he was appointed manager of the team and Simmons became low man on the totem pole.

Major changes were also brewing in Cincinnati, where Opie Caylor, disgruntled with the Reds' performance ever since their

Louisville Base-Ball Club. Season of 1885.

A nifty collage of the 1885 Louisvilles. Owing to the collapse of the UA and the many players thrown on the market, there were few openings for rookies in 1885. Norman Baker (10) was the lone AA yearling of consequence. A fine pitcher, Baker got into hot water everywhere he went. Manager Jim Hart (center) could endure him for only one year. In 1885, Pete Browning (6) and Guy Hecker (5) again endured each other as road roommates. Browning could only spell phonetically and wasn't too deft with numbers either. When he left a message for Hecker telling him what room they had at St. Louis's Lindell Hotel, he wrote "Aity Ate."

triumph in 1882, came out of the weeds and appointed himself field manager, general manager and everything but chief bottlewasher, after Aaron Stern resigned as club president on January 1, 1885, leaving the team to Caylor and city treasurer George Herancourt. One of Caylor's first acts was to garner Tony Mullane. When Caylor threatened to bolt the Association over Mullane's suspension for contract jumping, Outlaw Reds owner Justus Thorner, who was in suspense wondering what league would house his team in 1885, eagerly fell victim to a telegram from Billy Barnie inquiring whether he would take the Reds' place in the Association in the event they defected to the League. Thorner shot back a telegram that he most certainly would and was only awaiting further word. When Barnie announced that his offer was a hoax and let the baseball world know how Thorner had fallen for it, Thorner was made a laughingstock and his partner, *Cincinnati Enquirer* publisher John McLean, swore revenge. Caylor and the Reds, a prime target of McLean's ever since 1882, when both

he and Thorner had been bamboozled out of their stock in the team, now came under unrelenting attack in the *Enquirer*. Beginning in 1885, Caylor was almost never mentioned in its pages by name, instead being referred to most commonly as "skeleton head."

With Caylor, for the first time, openly at their helm, the Reds got out of the gate well, beating Louisville in their opener on April 19, 4–1. It jarred Cincinnatians that for the first time since 1877 someone other than Will White—Gus Shallix—occupied the box on launching day in the Queen City, but two afternoons later their nerves were soothed when the Reds won 2–1 over the Browns, much hated now in Cincinnati because Von der Ahe had spearheaded the campaign to have Mullane suspended for all of the 1885 season.

Missing from the Browns' lineup on April 21 was manager-first baseman Charlie Comiskey, who was out with an injury. Subbing for him was Sam Barkley, normally a second baseman, and Yank Robinson, a refugee from the collapsed Union Association, was at second. By April 23, Comiskey was back at his post to aid St. Louis in edging Cincinnati, 2–1, and on April 26 the Browns stood at 3–3, a game behind the Reds and Baltimore, which were tied for first with identical 4–2 records. A week later, the Browns had pulled into the top spot with a 6–4 mark, a slender half game ahead of Baltimore and Brooklyn, which were tied for second, and the Mets and Louisville, though tied for last, were just two games off the pace at 4–6. Judging from the first two weeks of the season, the Association was in for a tight pennant race from top to bottom. In any event, McKnight and the Board of Directors were congratulating themselves for getting rid of the dead wood by cutting back to eight teams, and even the Mets, given up for lost before the season started, were showing themselves to be still surprisingly spunky.

Just four weeks farther down the road, after each team had played some 15 more games, the race was essentially over. On May 31 the Browns were at 22–5, having swept all 14 contests with the four Eastern clubs on their first visit of the season to St. Louis. Five games back, at 19–12, was Cincinnati, and Baltimore, which had been tied for first only a month earlier, had slipped to 11–16 while the Mets had smashed any lingering illusions that they could still be competitive by tumbling into the cellar with just nine wins in their first 30 games.

In the remaining four months of the season, all that changed was that St. Louis continued to lengthen its lead and Baltimore and the Mets traded places as Billy Barnie's Orioles hit a horrid .219, a full 21 points below Pittsburgh, owner of the second-worst team average. By the most important measure, the Orioles trailed

the first-place Browns by 36 and a half games. All the more revolting to Barnie was the memory that his team had finished just three and a half lengths back of the Browns the previous year and forecasters had rated the two clubs about even going into the 1885 season. What had happened?

Two other questions need to be answered first. Why were Barnie's Orioles so often like a runaway train, rocketing ahead pell-mell one season and diving off the tracks into a ravine the next? And how did Von der Ahe, who only a year earlier had been considered too "erratic" ever to build a winning team, in a few short months assemble one that would not just become the fourth different club in four years to claim an Association flag but would go on to bag four straight pennants and rank as the greatest dynasty in the first half-century of professional baseball?

The Baltimore conundrum still perplexes students of the 1880s. Barnie knew probably fifty times as much about baseball as Von der Ahe even if he could never seem to convey it to his players. Or was it more that he did not have a clue how to handle difficult players in an era when there were few who were not difficult? Von der Ahe was no wizard with fractious players either, but he found a way out of having to be good at it. His solution to the problem is also the explanation most frequently offered for the success of his Browns. In 1882, Von der Ahe chose as his first manager Ned Cuthbert, figuring that a player could do the best job. But Cuthbert was nearly done as a player and no leader anyway, so Von der Ahe turned to Ted Sullivan. A rough sort, Sullivan could get results from such as Pat Deasley, Fred Lewis and Arlie Latham—the Browns came within a hair of winning the pennant in 1883—but he could not abide Von der Ahe. Thinking he'd learned his lesson, Von der Ahe hired Jimmy Williams, both a skilled executive and a sound baseball mind. But Williams was out of his bailiwick when he had to do business while sitting on the bench amid the Deasleys, Lewises and Lathams. Now Von der Ahe *really* had it. He found someone who combined Sullivan's steely presence and Williams's flair for organization. He found him right on his own club in the person of Charlie Comiskey.

Born in 1851 in the Westphalia province of Prussia, Von der Ahe immigrated to America when he was seventeen. After trying unsuccessfully to make his way in New York, he journeyed to St. Louis and worked for two years as a grocery clerk. At nineteen, the frugal youth had saved enough money to outfit his own store and have enough left over to buy a piece of property on a section of Grand Avenue that was then little more than wilderness. Within five years, Von der Ahe's undeveloped land became so valuable that the cash from its sale gave him the capital to expand

• • •

Injuries restricted Charlie Comiskey to just 83 games in 1885. Dave Foutz and Sam Barkley were his replacements when he was idled. Both contributed more offensively than Comiskey and were said to look nearly as good at first base. Comiskey responded by getting rid of Barkley and dumping Foutz two years later, when it grew apparent that Foutz would have to move to first base to keep his career alive after breaking the thumb on his pitching hand. As much of a demagogue as Chris Von der Ahe, Comiskey flirted with disaster for years after he too became an owner, before his tyrannical and miserly rule destroyed the morale of his Chicago White Sox and created the climate for eight members of the team to throw the 1919 World Series.

into the saloon trade. By the time he was in his mid-twenties, he was already an established beer baron as well as a minor political figure, serving as chairman of the Eighth Congressional District in Missouri, represented by John J. O'Neill.

Owning a baseball club at once gave Von der Ahe a certain cachet in the community and a natural venue for his beer. His suds could now be hawked both at Sportsman's Park, the Browns' home ground, and his Golden Lion Saloon two blocks away from the park, where his waiters all wore Browns caps and shirts. Von der Ahe had a huge red nose the size of a turnip and a tiny clump of whiskers under his lower lip that looked like something his razor kept accidentally missing when he shaved. He wore loud checkered suits and a flattened black derby, and with his thick German accent, every word he uttered sounded like it came from a mouth full of mush. Since he knew next to nothing about baseball when he first ventured into the game, Von der Ahe found it expedient to dress and act and talk like a buffoon, but he was really rat shrewd. As the years wore on, his cunning only increased. Von der Ahe never revealed the full strength of his hand. He claimed the city of St. Louis was squeezing him on the rental for his ballpark, even though he actually held the controlling interest in it. It was crucial to him that his fellow owners remain oblivious of how successful he really was or the true reasons for his success. The public saw a man who put the Browns' logo on cheap crockery but was never told that Von der Ahe led the crusade to suspend his former pitching ace Tony Mullane not out of spite, but because he foresaw danger if players were allowed to continue extorting enormous salaries by jumping from team to team. Von der Ahe also fought to curb the abuse of the free-pass system, and in 1888 he was the first to predict that baseball would one day have a single 12-team major league. His forecast came to pass four years later, though not in the form he hoped.

In the winter of 1881–82, Al Spink, an early partner of Von der Ahe's and later the founder of *The Sporting News*, snared Charlie Comiskey for the Browns when events made it appear the American Association would come to fruition. Comiskey had been playing with the Dubuque Rabbits, a semi-pro team run by Ted Sullivan. The relationship between Von der Ahe and Comiskey developed slowly, but by the fall of 1884 each understood that he had found a perfect counterpart in the other. Comiskey not only knew how to handle men on the playing field but how to handle Von der Ahe. As Von der Ahe was capricious, ready to fine players for the slightest offense, Comiskey would operate obliquely to rescind the fine by giving the guilty player a comparable financial reward for an outstanding play. From his perch in the

front office, Von der Ahe swore that he wanted to create competitive balance in the Association and seemingly sold many of his stars to achieve that end, but then replaced them with unheralded players just as good, whom he could pay substantially less money. On the field Comiskey stressed good baserunning, crisp fielding and, above all, trying to get an opponent's goat. The son of an Irish-born Chicago alderman, Comiskey had learned from his father how to survive in the Windy City's brawling political arena. He applied the same lessons to baseball. Comiskey loved to win, but he loved even more beating an opponent who had been riled into blowing the game. Moreover, he delighted in taking on players whom everyone else had given up as lost causes and molding them into stars. Prior to the 1885 season, Comiskey instigated the release of the problematic Deasley to the New York Gothams because he said Deasley was "a continual source of trouble to the team." But he then prodded Von der Ahe to sign Curt Welch, the bane of Toledo manager Charlie Morton in 1884. A daring base thief and an innovative centerfielder with an uncanny talent for turning his back to a batted ball in flight and racing to the exact spot it would descend, Welch nearly threw away his career in his rookie year at Toledo by swilling beer whenever there was a break in action—an argument with an umpire or a conference in the pitcher's box—from a stash he hid behind a loose board in the outfield fence at the Blue Stockings park. Comiskey was convinced that he could put a stop to Welch's drinking and that the Browns would then have the best outfielder in the Association. He was half right. Welch drank himself out of baseball by the time he was thirty-one, but in the interim he contributed heavily to three St. Louis pennants and tallied the run that gave the Association its lone undisputed World's Series victory.

In 1885, Welch played in every one of the Browns' 112 games and led all the team's regulars in hitting. His average was a lackluster .271, though, prompting yet another question. How did this team win the pennant by 16 games despite having no players among the top ten in batting, slugging, on-base percentage, total bases, home runs or hits? Unsurprisingly, the pitching half of the 1885 season leaders chart furnishes a likely answer. Between them, Bob Caruthers and Dave Foutz logged 73 victories and just 27 losses for a combined winning percentage of .730.

The year before, each had begun the season in the minor leagues. Foutz in 1884 was already twenty-eight years old but said he was twenty-two. Born in Maryland, in 1879 he went to Leadville, Colorado, where he worked as a gold miner. After claiming he had racked up 40 wins and only one loss for the semi-pro Leadville Blues in 1882, he was engaged by Bay City of the

The versatile Yank Robinson. In 1882 he broke in as a shortstop with Detroit. Two years later, he played primarily at third base for Baltimore of the UA. In 1885 the Browns used him mostly in the outfield and behind the plate, but the following season he grabbed their second-base post and hung on to it until he jumped to the PL in 1890. Robinson also pitched a bit, leading the UA in relief wins in 1884.

Northwestern League the following year. When the Northwestern League collapsed in July 1884, the Browns outbid several other teams and bought his contract from Bay City for $2,000. Had the Browns known Foutz's true age, they probably would have passed on him. Caruthers, who professed to be a mere twenty and really was, was nearly overlooked because he was so frail, carrying only 135 pounds on his 5'7" frame, and was reckoned to be a poor hitter besides, even for a pitcher. Owing to his .218 batting average and so-so 17–15 record in the box for Minneapolis of the extinct Northwestern League, the Browns were able to get him more cheaply a few weeks after they landed Foutz.

At the finish of the 1885 season, *Sporting Life's* assessment of Caruthers was that he was "a fair batsman and the best base-running pitcher in the profession." Furthermore, he had a quick and deceptive delivery with "a faculty for using his head and studying the weak points of a batsman." Deft baserunning and heady play—these were the attributes that were cited again and again by *Sporting Life* in summing up each member of the Browns except one. Leftfielder Tip O'Neill was not at all Comiskey's kind of player. Shaky in the field, O'Neill was aided partially by his strong arm, but there was no salvation for him on the bases. O'Neill was a poor base runner and atrocious at sliding. In June 1885 he was hitting close to .400 and leading the Association in batting by a wide margin, but then on June 13 he injured his right leg in a sliding collision with Mets second baseman Joe Reilly and was out of the lineup until early September. The mishap was but one of many that befell O'Neill on the basepaths during his ten-year career. His station-to-station style of running also contributed to his relatively low run and stolen-base totals for a player who consistently ranked near the top in every other offensive department.

The long stint on the disabled list in the summer of 1885 cost O'Neill the batting crown—he collected only 206 at bats for the season—but it afforded Comiskey an opportunity to utilize Yank Robinson in left field. The Union Association graduate had been expected to take over the Browns' catching job after Deasley was let go, but instead Doc Bushong, who had been picked up in the spring for insurance after he was cut by Brooklyn, beat out Robinson and several other backstopping aspirants. Robinson was too precious, however, to let languish on the bench. He had all of the skills Comiskey admired—in part because they were the same skills Comiskey had—plus one that made him a treasure. Along with being a great fielder, able to play any position and an exceptional base runner, Robinson was an artist at coaxing walks. His closest parallel in the twentieth century is Max Bishop, a second baseman who hit little but reached base so frequently he was

nicknamed "Camera Eye." Robinson was the original Camera Eye. In 1888 he became the first regular player ever to collect more walks than hits. The following year, although he batted just .208, he led the Association with 118 walks. Robinson, more than any other member of the Browns, was Comiskey's ideal team cog. A self-taught player whose skills were so rudimentary when he started his professional career that he batted cross-handed, by 1885 he had grown so invaluable that Comiskey used him at every position but shortstop, where the durable Bill Gleason held forth in every contest.

Two other Comiskey favorites were rightfielder Hugh Nicol and third baseman Arlie Latham. In 1885, Nicol hit a dismal .207 but paced all Association outfielders in total chances per game. He probably also led the Association in stolen bases. In 1887, soon after this important baserunning department was made an official statistic, Nicol, then with Cincinnati, set an all-time record by notching 138 steals. A marble cutter by trade, Nicol thought himself to be the strongest 5'4" man in the country. Cynics supposed the Browns kept him around because he was the only man on the team smaller than Von der Ahe. Comiskey fought to hold on to Nicol but could no longer afford that luxury when he continued to bat in the low .200s in 1886 and both Caruthers and Foutz had developed enough as hitters to play the outfield on days they didn't pitch.

Before becoming a professsional ball player in 1879, Latham was a shoemaker. As late as 1885, it seemed he might soon have to return to his original trade. Even as the Browns sprinted to an easy pennant, Latham hit below .200 much of the season, before finishing at .206. The following year he hiked his average to .301 but led all third basemen in errors. Latham's career was marked by that sort of wild performance swing. During the 1880s he would have been a nonentity on most teams, but the Browns were the ideal vehicle for him. Comiskey catered to Latham's style of play and encouraged his antics. When the Browns were at bat, Latham operated as a base coach, where he achieved so much notoriety that fans came to the park solely to watch him torment opponents. Because of Latham's vociferous coaching, a rule was introduced limiting the type and amount of verbal haranguing a base coach could employ, but Latham was such a gate-attraction that the rule was usually ignored.

During his heyday, Latham had a song written about him called "The Freshest Man on Earth" and was known as "Jimmy Fresh," but cracks began to appear in his image as the Browns' popular sparkplug. In October 1885, Latham issued a formal challenge to race any other player in the game 100 yards for any amount from $50 to $500. His taker was Billy Sunday, a speedy outfielder with the Chicago White Stockings and later a famous evangelist. When Latham was beaten by Sunday in the big race on November 8, he was accused of giving "his friends and backers the dumps." Two months later Latham was thwarted by Circuit Court Judge Horner when he tried to get a divorce from his wife Emma, who had attempted to commit suicide a year earlier. Horner turned down the plea and ordered Latham to pay Emma $100, plus $25 per week. This airing of his dirty linen was just the first indication that Latham's personal life was a nightmare. Eventually successful in divorcing his first wife, he married one Ella Garvin on June 14, 1886, and soon found himself fending off her charges that he was a pervert, a philanderer and physically abusive. In the meantime Latham had ruined his arm in a throwing contest with Bushong. Always ready to test himself in every physical arena, Latham did not bother to warm up when Bushong challenged him. Even though he won the contest with his first throw, he so severely damaged his arm that he was never again more than an average third baseman.

Latham somehow survived all these injuries and character assassination attempts to become the first big leaguer to play 1,500 games at third base, and to outlive all of his teammates on the Browns and most other 19th-century players, as well. In 1880, his rookie season, the pitchers' box was still only 45 feet from home plate. By the time Latham died in 1952 at ninety-three, he was the last to have batted in a major league game against a pitcher who threw from so short a distance.

A major pitching rule change in 1885 that was perhaps the most significant rule revision during the decade impacted on Latham and accounted, more than any other single factor, for his lowly batting average that year—and for the Browns' commitment to win via defense and aggressive baserunning. At a loop meeting on June 5, at the Girard House in Philadelphia, the Association's Board of Directors voted to lift all restrictions on where a pitcher's arm had to be in relation to his shoulder when he released the ball, to eliminate the foul-bound out rule and to give the choice of whether to bat first or last to the captain of the home team. This was a weird set of rule changes to implement in any case after the season had already started, but licensing pitchers to throw with whatever style of delivery they pleased, ranging from underhand to straight overhand, was particularly influential on play for the rest of the year. The National League had abandoned all attempts to monitor pitching deliveries in 1884 and then had tried to restore a rule against overhand pitching when batting averages tumbled accordingly. But it proved so difficult for umpires to gauge whether a pitcher's arm was above his shoulder at the moment he released the ball that the rule was scrapped again a few weeks into the 1885 season, and this time the Association, which had held fast against overhand pitching in 1884, went along with the change. The effect on batting averages was almost instantaneous and would become still more devastating the following year after pitchers who heretofore had been sidearmers worked during the off-season on learning how to throw overhand.

Other teams besides the Browns saw the hitting decline coming and strove to prepare for it. In late June, centerfielder Dennis Casey was benched in Baltimore for his poor baserunning and also for swinging too often at pitches outside the zone where he called for them to be delivered. A month later Casey was released when he could not remedy his deficiencies, even though he was leading the Orioles in hitting. In September, Barnie also released Oyster Burns, the team home-run leader and the only pitcher on the club with a winning record. Along with being freeswingers, Casey and Burns created a morale problem for Barnie, but never so severe as the one that plagued Charlie Byrne in Brooklyn. The team in the City of Churches was divided into two groups, one comprised of holdovers from 1884 and the other players who had been with Cleveland. Adonis Terry, Byrne's leading winner in 1884, fell to a 6–17 record that he blamed on a lack of support from the "Cleveland clique." The rest of the team faulted manager Charlie Hackett for their weak showing. When Hackett started Phenomenal Smith, just up from Allentown, against the Browns on June 17 rather than John Harkins, one of the Cleveland ringleaders, the team retaliated by making 28 errors behind Smith in an 18–5 loss. After the game, Byrne read the riot act, but when Brooklyn continued its shoddy play he eventually took over the field reins himself and elevated the Grays to a fifth-place tie with Louisville. Picked to finish last, the Falls City club, now known as the Colonels, parlayed a great year by Pete Browning, whose .362 batting average was 129 points above the combined mark the rest of his teammates registered, and the field leadership of Jim Hart to overcome the lack of a decent catcher after Dan Sullivan was released for his own protection. In mid-June, Sullivan got into a row with a local reporter who swore revenge and had a big family in the Louisville area to help him carry out the threat. Fearing for his life if he went back to "the dark and bloody ground of Kentucky," Sullivan gladly accepted a transfer to St. Louis.

Fourth in 1885 were the Athletics, which slipped below .500 at 55–57 despite all the front-office retooling. The Allegheny club, in its first full season under Horace Phillips's tutelage, surprised pleasantly, breaking .500 for the first time, albeit by a narrow one-

• • •

Dennis Casey, Baltimore's leading hitter in 1885 who nevertheless was released in mid-season. Was he "Casey at the Bat"? His brother, Dan, later insisted he was, and when that didn't fly, Dan tried to maintain that he himself was the great Casey.

game margin, to nail down third place. Cincinnati, though it finished second, disappointed Ohioans, who'd had five major league teams to spread their affection among in 1884 but now had only the Reds. Caylor contended that what with Mullane's suspension and White's slip from stardom, the problem had been not enough pitching, and the *Enquirer* contended that the problem was too much Caylor.

After ending the season in New York, the victorious Browns traveled home in a special car decorated with flags and a gargantuan banner bearing the words "St. Louis Browns, Champions 1885." The team was greeted at Union Depot in St. Louis on the evening of October 7 by an enormous crowd. There then followed a parade through the city that included many luminaries, local amateur nines and even several other major league teams, namely Cincinnati and Jim Mutrie's New York Gothams, which by this time were nicknamed the Giants. The triumphant night culminated in a grand banquet, dozens of speeches and a massive fireworks display. Browns fans got a double treat at Sportsman's Park the next day—a performance of Buffalo Bill's Wild West Show along with an exhibition game against Cincinnati, with Tony Mullane pitching for the Reds after being held off-stage all summer while he served a season-long suspension.

A week later, the Browns and Chicago White Stockings squared off in Chicago for the opening game of the second sanctioned World's Series between the champions of the American Association and the National League. In 1885 the postseason match was expanded to seven games, it was agreed to split the gate receipts 50/50 and each team put up $500 in addition, with the $1,000 kitty to go to the winner. The battle commenced on October 14 with a 5–5 tie that was preceded by throwing and base running contests among the members of both teams. In St. Louis the next afternoon, Comiskey pulled the Browns off the field in the sixth inning when umpire Dave Sullivan called a ball White Stockings third baseman Ned Williamson tapped down the first baseline fair after it had started out foul, then hit something outside the line and ricocheted back into fair territory subsequent to Sullivan's initial call of foul. Sullivan denied he had uttered any such call, claiming White Stockings first baseman Cap Anson was the one who had shouted foul from the bench, and several hours later, from the safety of his hotel room, he forfeited the game to Chicago after St. Louis, trailing 5–4 at the time, refused to play on.

For the third game Harry McCaffrey replaced Sullivan, who never again worked as a regular umpire in the majors, but a dispute raged for several weeks over whether Sullivan's forfeit ruling should stand. The issue took on critical significance when the Browns won two of the next four games and then, prior to the seventh and final contest, Anson and Comiskey agreed to call the first two engagements draws and play Game Seven for all the marbles. After St. Louis won 13–4 over a tired Jim McCormick, *Sporting Life* reported, "The Chicago club is much chagrined at the defeats inflicted by St. Louis, a club they underrated, and the loss of the 'world championship,' a title which amounts to little, is yet irritating to the white-hosed lads." The comment suggests that the players and the press did not take these fall clashes all that seriously as yet, which was probably the case. For that matter, the fans were not exactly in a frenzy either over the postseason spectacle. While the three World's Series games played in St. Louis drew a total attendance of around 7,000, an exhibition game between the Browns and the Maroons, which took place in the midst of the postseason battle, pulled some 10,000. But if the action of the field failed to stimulate St. Louisans, Al Spalding evoked their wrath when he declared that, contrary to Anson's concession, the White Stockings still viewed the forfeit in Game Two as valid and considered the Series drawn. In late November, *Sporting Life* further roused the ire of Browns fans when it declared the Series a tie at 3–all, with St. Louis the loser in the disputed game, and said all bets were therefore off "while the championship of the United States for 1885 remains in abeyance."

Von der Ahe still felt he was entitled to the $1,000 purse. There had never been a more serious event to him than the 1885 World's Series. The disputed game of October 15 still fresh in his craw, he was in New York the following evening attending a joint Association and League meeting, when he was handed a telegram from White Stockings owner Al Spalding. Opening it, he read that in the World's Series game that afternoon at St. Louis, Cap Anson and Comiskey had fought on the field while the crowd rioted. Comiskey, Spalding reported, had been fearfully beaten in the brawl and both he and Anson were now in jail with an angry mob milling about outside, threatening to lynch Anson. The telegram was Spalding's idea of a joke, and when Von der Ahe bought it hook, line and sinker, "his distress and worstment were comical to witnesses and afforded much amusement to all in the secret."

It was the only moment of levity at the New York meeting, for the two sides were there to adopt a new National Agreement that would limit player salaries to $2,000. The players were incredulous at first when they heard of the proposed ceiling on salaries, and then were up in arms as the possibility grew that the owners might be serious. In its October 28, 1885, issue, *Sporting*

• • •

Ferdinand "Gus" Abell, who once said, "Whenever I go to a baseball meeting, I never forget to check my money and valuables at the hotel office before entering the session chamber." A gambler by profession, Abell helped Charlie Byrne bankroll the Brooklyn team and engineered the purchase of the NL Cleveland club's assets prior to the 1885 season. Two years later, Abell put up most of the cash to buy three St. Louis Browns stars. After Byrne died in 1898, Abell became Brooklyn's principal owner before giving the club over to Charlie Ebbets.

THE BEER AND WHISKY LEAGUE

Life posited, only half jestingly, several ways in which the salary limit could be circumvented, such as Spalding offering Chicago's 53-game winner John Clarkson $1,000 on top of his regular salary for his old uniform if he would don a new one in 1886 and Mutrie agreeing to pay Buck Ewing $1,400 for the kid gloves he was wearing if he would wear a catcher's mitt next season.

But though the action taken at the joint meeting ended the 1885 season on something of a down note for many players, most of the owners were highly pleased with the way the year had gone. Association moguls could point to *Sporting Life's* opinion that their loop was now a "formidable rival" to the League and its further assessment that the Association's 25¢ admission price "has popularized the game in that it has brought it within the reach of thousands who were unable to meet the demands of the League, and thus gave the game the go-by altogether." League magnates, while appearing to be conciliatory, and even as if they had accepted the Association as an equal, covertly met to draft a new plan when the Browns came to power. Back in the spring the hope had been to undermine Von der Ahe by giving Henry Lucas a League berth in St. Louis, but that had fallen flat when Lucas's Maroons finished last in their initial League season and drew poorly. Since the Browns were above being destroyed, at least for the moment, the League began to work a different vein. It shifted its pickax to the Association towns where Von der Ahe was loathed.

• • •

Hick **Carpenter had one of his better seasons in 1885, hitting .277. As usual, he collected few walks or extra base hits, but it was a rare third baseman then who did. In the 1880s the position was made for hard-bodied durable sorts who were pretty much a load on offense. One such was Jim Donnelly, who held a steady job for three years even though he never hit above .201.**

1885 FINAL STANDINGS

	W	L	PCT	HOME	ROAD	GB
1. St. Louis Browns	79	33	.705	44–11	35–22	
2. Cincinnati Reds	63	49	.563	35–21	28–28	16
3. Pittsburgh Alleghenys	56	55	.505	37–20	19–35	22.5
4. Philadelphia Athletics	55	57	.491	33–23	22–34	24
5. Brooklyn Grays	53	59	.473	36–22	17–37	26
Louisville Colonels	53	59	.473	37–19	16–40	26
7. New York Metropolitans	44	64	.407	28–24	16–40	33
8. Baltimore Orioles	41	68	.376	29–25	12–43	36

Ed Morris's left arm never recovered after he won 80 games in 1885–86, as Pittsburgh put on a show to convince both its skeptical populous and the NL that it was verging on becoming a force. But a sore wing never stopped Morris from pursuing nocturnal pleasures. A terrific billiards player, among other things, he often teamed up with his buddy, Willie Kuehne, to hustle rubes. In later life, Morris worked as a deputy warden at a Pennsylvania prison and remained a close follower of the game until his death in 1937.

1885 SEASON LEADERS*

BATTING

BATTING AVERAGE (300 ABs)

1. Browning, Louis	.362
2. Orr, NY	.342
3. Larkin, Phila	.329
4. C. Jones, Cinci	.322
5. Stovey, Phila	.315
6. T. Brown, Pitts	.307
7. Phillips, Brook	.302
8. Coleman, Phila	.299
9. Reilly, Cinci	.297
10. Purcell, Phila	.296

SLUGGING AVERAGE

1. Orr, NY	.543
2. Browning, Louis	.530
3. Larkin, Phila	.525
4. Stovey, Phila	.488
5. C. Jones, Cinci	.456
6. Fennelly, Cinci	.445
7. T. Brown, Pitts	.426
8. Phillips, Brook	.422
9. Wolf, Louis	.416
10. Coleman, Phila	.415

ON-BASE PERCENTAGE

1. Browning, Louis	.393
2. Larkin, Phila	.372
3. Stovey, Phila	.371
4. T. Brown, Pitts	.366
5. Phillips, Brook	.364
6. C. Jones, Cinci	.363
7. Orr, NY	.358
8. Nelson, NY	.353
9. Fennelly, Cinci	.351
10. Hotaling, Brook	.350

TOTAL BASES

1. Browning, Louis	255
2. Orr, NY	241
3. Larkin, Phila	238
4. Stovey, Phila	237
5. C. Jones, Cinci	222
6. Fennelly, Cinci	202
7. Wolf, Louis	201
8. Reilly, Cinci	198
9. T. Brown, Pitts	186
10. Roseman, NY	167

HOME RUNS

1. Stovey, Phila	13
2. Fennelly, Cinci	10
3. Browning, Louis	9
4. Larkin, Phila	8
5. Orr, NY	6
6. O. Burns, Balt	5
Reilly, Cinci	5
8. G. Smith, Brook	4
T. Brown, Pitts	4
C. Jones, Cinci	4

RUNS

1. Stovey, Phila	130
2. Larkin, Phila	114
3. C. Jones, Cinci	108
4. Nelson, NY	98
Browning, Louis	98
6. Reilly, Cinci	92
7. Carpenter, Cinci	89
8. McClellan, Brook	85
P. Smith, Pitts	85
10. Welch, StL	84
Sommer, Balt	84
Latham, StL	84

HITS

1. Browning, Louis	174
2. C. Jones, Cinci	157
3. Stovey, Phila	153
4. Orr, NY	152
5. Larkin, Phila	149
6. Reilly, Cinci	143
7. Wolf, Louis	141
8. T. Brown, Pitts	134
9. Carpenter, Cinci	131
10. Brady, NY	128

*Stolen Base and RBI leaders unavailable.

PITCHING

WINS

1. Caruthers, StL	40
2. Morris, Pitts	39
3. Foutz, StL	33
Porter, Brook	33
5. Mathews, Phila	30
Hecker, Louis	30
7. Henderson, Balt	25
8. Lynch, NY	23
9. McKeon, Cinci	20
10. White, Cinci	18

LOSSES

1. Henderson, Balt	35
2. Morris, Pitts	24
3. Hecker, Louis	23
4. Porter, Brook	21
Lynch, NY	21
Cushman, Phila-NY	21
7. Harkins, Brook	20
8. Terry, Brook	17
Mathews, Phila	17
10. White, Cinci	15

INNINGS

1. Morris, Pitts	581
2. Henderson, Balt	539.1
3. Caruthers, StL	482.1
4. Porter, Brook	481.2
5. Hecker, Louis	480
6. Mathews, Phila	422.1
7. Foutz, StL	407.2
8. Lynch, NY	379
9. Harkins, Brook	293
White, Cinci	293

COMPLETE GAMES

1. Morris, Pitts	63
2. Henderson, Balt	59
3. Porter, Brook	53
Caruthers, StL	53
5. Hecker, Louis	51
6. Mathews, Phila	46
Foutz, StL	46
8. Lynch, NY	43
9. Harkins, Brook	33
White, Cinci	33

STRIKEOUTS

1. Morris, Pitts	298
2. Mathews, Phila	286
3. Henderson, Balt	263
4. Hecker, Louis	209
5. Porter, Brook	197
6. Caruthers, StL	190
7. Lynch, NY	177
8. Cushman, Phila-NY	170
9. Foutz, StL	147
10. Harkins, Brook	141

WINNING PCT. (25 DECISIONS)

1. Caruthers, StL	.755
2. Foutz, StL	.702
3. Mathews, Phila	.638
4. Morris, Pitts	.619
5. Porter, Brook	.611
6. McKeon, Cinci	.606
7. Hecker, Louis	.566
8. White, Cinci	.545
9. Lynch, NY	.523
10. Baker, Louis	.520

ERA (112 INNINGS)

1. Caruthers, StL	2.07
2. Hecker, Louis	2.18
3. Morris, Pitts	2.35
4. Mathews, Phila	2.43
5. Foutz, StL	2.63
6. Mays, Louis	2.76
7. Porter, Brook	2.78
8. McKeon, Cinci	2.86
9. Cushman, Phila-NY	3.01
10. Henderson, Balt	3.19

LOWEST ON-BASE PCT.

1. Morris, Pitts	.243
2. Caruthers, StL	.251
3. McGinnis, StL	.258
4. Hecker, Louis	.260
5. Mathews, Phila	.262
6. Porter, Brook	.269
Foutz, StL	.269
8. McKeon, Cinci	.270
Cushman, Phila-NY	.270
10. Mays, Louis	.276

• • •

Hardie Henderson, the AA pacemaker in 1885 in losses, walks, and hits surrendered. He averaged 30 setbacks a year in his first three AA seasons, all with Baltimore. Sent to Brooklyn after a 3–15 start in 1886, Henderson went 10–4, experiencing the usual turnaround that good pitchers enjoy when they move from dismal teams to decent ones. His arm betrayed him, though, early the following year.

SIX

1886

• • •

The 1884 Hudson club had two future big leaguers, Wilbert Robinson (seated, center) and Jimmy Ryan (seated, far left). Later a portly member of some great Baltimore Orioles teams, Robinson in 1886 was a stringy rookie catcher with the Athletics who couldn't hit a lick. In 1892 he collected a record seven hits and 11 RBIs for Baltimore in a game against St. Louis. Then in his seventh season, Robinson had begun the year with a .226 career batting average.

The Beer and Whisky League Attains Its Pinnacle

BY THE CLOSE OF 1885, THE BASEBALL WORLD seemed to have made a full 180-degree turn on its axis during the past year. Whereas the Association had looked to be on the verge of collapse after the frenetic 1884 campaign, now the League's health was in doubt. Throughout the fall of 1885, the League stewed over whether to take on Washington and another new club to replace Providence and Buffalo, which had both folded after the 1885 season due to poor attendance, or to try to go it as a tottery six-team alliance. The indecision finally drove Washington's main backer, Mike Scanlon, to solicit the Association once again for membership.

Scanlon's plea bade McKnight and the Board of Directors to take fresh stock of the Mets' situation. The Manhattan-based team had recently been sold by the Metropolitan Exhibition Company for a reported $25,000 to Erastus Wiman, owner of the Staten Island Amusement Company, which numbered among its properties the Staten Island ferry. Wiman proposed moving the team to

Staten Island, where it would play at the St. George Cricket Grounds in his "Palace of Eden" amusement park. The plan did not appeal to McKnight, who felt it was essential that the franchise keep its foothold in Manhattan. In December 1885, he and the Board voted to oust the Mets and admit Scanlon's Washington team in their place. When Wiman got an injunction to stop the eviction, McKnight argued in his defense that "the Association has no legal existence, that is to say, it is not an incorporated body, and the clubs composing it can, by common consent, refuse to play with the Mets or any other lot of players." On December 19, however, a Philadelphia court found for the Mets, stating that holding a membership in a baseball league is "as sacred as any property," and the club was reinstated after Wiman established that he had bought it on the understanding that he could move it to Staten Island and had already sunk considerable money into the venture.

The tortuous legal wrangle prevented Mets manager Jim "Gift Show" Gifford from beginning work to rebuild the team until after the other clubs had already vacuumed up most of the loose talent. A further impediment was put in Gifford's path by Charlie Byrne. The Brooklyn owner signed first baseman Dave Orr and centerfielder Chief Roseman, when it seemed the Mets would fold, and refused to give the two stars back after the New York club was saved. At McKnight's insistence, Byrne eventually acquiesced, but by then the spotlight had shifted to McKnight himself for the manner in which he sought to unravel the dispute over the rights to second baseman Sam Barkley.

Unable to endure St. Louis's player-manager, Charlie Comiskey, Barkley was put on the block by the Browns. When Baltimore offered St. Louis $1,000 for his contract, topping Pittsburgh's offer of $750, Barkley signed with the Orioles. Pittsburgh then upped its bid to $1,000 and Barkley chose to join the Allegheny club in defiance of McKnight, who told him that while his Baltimore contract was not binding, the honorable thing was to stick with the Orioles. When Baltimore formally protested Barkley's apostasy, Pittsburgh threatened to bolt the Association if the decision went to the Orioles, and McKnight came under fire from every direction. At a special Association meeting on March 4 at the Louisville Hotel, Philadelphia co-owner Lew Simmons and Zach Phelps, a Louisville attorney who now had a part interest in the Colonels, were appointed a two-man committee to decide the Barkley case. Upon hearing the evidence of all parties concerned, they adjourned for the night. The following day they returned a decision to suspend Barkley for one year and reserve him for Pittsburgh in 1887. Their ruling was based largely on the fact that Barkley had signed a Pittsburgh contract after conferring with Mc-Knight, who was acting at dual purposes as both a supposedly impartial Association president and a partner in the Pittsburgh club.

Unlike Tony Mullane, who had been handed an almost identical suspension the previous year after jumping his contract for the third time in three seasons, Barkley forestalled the action against him by getting an injunction in a Pittsburgh court to prevent all the other Association clubs from playing the Alleghenys unless he was on the team. When it grew apparent that Barkley had the Association in a bind, McKnight was asked to resign as loop president on March 20 by every club but Pittsburgh and St. Louis over his inept handling of both the Barkley case and the Mets' ouster attempt. The Browns then added their vote to the groundswell, but McKnight would not go peacefully. Instead, he locked himself in his office and refused to hand over the Association's papers. His elected replacement, Wheeler Wyckoff, moving up from secretary to the top job, eventually was able to take command but not before the incident squirted everyone involved with embarrassment. McKnight's reward for his four years of presidential service was to be stripped, not only of his office, but also of his interest in the Pittsburgh team, which passed completely into the hands of Horace Phillips and William Nimick.

• • •

Sam Barkley, the culprit in the AA's greatest internecine legal feud. On the field, Barkley had a feud raging too. Barkley and Tony Mullane hated each other after Mullane stole Barkley's woman while the two were with Toledo in 1884. The feud quieted in 1885 after Mullane was suspended for the season but flared again in 1886 whenever Pittsburgh and Cincinnati met.

• • •
Lee Richmond, the first left-handed pitcher of note. In 1886, he made a comeback bid with Cincinnati after being out of the majors for nearly three years. Hammered in two starts, Richmond was then tried as an outfielder by Opie Caylor, who would explore every avenue before admitting that he might have made a mistake. Later in the 1886 season Caylor signed Bill Irwin—a one-eyed pitcher—and then applauded his own perspicacity even after Irwin was racked in his only two appearances.

Over the winter, the Cincinnati club also had a change in ownership. In February 1886, Caylor reported that John Hauck, the "wealthiest brewer in Cincinnati," had bought the Reds and put the club completely in his charge, with a policy "to elevate the tone of it and cater especially to the best classes." Given this financial shot in the arm, Caylor rated Cincinnati the team to beat in 1886. So he could get the club off to a flying start, he arranged for the Reds to train in the spring under a British professor Chatfield, a former gymnastics instructor at Oxford University. But either Chatfield's regimen was a failure or else the Reds were still under the early-season jinx that had marred even their 1882 pennant dash. In May, Hick Carpenter sprained his ankle in a basepath collision with Browns catcher Rudy Kemmler, first baseman Long John Reilly broke his ankle, catcher Jim Keenan bruised his knee, rightfielder Pop Corkhill was idled by a fractured finger and centerfielder Fred Lewis, the scourge of former Browns manager Jimmy Williams, got roaringly drunk. Lewis, of whom it had been written only a few days earlier that he was "making hosts of friends with his quiet and unobtrusive ways and manners," came around in time to lead the team in hitting, but the absence of the others—Reilly and Carpenter in particular—knocked Cincinnati out of the race early. By June 9, the Reds were mired in seventh place, and to the *Enquirer* the culprit was not all the injuries, but Caylor. In its pages the team was referred to as "Caylor's Crabs," and McLean jeered, "The present manager of the team wore dresses until he was twelve years old, and if he had his own way, he would be strutting around today in a Mother Hubbard . . . What is wanted is a manager with a backbone, and not one with a spine no larger than a thread." When McLean was refused admission to the Reds park in June after his scalding attacks on his former employee, the *Enquirer* claimed that it had been given affidavits from two Indianapolis men, purportedly private detectives, that Tony Mullane had written letters telling them to bet money on certain Cincinnati games. This accusation seemed so rank, especially when McLean would not produce the letters in question, that other writers rallied to Caylor's cause. At a June 30 meeting in Cincinnati, with Caylor and Charles Phares acting as his counsel, Mullane was exonerated of any wrongdoing. The unanimous vote once the evidence was reviewed was to acquit him of all charges and move to recover damages from the *Enquirer* unless the paper could prove its case.

No sooner had the Reds struck down this challenge to the team's integrity than they had to defy the local "Law and Order League" in order to play their first Sunday home game of the season on July 4 against the Athletics. Convinced the game would be canceled, the A's brought only a skeleton crew to the park and had to draft Ed Clark out of the stands to pitch. Clark, a Cincinnati amateur, came out on the wrong end of an 8–0 shutout in his only major league start, but it was one of the rare high spots in a tedious season that rendered Caylor fed up with the Queen City's politics long before it ended.

He at least finished out the year at the Reds helm. Jim Gifford, in contrast, was fired by the Mets only 17 games into the season when the club got off to a 5–12 start. One New York reporter traced the Mets' decline to "the spirit of good little Eddie Kennedy, the old left-fielder of the club, [which] still hovers over the nine, and believers in omens say that Manager Gifford allowed the club's 'Mascot' to escape when Kennedy was released." Other writers blamed the location of the Mets park, grumbling that transportation to it was too expensive and the trip was too long to make just on the chance the weather would be decent. But even when the day was windy and foggy, as it often was, and

•••
Henry Larkin led the Athletics in almost every offensive department in 1886. He also paced all AA outfielders in errors with 44. In 1888, when the A's got Curt Welch, Larkin was moved to first base, where he remained until his retirement in 1893. Larkin was one of the hardest hitters in the game, but his lack of speed kept him from becoming a star of the first order.

•••
Pop Corkhill was second only to Curt Welch among AA flychasers. He also could play every infield position and, in 1886, filled in at third base while Hick Carpenter was out with a sprained ankle. Corkhill even took an occasional turn in the box. In 1885 he was the Reds' top relief pitcher.

OLD JUDGE CIGARETTES Goodwin & Co., New York.

• • •

Nat Hudson staged a turbulent holdout after his stellar rookie season in 1886 but was otherwise one of the Browns' more peaceful players. In early May of 1886 the mere prospect of having to work a series of games involving the Browns drove heralded rookie umpire Ben Young out of the AA.

the team played execrably, as it usually did, there were other attractions. Early in the year, a gorgeous and "handsomely dressed" mystery woman occupied a prime grandstand seat at every game. Seen to weep openly when the Mets lost, she was never identified and eventually stopped coming, but grandstand occupants soon were given another visual perk. In addition to the splendid view they had of New York harbor to the south, from July 12, 1886, to the end of the season they could stand on the top row, spin their heads back to the north, and watch the Statue of Liberty, then under construction, slowly ascending skyward.

In Pittsburgh, the perk, for the first time, was a contending team. Even though the Alleghenys started poorly, Horace Phillips stuck to his belief that having Pud Galvin for a full season to pair with Ed Morris would give his club the necessary strength to compete with the Browns' duo of Caruthers and Foutz. The fans too were buoyed. A local record total of 17,159 came out to a morning-afternoon doubleheader on Decoration Day, giving Baltimore a $2,145 half share of the holiday gate, the largest single-day windfall for a visiting club to that time. By June 16, Phillips had pulled the Alleghenys to within a game and a half of the first-place Browns. Having observed that Comiskey was winning now with three pitchers, after adding rookie Nat Hudson to the Browns' rotation, Phillips tried to buy Jumbo McGinnis from St. Louis. Between an ailing shoulder and the death of his three-year-old daughter in January, McGinnis had fallen into the doldrums and was rarely used by Comiskey once Hudson began to assert himself.

Von der Ahe was wary, though, of selling McGinnis to a contending team and on July 8 peddled him to Baltimore instead, even though Pittsburgh had offered more for his contract. McGinnis made little difference to the Orioles, which were headed for a basement finish in any event, but Phillips and Nimick were convinced—and not unjustifiably—that the Browns had roadblocked them from a shot at the pennant. In the final three months of the season McGinnis beat the Browns four times, and though he only posted an 11–13 record overall with the Orioles, he and rookie sensation Matt Kilroy collected 40 of the Orioles' 47 wins. To augment them, Billy Barnie used seven other hurlers at various junctures, including Dick Conway, who formed the second sibling battery in Association history with his older brother Bill, and one Zay (first name unknown), whose entire major league career was encompassed in the two innings he lasted in a lamentable start against Cincinnati on October 7. The seven second-liners combined for just eight wins in 44 decisions, as even Kilroy and his all-time record 513 strikeouts could do little for a nine that hit .204, the lowest average ever by a team that played a full schedule.

Yet Baltimore finished just four and a half games behind the seventh-place Mets and probably would have overtaken them but for Dave Orr. In 1886 the burly first sacker outhit every one of his Staten Island teammates by 97 points, finishing at .338 to third baseman Frank Hankinson's .241. The dearth of offense wrecked an attempt by Wiman's new manager, Bob Ferguson, to emulate the Browns. While the St. Louis trio of Caruthers, Foutz and Hudson was winning 87 games, Ferguson's three-man rotation of Al Mays, Jack Lynch and Ed Cushman made the Mets the first team to have three 20-game losers.

Even the traditionally strong-hitting Athletics sagged to a .235 average in 1886. Moved to left field to make room for rookie center gardener Ed Greer, Henry Larkin was fast emerging as one of the Association's new stars, but Harry Stovey skidded below .300, though with hitting on the wane everywhere he still managed to finish among the loop's top ten batters. In mid-June, following a 5–4 loss at home to Baltimore, co-owner Lew Simmons stomped into the A's clubhouse and fined shortstop Joe Quest $50 for a misplay that had cost the A's the game. Simmons then threatened to suspend practically the entire squad and relieved Stovey of all command over the team, snarling that he was too lax. For a while, Simmons took over the field operation of the club himself, but when the A's began to slide toward the cellar, Bill Sharsig regained control in time to bring them home sixth.

Simmons's clubhouse tirade had come at a juncture when the A's were only two games out of first place at 22–19, while Pittsburgh was in third at 25–21, Brooklyn held second at 24–19 and the Browns led with a 28–21 record. Louisville, which had beaten the Browns for the fifth time in the young season just a few days earlier and would up winning the season series with Comiskey's club ten games to nine, could have made it a five-team race but for an inability early on to beat the other contenders. By August, the Colonels were in full gear and for most of the month held second place. The highwater mark of the season in the Falls City came in a doubleheader against Baltimore on August 15. In the morning game, a replay of a tie that had been ended by darkness the previous day, Louisville southpaw Toad Ramsey beat the Orioles' Matt Kilroy 13–6 in a battle of the two greatest rookie strikeout artists in history. Neither hurler was on his game that day, and the hitting deluge continued in the afternoon contest, a matchup between Guy Hecker and the Conway brothers. An outstanding hitter for a pitcher, Hecker was put in the second slot in the batting order by Louisville skipper Jim Hart. In the resulting 22–5 Louisville win, he tallied a record seven runs, rapped six hits and became the one and only Association

A cabinet card of the players that Jim Hart piloted in California during December, 1886. To Hart's right, above the crossed bats, is Hub Collins, who joined Louisville too late in the 1886 season to be led astray as yet. So exhausted was Hart from having had to cope with the likes of Toad Ramsey and Pete Browning during the regular season that he left most of the Colonels' stars behind when he went West to head the tour team.

player to belt three home runs in a game. Hecker was awarded the lone batting title ever given to a pitcher, but a September slump dumped the Colonels into fourth place and cost Hart his job. Upon being bounced, Hart said he had only himself to fault for raising false hopes by spurring a club into second place that had no business being that high. Time would demonstrate that Hart's gripe was not just sour grapes, for the Colonels would soon become the most poorly run franchise in the majors.

A solid third-place finish further persuaded Brooklyn owner Charlie Byrne that he was the right man to pilot his own team, but others ascribed the Grays' ascension to their outfield of Ed Swartwood, Jim McTamany and Ernie Burch. Swartwood was back on track after a mediocre year in 1885 following his purchase from Pittsburgh, and the other two were fine rookie additions. Burch had been awarded to Brooklyn after a vicious dispute back in the spring that for a while eclipsed even the war over Sam Barkley's services, but McTamany, up from Lancaster of the Eastern League, was actually the more valuable of the two. In 1886, he topped all Association fly chasers in total chances per game and was the loop's premier frosh outfielder, an honor that meant something in a season that was rich with yearling stars. Baltimore produced Kilroy; Louisville unveiled Ramsey and third baseman Joe Werrick; Cincinnati introduced pitcher George Pechiney; and the A's had the biggest harvest of all in second baseman Lou Bierbauer, catcher Wilbert Robinson and pitcher Bill Hart, purchased in July from Chattanooga a few weeks after he set a Southern League record by hurling in four straight games.

Another Southern League recruit, Atlanta third baseman Denny Lyons, who joined the A's near the tail-end of the season, would become the best of the rookie bumper crop with time and Hudson would become both the most coveted and the most controversial. But, for the time being, the Browns' only new acquisition of consequence was content to help the club snare its second straight easy pennant.

A 9–3 homestand to launch the season vaulted the Browns to an 11–4 start. Before a home game with St. Louis on May 29, in an effort to take away the Browns' chief weapon, their superb

• • •
The only known picture of Jim McTamany, Brooklyn's new star in 1886, without a mustache. He stands at left with two Kansas City teammates in 1888. McTamany is the only player to tally both 100 walks and 100 runs in his final big league season (1891). A very enigmatic figure, McTamany could run, field and get on base but was constantly being sold or traded. The natural supposition is that he must have been a troublemaker, but the available testimony portrays him as being on the quiet side and so well regarded by his managers that he was often named field captain.

John Kerins had a solid year in 1886 for Louisville. He was headed for an even better one in 1887 before breaking his right hand in a July collision at home plate. Kerins returned to action too soon and was never the same player. In 1889, Chris Von der Ahe swore that Kerins, by then an AA umpire, had told Charlie Comiskey that Darby O'Brien had offered him a $1000 bribe. Kerins claimed he'd been misunderstood; O'Brien had said he'd gladly give $1000 out of his own pocket if Brooklyn could win the championship. O'Brien's version was that Kerins was a tremendous "guyer" who had invented the whole thing just to rile Comiskey.

baserunning, the A's spread loose gravel around each base, but Comiskey's men simply hauled out a few brooms during pregame practice, swept the gravel away and then ran wild. In Pittsburgh, the Browns were given a major scare when Comiskey crashed into a railing while chasing a pop foul and was knocked out, but he suffered only a lacerated mouth and quickly returned to the lineup. It was virtually the only injury the team sustained in 1886, as all eight regulars except rightfielder Hugh Nicol, who was benched for weak hitting, played nearly every game, and Doc Bushong became the first catcher to work over 100 contests in a season.

A brief slump in mid-May, during which the Browns lost four games in a week for one of only two times all season, forced them to surrender first place momentarily to Brooklyn, but after that they never again relinquished the lead. The final margin of victory was 12 games, thanks largely to a 59–20 record against the four second-division teams—Cincinnati, Philadelphia, the Mets and Baltimore. Against their three top rivals—Pittsburgh, Brooklyn and Louisville—the Browns compiled a much less spectacular 34–25 mark but were the only team to win a season series from Pittsburgh.

Notwithstanding the Allegheny club's newly gained respectability, Phillips and Nimick advanced only reasons to find grievance with the Association when they met with their stockholders at the end of the season. The Browns meanwhile tuned up for their second consecutive World's Series confrontation with the White Stockings by taking four straight games from the Maroons in mid-October to snare the St. Louis city series. A pall was cast over their victory, however, when Caruthers wrenched his knee on the bases in the first contest on October 14 and seemed likely to miss the World's Series. By the opener Caruthers had recovered sufficiently to man right field, but he was of little help as the Browns got just five hits, two each by Comiskey and Robinson, off John Clarkson, who cakewalked to a 6–0 win before 6,000 Chicago rooters, ecstatic to see their white-hosed wonders establish their superiority from the outset.

The following day it was Caruthers's turn to glow after he spun a 12–0 shutout over Jim McCormick in the first Series game ever to have two umpires. Prior to the first pitch Honest John Kelly was designated to be the referee and work the bases when his name was chosen by lot, and Joe Quest, released by the A's a couple of months earlier, and John McQuaid were selected to alternate behind the plate, Quest officiating when the Browns were up and McQuaid taking over each time Chicago batted. Bizarre as the arrangement seems now, it was regarded in 1886 as an impressive innovation and the first major step toward the two-umpire system Caylor and several other Association leaders had been touting for several years.

In the rubber game at Chicago, Caruthers essayed to pitch for the second day in a row, and got off to a bumpy start when he walked George Gore and King Kelly to open the game. After Cap Anson sacrificed, Caruthers walked Fred Pfeffer and then gave up his fourth free pass of the inning to Ned Williamson, forcing home Gore. When Tom Burns grounded to Yank Robinson, Kelly scored on the throw to first. Though Comiskey whipped the ball to Arlie Latham, nailing Pfeffer off third base to end the rally, that was the game. Down 2–0 before they came to the plate for their first at bat, the Browns never caught up and finally lost 11–4 to Clarkson for the second time in three days. Anson removed his ace in the eighth inning for Williamson when the victory seemed secure, but Comiskey let an exhausted and dispirited Caruthers go the route.

The two teams then piled into a train to St. Louis, where the next three games were slated to be played; a seventh contest, if necessary, was booked for a neutral site—Cincinnati's American Park. Nowadays there would be a day's break for travel, but in the 1880s players were expected to hop off an overnight coach and be ready for immediate action. As a result, the six games of the 1886 World's Series were crammed into only six days. The Browns knotted the fray at 2–all by taking their home opener, 8–5, when Anson consented to umpire Quest's wish to call the game on account of darkness after only six and a half innings were played. Anson's compliance was based in part on a desire to spare Clarkson, working his third game in four days, so that he would be rested enough to come back in Game Six. For Game Five on October 22, Anson planned to start Mark Baldwin, the Northwestern League's leading hurler in 1886 who had been signed by Chicago just two days earlier. But Comiskey vetoed Baldwin, even though Anson protested that Clarkson and McCormick were both too weary to pitch and that sore-armed rookie 24-game winner Jocko Flynn had been left behind in Chicago on the assumption Baldwin would be approved. Lacking a bonafide pitcher, Anson was made to start third baseman Williamson in the fifth game and then replace him with rightfielder Jimmy Ryan after the Browns chalked up three quick runs to send Hudson off to an easy 10–3 win.

Now down three games to two in the best-of-seven affair, Anson called on Clarkson again. Comiskey turned to a somewhat regenerated Caruthers, who had not pitched in three days though his arm had been used in right field. The all-important umpire's job went to the "stout, broad-shouldered" Gracie Pierce, who had been through as a player for more than two years. Pierce had not umpired a major league game since 1882 and would not work one

FULLMER, C., Baltimores
OLD JUDGE
CIGARETTE FACTORY

• • •
Chris Fulmer, one of the few Washington UA members to play again in the majors. After spending 1885 in the Eastern League, Fulmer led all Baltimore regulars in 1886 with a .244 batting average. He still lost his first-string catching post the following year to Sam Trott. Fulmer groused that Billy Barnie favored Trott so that Trott, a great roller skater, would continue to give free exhibitions at Barnie's rink.

again until 1890. Nevertheless, his officiating presumably was adequate. At any rate, it went unmentioned in most accounts of the game, which began disastrously for the Browns and ended with the event that flew the Association to its absolute pinnacle. Never again would the Beer and Whisky League soar as high as it did on October 23, 1886.

At 2:18, Pierce called "Play," and both Caruthers and Clarkson completed the first inning unscathed. Chicago then punched home a single run in the top of the second and added another in the fourth. Trailing 2–0, Comiskey pulled his players over to the sidelines and began prodding Pierce to call the game before it went five innings and became official because a steady drizzle was falling. But Von der Ahe, fearing a crowd riot, ordered Comiskey to send the players back to their places.

Comiskey mentally conceded the game when Chicago took a 3–0 lead in the sixth, which was still intact as the bottom of the eighth began. St. Louis then tied the count by scoring three runs, the latter two coming on a triple by Latham that Anson would always swear was no more than a fly ball that White Stockings leftfielder Abner Dalrymple should have had in his hip pocket. The 3–3 tie lasted into the bottom of the tenth. Curt Welch led off by singling to center for only the Browns' fourth hit off Clarkson. He darted to second on Dave Foutz's infield hit and then was sacrificed to third by Yank Robinson. With Bushong at bat and Welch jockeying up and down the baseline, threatening at any instant to steal home, Clarkson grew rattled. He unleashed an upshoot that eluded King Kelly, who had been looking for a low pitch, and Welch sprinted home with the run that sealed the Association's first and only undisputed championship win over its arch rival. Though game accounts indicate that Welch scored standing up on the wild pitch, his dash was later labeled "The $15,000 Slide," but even the sum is specious. The Browns' spoils from their victory actually came to just $13,920. Half of it was divided equally among the team's 12 players at $580 apiece, which amounted, for most, to about a third of their 1886 salaries. The other half went to Von der Ahe, who paid the umpires and expenses out of his share. Because the 1886 World's Series was a winner-take-all affair, the White Stockings got zip for their work, prompting a reversion the following year to the 1885 format, which called for both contestants to split the gate receipts 50/50.

Though Welch drew most of the accolades in the press for the Browns' gritty comeback win, those closest to the team knew its true catalyst was Caruthers. The son of a prominent Memphis lawyer who had moved his family to Chicago in the late 1870s, the little pitcher grew up accustomed to having the best in life.

• • •
Arlie Latham personified the "down and dirty" Browns. In June 1886, Billy Barnie and Charlie Byrne forced the collection of fines imposed by AA umpires on Latham and Charlie Comiskey to the tune of $260. They then tried to have Latham and catcher Doc Bushong suspended for an on-field fight in early June. AA president Wheeler Wyckoff first ordered the pair to the sidelines for thirty days and then changed it to $100 fine when he was accused by Chris Von der Ahe of trying to keep the Browns from winning the pennant.

• • •

The 1886 NL champion Chicago White Stockings. The banner at rear was premature. In the national championship series with the Browns, Chicago lost. Jimmy Ryan (top row, fourth from left) had the kind of career that many AA players who missed out on the Hall of Fame did, but he too has been denied enshrinement. To Ryan's left is Jocko Flynn, the rookie sensation who blew out his arm on the eve of the World's Series, making the Browns' task easier.

But if Caruthers never lacked for wealth, his health was precarious almost from birth. Sickly all during childhood, he had been encouraged to participate in light outdoor exercise but was warned to stay away from vigorous activity. To his mother's consternation, Caruthers took up baseball and quickly achieved local eminence playing for various Chicago amateur teams. Over his family's violent objections, he signed a professional contract with Grand Rapids in 1883. Within three years, however, Caruthers had allayed even his mother by attaining both fame and fortune as a ballplayer. Though just twenty-two in the fall of 1886, he was already a national hero and arguably the game's most versatile player, good enough to lead the Association in slugging average and to rank near the top in virtually every pitching department.

The post-Series victory parade, in which most of the Browns and Von der Ahe were shouldered by adoring fans, seemed as if it would be only one of many such occasions for the Association. When the two major leagues met that fall to hammer out some lingering wrinkles in the National Agreement and draft a uniform set of playing rules, it was as equals. But Association leaders had yet to grasp that the League was girding itself for war even as it behaved

• • •

The 1889 Pittsburgh Alleghenys. Three years after leaving the AA, Pittsburgh still had many of its old Association stars, but none helped more in 1889 than Fred Carroll, who batted .330. Catchers who could hit were scarce then. Carroll's bat was so potent that room had to be found for him on days when his hands were too sore to catch. First base, as Pittsburgh learned in 1886, wasn't a great spot because Carroll's aching hands made him drop too many throws. He was subsequently tried with success in the outfield.

like a dove. Soon after that grand meeting in which it had been almost servile, the League twisted the spat between Pittsburgh and the Association to its own ends and enticed the Allegheny club into its camp. Had it played its cards better and waited a few more weeks, the League might have netted a second, even bigger fish. Over the winter, Cincinnati owner John Hauck sold his stake in the Reds to Aaron Stern. Caylor said it was done because Hauck was "an old man" who was worried that as a churchman, pressure to stage Sunday games in Cincinnati would damage his business interests in the German National Bank. With Stern back in the saddle and the *Enquirer* still giving him a merciless emotional pounding, Caylor decided that it was time for him to go too. He announced that he was leaving baseball and heading east in 1887 to work again as a journalist, probably in Philadelphia.

John J. Fields, l. f.   G. F. Miller, c.   W. J. Kuehne, 2b.   H. E. Staley, p.   E. Morris, p
F. H. Carroll, c.   J. P. Beckley, 1b.   Capt. Ed Hanlon, c. f.   Jas. White, 3b.   J. Rowe, s. s.

THE PITTSBURG BASE BALL CLUB.

1889

Caylor's imminent departure meant that the Association would soon be shorn of its two primary sires. By the time the 1887 season began, Horace Phillips and his Pittsburgh Alleghenys would be a League affiliate and Caylor would be out of the game altogether. Phillips would be little missed. He was considered remarkably quick for his years and "a prince of a schedule maker" but otherwise kind of a pain whose overzealousness "won for him the name of meddler or disturber." Phillips would continue to manage the Pittsburgh club for a salary and a percentage of the profits until July 1889 when he began having delusions that he was a wealthy tycoon and tried to buy all sorts of businesses including several major league teams. Believed by doctors to be in the advanced stages of paresis, on August 1, 1889, he was locked up at his wife Anna's urging in an insane asylum near Merchantville, New Jersey. Five years later, however, Phillips was reported to be still alive, apparently suffering from a mental affliction rather than syphilis. Only forty-one years old at the time, in any case he was never heard from again.

Caylor would continue to be heard from until his death in 1897. He would even return to the Association soon after the 1887 season began, when the itch to be in the thick of the action again overcame him. But then something occurred that would forever turn him against the Association and transform him from its greatest champion into one of its most implacable foes. It would be this parting of the ways, more than any other single event, that knocked the Association from its lofty perch and in the end doomed it to near oblivion.

• • •

In 1886, Bob Caruthers tussled Guy Hecker for the AA batting crown while winning 30 games. A high-ball hitter, Caruthers suffered when the high-low rule was abolished in 1887. However, he had craftily concealed his weakness for low pitches to an extent by occasionally calling for low ones, especially against hurlers he knew he couldn't hit anyway. As a result, pitchers did not catch on to Caruthers's game immediately. It was not until 1888 that the rule change really impacted him.

1886 FINAL STANDINGS

	W	L	PCT	HOME	ROAD	GB
1. St. Louis Browns	93	46	.669	52–18	41–28	
2. Pittsburgh Alleghenys	80	57	.584	46–19	34–28	12
3. Brooklyn Grays	76	61	.555	43–25	33–36	16
4. Louisville Colonels	66	70	.485	37–19	16–40	25.5
5. Cincinnati Reds	65	73	.471	40–31	25–42	27.5
6. Philadelphia Athletics	63	72	.467	37–32	26–40	28
7. New York Metropolitans	53	82	.393	30–33	23–49	38
8. Baltimore Orioles	48	83	.366	30–31	18–52	41

● ● ●

Baltimore rookie Matt Kilroy fanned an all-time record 513 batters in 1886 thanks in part to being allowed to use a running start. Strangely, Kilroy was not known as a strikeout pitcher in the minors. For example, on September 17, 1885, when he beat Nashville to clinch second place in the Southern League for Augusta, he had just one whiff.

BATTING

BATTING AVERAGE (300 ABs)

1. Hecker, Louis		.341
2. Browning, Louis		.340
3. Orr, NY		.338
4. Caruthers, StL		.334
5. O'Neill, StL		.328
6. Larkin, Phila		.319
7. Lewis, Cinci		.318
8. Latham, StL		.301
9. Stovey, Phila		.294
10. F. Carroll, Pitts		.288

ON-BASE PERCENTAGE

1. Caruthers, StL		.463
2. Hecker, Louis		.402
3. Larkin, Phila		.390
4. Browning, Louis		.389
5. O'Neill, StL		.385
6. Stovey, Phila		.377
Swartwood, Brook		.377
Robinson, StL		.377
9. Latham, StL		.368
10. T. Brown, Pitts		.365
Lewis, Cinci		.365

HOME RUNS

1. McPhee, Cinci		7
Stovey, Phila		7
Orr, NY		7
4. Fennelly, Cinci		6
5. F. Carroll, Pitts		5
Roseman, NY		5
C. Jones, Cinci		5
Milligan, Phila		5
9. Caruthers, StL		4
Kerins, Louis		4
Hecker, Louis		4
Reilly, Cinci		4
Corkhill, Cinci		4

HITS

1. Orr, NY		193
2. O'Neill, StL		190
3. Larkin, Phila		180
4. Latham, StL		174
5. Phillips, Brook		160
6. Browning, Louis		159
7. Welch, StL		158
8. Pinkney, Brook		156
9. McClellan, Brook		152
10. McPhee, Cinci		150

SLUGGING AVERAGE

1. Orr, NY		.5271
2. Caruthers, StL		.5268
3. Larkin, Phila		.450
4. Hecker, Louis		.446
5. Browning, Louis		.441
6. O'Neill, StL		.440
Stovey, Phila		.440
8. F. Carroll, Pitts		.422
9. Lewis, Cinci		.417
10. McPhee, Cinci		.393
Welch, StL		.393

TOTAL BASES

1. Orr, NY		301
2. O'Neill, StL		255
3. Larkin, Phila		254
4. Welch, StL		221
5. McPhee, Cinci		217
6. Phillips, Brook		216
Latham, StL		216
8. Stovey, Phila		215
9. Browning, Louis		206
McClellan, Brook		206

RUNS

1. Latham, StL		152
2. McPhee, Cinci		139
3. Larkin, Phila		133
4. McClellan, Brook		131
5. Pinkney, Brook		119
6. Stovey, Phila		114
Welch, StL		114
8. Kerins, Louis		113
Fennelly, Cinci		113
10. O'Neill, StL		106
T. Brown, Pitts		106

STOLEN BASES

1. Stovey, Phila		68
2. Latham, StL		60
3. Welch, StL		59
4. Robinson, StL		51
5. McClellan, Brook		43
6. Comiskey, StL		41
7. McPhee, Cinci		40
8. P. Smith, Pitts		38
Nicol, StL		38
10. Swartwood, Brook		37

*RBI leaders unavailable.

PITCHING

DAVIS, 3d B Kansas City

OLD JUDGE
CIGARETTES
GOODWIN & CO. New York

• • •

In 1886, Baltimore's four regular infielders—Milt Scott, Mike Muldoon, Jimmy Macullar and rookie third sacker Jumbo Davis (above)—hit below .200 as a unit, and backups Joe Farrell and Sadie Houck were just as bad. Scott drew raves early on. "Great Scott! Who would give our Scott for Barkley!" cackled one Baltimore writer. "The graceful first baseman is playing great ball, besides hitting very well." Scott ended the season at .190, the lowest batting average ever for a first sacker with over 400 at bats.

WINS

1. Morris, Pitts	41
Foutz, StL	41
3. Ramsey, Louis	38
4. Mullane, Cinci	33
5. Caruthers, StL	30
6. Kilroy, Balt	29
Galvin, Pitts	29
8. Porter, Brook	27
9. Hecker, Louis	26
10. Atkinson, Phila	15

LOSSES

1. Kilroy, Balt	34
2. Lynch, NY	30
3. Mays, NY	28
4. Mullane, Cinci	27
Ramsey, Louis	27
6. Hecker, Louis	23
7. Galvin, Pitts	21
Pechiney, Cinci	21
9. Cushman, NY	20
Morris, Pitts	20

INNINGS

1. Ramsey, Louis	588.2
2. Kilroy, Balt	583
3. Morris, Pitts	555.1
4. Mullane, Cinci	529.2
5. Foutz, StL	504
6. Galvin, Pitts	434.2
7. Lynch, NY	432.2
8. Porter, Brook	424
9. Hecker, Louis	421
10. Atkinson, Phila	396.2

COMPLETE GAMES

1. Ramsey, Louis	66
Kilroy, Balt	66
3. Morris, Pitts	63
4. Mullane, Cinci	55
Foutz, StL	55
6. Lynch, NY	50
7. Porter, Brook	48
8. Galvin, Pitts	47
9. Hecker, Louis	45
10. Atkinson, Phila	44

STRIKEOUTS

1. Kilroy, Balt	513
2. Ramsey, Louis	499
3. Morris, Pitts	326
4. Foutz, StL	283
5. Mullane, Cinci	250
6. Lynch, NY	193
7. Cushman, NY	167
8. Caruthers, StL	166
9. Mays, NY	163
Porter, Brook	163

WINNING PCT. (25 DECISIONS)

1. Foutz, StL	.719
2. Caruthers, StL	.682
3. Morris, Pitts	.672
4. Hudson, StL	.615
5. Atkinson, Phila	.595
6. Porter, Brook	.587
7. Ramsey, Louis	.585
8. Galvin, Pitts	.580
9. Mullane, Cinci	.550
10. Hecker, Louis	.531

ERA (140 INNINGS)

1. Foutz, StL	2.11
2. Caruthers, StL	2.32
3. Ramsey, Louis	2.45
Morris, Pitts	2.45
5. Galvin, Pitts	2.67
6. Hecker, Louis	2.87
7. C. Miller, Phila	2.97
8. Hudson, StL	3.03
9. Terry, Brook	3.09
10. Cushman, NY	3.12

LOWEST ON-BASE PCT.

1. Morris, Pitts	.255
2. Caruthers, StL	.259
3. Ramsey, Louis	.269
4. Foutz, StL	.270
5. Kilroy, Balt	.272
6. Cushman, NY	.277
7. Hecker, Louis	.285
8. Hudson, StL	.287
9. Galvin, Pitts	.288
10. Mullane, Cinci	.294

• • •

Elmer Smith sits in the middle row, second from left, in this picture of the 1895 Pittsburgh Pirates. In 1887, Smith and Tony Mullane had a combined 64–35 record for Cincinnati while the team's other pitchers went 17–19, explaining why the Reds finished a distant second. Smith denied Opie Caylor's allegation that booze caused his decline the following year, saying he had rheumatism in his shoulder and had ceased "rushing the growler." (A growler in the 1880s was a nickel pail of beer.) When his arm failed him for keeps in 1889, Smith dropped back to the minors, worked on his hitting, and in 1892 returned to the majors, where he carved a lustrous new career as an outfielder.

BREAK UP
THE BROWNS

EVERYONE THOUGHT THE BROWNS WERE IN-credibly lucky, especially with their pitchers. As minor leaguers, Foutz and Caruthers had seemed promising but nothing extraordinary. Yet, in little more than two and a half seasons, they had won 166 games between them, and now Von der Ahe had, in Nat Hudson, a third pitcher who appeared to be nearly as good. It was an excess of riches. It was too much. It was so unfair that the other Association owners understandably were less than sympathetic when Hudson refused to sign his contract for 1887 and became one of the game's first great holdouts.

Hudson later denied the issue was money. When he finally joined the Browns in June, he said he'd been kept away from baseball by his father's death and his mother's illness, but most of his teammates figured he was putting the screws to Von der Ahe, much as Caruthers had done the previous year. In the winter of 1885–86 Caruthers ran a shoe store in St. Louis and vowed he'd sell shoes forever rather than sign for a mere $2,000 pittance

... The AA didn't keep reliable RBI data in 1887, so we can't determine RBI totals for that season. Almost certainly, however, Tip O'Neill was the runaway RBI leader, as he was in just about every other batting department. In 1887, O'Neill became the only player ever to top a major league in hits, runs, doubles, triples, home runs, total bases, slugging average and batting average.

when he learned that Von der Ahe intended to try to impose the new salary max the National Agreement had passed. He then threatened a trip to Scotland, England, and maybe Australia if he didn't get a contract offer more to his taste. Soon after that he disappeared. Eventually, Von de Ahe got a cable that his star pitcher was in Paris and would return on April 1. But when Von der Ahe had the passenger lists for transatlantic ships checked, he could find no one named Caruthers. On his reappearance in St. Louis, Caruthers claimed he'd gone abroad with Doc Bushong, but many still thought he'd never really left the country and had just bluffed Von der Ahe into paying him what he wanted. Lending a smidge of credibility to Caruthers's tale is the fact that in the winter of 1883–84 Bushong studied dentistry in Bordeaux, France, so if nothing else, the pitcher embellished his story with a plausible travel companion. In any case, the maneuver earned him the nickname "Parisian Bob." It also gained the Browns another pitcher. Against the possibility that Caruthers would not return from Paris or wherever he was, Von der Ahe had procured Hudson as insurance.

Now that Hudson was apparently pulling the same stunt, Von der Ahe saw no reason to change a formula that had already worked so well once. He signed a young St. Louis native, just turned nineteen, who was born under the name of Charles Koenig. The previous year, Koenig had made his professional debut with St. Joseph of the Western League and late in the summer had caught the eye of the Kansas City Cowboys. Koenig joined the Cowboys in time to hurl in five games, including the final contest Kansas City played as a member of the League. On the closing day of the 1886 season, Koenig beat Washington for his first major league victory.

Sportswriters had already translated the pitcher's Germanic surname to "King" by the time he joined the Browns. Owing to his almost albino white hair, he was nicknamed "Silver." As Silver King, Charles Koenig won 112 games for St. Louis over the next three years and staked his claim to being the best pitcher ever to perform in the Association.

King made his Beer and Whisky League entrance on April 26, 1887, with a 19–6 win over Cincinnati's Mike Shea, who that afternoon hurled his second and last major league game. Six days earlier, Shea had been victorious in his debut, helping the Reds to get off to a 5–0 start and the early lead in the pennant race. Even after Shea's release following the April 26 debacle, another rookie hurler named Elmer Smith and White Wings Tebeau, a freshman who was trying to wrest the leftfield post away from long-time incumbent Charley Jones, together with the Reds new manager

Gus Schmelz infused the club with enough fresh blood that even the *Enquirer* waxed enthusiastic about the Queen City's prospects for 1887. Opie Caylor, it began to seem, really had been the problem after all.

In the Reds opener on April 16, a 16–6 pasting of the new Cleveland entry, Tebeau hit a home run in his first major league at bat. Nothing was made of it at the time—no one cared in 1887 about such things, or even noticed. A century later, however, after researchers had noted that on April 16, 1887, Baltimore rookie Mike Griffin homered in his initial major league at bat and so became apparently the first ever to do so, someone spotted that, on the same day no less, Tebeau had also done it. But on the afternoon that odd confluence occurred, the press was far more interested in the action at Louisville, where Toad Ramsey hurled the Colonels to an 8–3 win over the defending world's champion Browns.

Three days later, the Browns bagged their first victory of the season when Caruthers bested Ramsey, but the wins in the early going were few and far between for Comiskey's crew. Part of the reason was a patch of miserable weather that caused many games in the first weeks of the season to be postponed, but in any event Brooklyn occupied first place on April 29 with a 6–1 record, Cincinnati and St. Louis were tied for second at 6–3, and the Mets, winless in their first eight games, were last albeit only half a game behind Cleveland, which had won just once in nine outings.

Brooklyn's fast start made Charlie Byrne think himself a genius for hiring Jack McMasters, a former boxing trainer, to whip his club into playing trim, but fans in the City of Churches wished he had hired some new players. Alone among the eight Association teams, Brooklyn had unearthed no rookie finds, a failing that would help drag the club all the way down to sixth place by the end of the season. Even the abysmal Mets had added Darby O'Brien, the 1886 Western League batting champion, and John Shaffer, a hard-throwing pitcher who had joined the team late in the previous campaign and won his first four starts, two of them over the Browns. Shaffer was grounded by arm trouble, winning just two of 13 decisions in 1887 before the Mets dropped him, but O'Brien was the McCoy, leading the team in most batting departments and vying with Griffin, King and Elmer Smith for rookie honors.

Other meritorious yearlings were Philadelphia's two young pitching nuggets, 25-game winner Ed Seward and 26-game winner Gus Weyhing; Cleveland shortstop Ed McKean; Louisville's new leftfielder Hub Collins; and Baltimore first sacker Tommy Tucker, who was instrumental in transforming the Orioles in the space of

• • •

In 1887, Mets rookie Darby O'Brien got off to a slow start. The front office wanted him benched, but manager Bob Ferguson saw his talent and refused. O'Brien spent his freshman season helping Dave Orr keep the Mets out of the AA basement. The following year he crossed the Gowanus Bay, when Brooklyn owner Charlie Byrne bought the Mets in order to garner their few remaining decent players. O'Brien was a Brooklyn mainstay until his health declined in 1892. He died the following summer at his Peoria home.

one year from the worst-hitting team of all time into one of the best in the Association. Tucker was a real rarity in his day, a switch-hitter. One of the first of note, Tucker confounded Tony Mullane, who was even more of a rarity—a switch-pitcher. Although normally a righthander, Mullane could throw effectively with either arm. Since many players in the mid-1880's still did not use gloves in the field, Mullane would sometimes hide his hands behind his back as he began his delivery, keeping a batter guessing until the last instant as to which arm would launch the ball. But Tucker had the weapon to thwart Mullane. Inasmuch as the rules in 1887 permitted a hitter to jump from one batter's box to another at will, Tucker was free to leap to the opposite side of the plate as soon as he saw with which arm Mullane would pitch.

The 1887 season in both major leagues saw a panoply of rules and customs that seem archaic now. It was the first year that batters no longer had the privilege to call for either a high or a low pitch. Afraid the change would give pitchers too great an advantage, the Rules Committee shaved the number of balls needed to walk to five and hiked the number of strikes needed for a strikeout to four. For reasons that will probably never be wholly comprehensible, the rulesmiths then decided to count a walk as both a time at bat and a base hit. This unprecedented gift to batters enabled Tip O'Neill to hit .492 in 1887 when his walks were added to his hits and meant that anyone who batted under .300 was considered a pudding.

The 1887 season was also the first in which an umpire was no longer permitted to change his mind if a player or a spectator convinced him that he had made the wrong call. He was still at liberty, though, to consult with players before he rendered a decision. By 1887, umpires in both the League and the Association were contracted for the full season at salaries that were comparable to what substitute players received. John McQuaid, the Association's senior arbiter by dint of the fact that he was serving in his second full season in the loop, was paid a reported $1,400, and Bob Ferguson, hired to officiate after he was canned in May as the Mets manager, got $1,200. Ferguson's salary was pro-rated, as was that of former Association pitcher Al Bauers, who drifted into umpiring when he could no longer find work as a player, even in the minors. Wesley Curry, a young Philadelphian who had apprenticed in several eastern minor leagues, rounded out the four-man staff, which also included at various points in the season former Browns manager Ted Sullivan, John Valentine and another former Browns manager, Ned Cuthbert. Valentine bolted to the League early in the 1887 season for more money but lived to regret it when he was hit by a pitch while working behind the plate

From Walzl's Imperial Portrait Studios.

{ N. E. Cor. Eutaw & Franklin Sts. } BALTIMORE

• • •

Mike Griffin, one of the two AA rookies who homered in their first major league at bats in 1887. After a sophmore slump, Griffin grew into a superb outfielder. In 1890, Griffin, Jim Fogarty and Curt Welch were rated the best defensive gardeners in the game by *The Sporting News*, with Griffin given the nod as the most valuable overall because of his superior hitting.

and had his arm broken. Since the League refused to pay an umpire if he lost time to an injury, Valentine tried to officiate with his arm in a cast but had to stop when the pain grew unbearable. Cuthbert also was sidelined in June 1887 by an injury. In September he tried, without success, to sue the Association for his full year's salary.

The travails of Valentine, Cuthbert and other umpires of the period no doubt contributed to Honest John Kelly's decision to put aside his umpire's mask for a safer post. In 1886, Kelly, then in his fourth season as an Association arbiter, had turned down an offer to manage the Louisville club, saying, "Of course it will pay better than umpiring, but when you have umpired the game your work is over, while that of the manager continues almost year round." Upon reconsideration, though, Kelly took the Falls City job. He even toyed for a while with the notion of playing. Accustomed to being in the thick of the action, Kelly had trouble adjusting to a seat on the bench. Constantly in motion, he rode his players hard, perhaps too hard. On Pete Browning, who literally turned a deaf ear when he was chastised, Kelly despaired of effecting any change. In early May, Browning was arrested after an argument over whether a pass he tendered to board a Louisville streetcar was good after 6 PM when passes were no longer honored. Kelly let the local police handle that one, but in July he fined Browning $110 for getting "howling drunk" at a picnic after being excused from a Monday afternoon practice to attend it. With Toad Ramsey, Kelly at first took a similar tack, fining him $50 in mid-May for going on a bender with a "scarlet woman" after he pitched a "bum" game against Baltimore. But the temperamental southpaw, whose sinker balls Kelly rated the most arduous test for an Association umpire trying to call balls and strikes accurately, ignored the standard methods to curb his misbehavior. Compounding Kelly's headache was Ramsey's attitude toward Guy Hecker. In 1886, Ramsey's claim that Hecker was jealous of him had caused a schism in the team that resulted in Hecker being relieved of his captaincy and catcher John Kerins, once Ramsey's greatest champion, to stop talking to Toad. When the acrimony between the two stars flared again in 1887, Kelly finally had to resolve the problem by keeping Hecker on the bench when Ramsey was pitching, as Ramsey was convinced that every error Hecker made at first base was an attempt to sabotage him. With all the havoc going on around him, some of which he created, Kelly still guided the Colonels home fourth and even had them in second place for a spell. But the experience so burned him out that two months into the 1888 season, though he was just thirty-one years old, he quit the Colonels, never again to work regularly in the majors except for special guest-umpiring appearances in the World's Series.

Gus Schmelz could also have been discombobulated by events in 1887, but instead he rode out the tempest and rallied Cincinnati to its highest finish since 1882. The bearded ex-Columbus Buckeyes skipper appeared to be nurturing a possible pennant winner in early May, when Tony Mullane suddenly rebelled and refused to pitch after being listed to start a game against Brooklyn. Fined $100 by Schmelz and suspended indefinitely, Mullane accelerated the dispute when he threatened to shoot Mike Arnold, a security guard Schmelz and Cincinnati owner Aaron Stern had ordered to keep Mullane out of the Reds ballpark. The suspension lasted more than a month while the Reds tried to pry Nat Hudson loose from the Browns. When the holdout hurler finally announced he was signing with St. Louis, Schmelz capitulated on June 11 and cabled Mullane to return to the team. In his first game back, Mullane beat the Browns, 8–4. Attention in Cincinnati then shifted to the other end of the points, where Kid Baldwin was embarked on a durability kick that would not end until he had caught in a record 49 straight games. Baldwin worked behind the bat in game after game because he was one of the top catchers in the Association, but St. Louis rookie Jack Boyle, who in the summer of 1887 caught in 41 straight games, donned the mask and chest protector so often because Comiskey had no one else after Doc Bushong, the game's sturdiest receiver in 1886, broke a finger on July 1. Boyle was badly overmatched at the plate, hitting just .189, some 84 points below the loop average, but he showed enough promise defensively that Von der Ahe felt comfortable selling Bushong to Brooklyn over the winter.

Among the many teams that entered into the bidding for Hudson during his lengthy holdout was the Association's newest member, the Cleveland Blues. Cleveland was accepted in late November 1886, after Detroit manager Bill Watkins had crashed an Association meeting to sound out the possibility that his Wolverines could desert the League and join the Association. He was told that, if he was really in earnest, he should make a formal bid for admission. Watkins then cabled Detroit owner Frederick Stearns for authorization to do so, but got a return cable saying that the League had acceded to all of Detroit's demands and the club would stay put. The likelihood is that Watkins and Stearns importuned the Association only to pressure the League into giving the Detroit club a better deal, but it is worth a moment to speculate what might have happened if the Association had jumped on the feeler Watkins put out and corralled Detroit even as it was losing Pittsburgh to the League. In 1887, the Wolverines proved to be the

• • •

In 1887, Topeka—the class of the Western League—glittered with both future and past AA performers. Everyone in this snazzy cabinet card except catcher Jake Kenyon played in the majors during the 1880s. "Hafner" is Bill Hoffner, who was with Kansas City in 1888. W.H. Goldsby is Walt Goldsby, one of the first great minor league stars to wash out in the majors.

THE BEER AND WHISKY LEAGUE

strongest club in the game. A season-long battle between Detroit and the Browns would almost certainly have sent profits soaring throughout the Association. The tragedy, for Detroit, was that the League reneged on most of the concessions it promised and Stearns was forced to move the club anyway after the 1888 season.

For the Association, the tragedy was that instead of taking on the majors' strongest team in 1887 it saddled itself with the weakest. The Cleveland club had money and brains behind it but little luck. Principal backer of the Blues was Frank DeHaas Robison, who owned the Payne and Superior Avenue streetcar lines in Cleveland and built his park at Payne and East Thirty-ninth Street on the Payne branch. Robison's brother, Stanley, later helped him run the club, but for the moment he entrusted personnel decisions to his secretary, Davis Hawley.

• • •
The 1886 Poughkeepsies furnished the AA with numerous players, including Mike Lehane, Tom and Mike McDermott, Sam Shaw and Chief Zimmer. Zimmer, who had already muffed an NL test with Detroit, muffed another in 1886 with the Mets. The following year, though he was past twenty-six, Cleveland gave him one last shot at the majors. Zimmer then proceeded to catch in top company until he was in his mid-forties.

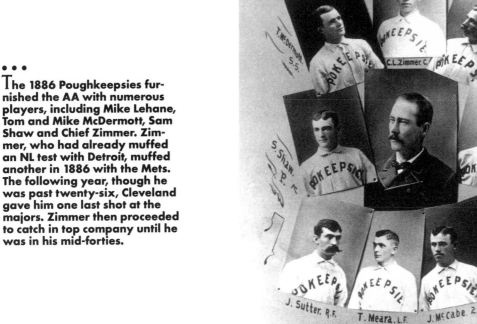

Hawley seemingly did a miserable job in the club's inaugural season, but the fault was scarcely his. In 1887 when a new team came on board it was entirely on its own. There was no draft pool of players contributed by existing teams, no effort at all to see that the newcomer was stocked with enough talent to make a go of it. One thing that Hawley could do was hire an experienced manager. He picked Jimmy Williams for the task. Williams was no better at handling hard cases in Cleveland than he had been in St. Louis, and he was tested almost immediately by Charlie Sweeney. His arm now gone just three years after he had won 41 games at age twenty-one, Sweeney was hired to man first base and give the club at least one name player, only to be dumped two months into the season after he punched out a teammate. Also jettisoned was One Arm Daily, no fighter, but in other ways an even nastier specimen. The previous May, when Mike Scanlon, owner of the Washington League team, had announced at a press conference that he was releasing the churlish Daily, all the writers present had stood up and cheered. Glad as he was to get rid of Sweeney and Daily, Williams could not be happy with the players he found to take their places. He griped that the other Association clubs were bent on keeping his Blues from improving. Seconding his grievance was Cleveland sportswriter Frank Brunell, whose protestations in various journals, though highly prejudiced, were so well drafted they made readers think Opie Caylor might be penning them under an alias.

Meanwhile, the real Opie Caylor was working for *Sporting Life* in Philadelphia and trying to adapt to his new role as no more than a detached observer of Association affairs. On May 6, he observed that Cleveland and the Mets were deadlocked for last at 1–12. Ten days later, at Cleveland's Payne St. park, in the first battle of the season between the two tail-enders, the Mets withstood Fred Mann's grandslam homer in the ninth inning to triumph 9–8. The game marked one of Joe Gerhardt's first appearances with the Mets and was expected to be a turning point in their fortunes. An enormous favorite of the New York sporting crowd, Gerhardt had requested his release from the Giants a few days earlier, claiming that Buck Ewing and Monte Ward had turned the team against him, and was cheered wildly as he left the Polo Grounds for the final time after cleaning out his locker. Soon after joining the Mets, though, he was laid low by a bad back and then contracted malaria. In early June, when Dave Orr, who had replaced Bob Ferguson as manager, also was hurt, breaking a blood vessel and losing two teeth in a collision with catcher Peter Sommers while chasing a pop foul, the Mets tumbled into the basement and seemed certain to stay there. After Orr lost his appetite

The picture labels read: CAPT. R. FERGUSON, 3rd B.; THOS. BARLOW, C.; JAS. BRITTON; R. J. PEARCE, SS.; ATLANTIC.; CHAS. PABOR L.F.; J. J. REMSEN, C.F.; H. DEHLMAN, 1st B.; Wm. BOYD, R.F.; J. BURDOCK, 2nd B.

• • •

The 1873 Brooklyn Atlantics, featuring captain Bob Ferguson, the first switch-hitter of note. Disliked as a manager and maligned as a player, Ferguson did not find his metier until he became an umpire in 1887 after he was fired as the Mets pilot. Ferguson's cocky and aloof manner made him the AA's most esteemed umpire in the late 1880s. Also in the Atlantics picture is Jack Remsen, who played in the AA in 1884 with a full set of whiskers, making him the last bearded big leaguer until the 1970s.

for the job, the Mets voted for catcher Bill Holbert to run the team, but the brass vetoed him because they didn't want another player in charge. Instead, club president Walter Watrous, with owner Erastus Wiman's approval, went outside the organization in search of a savior.

His choice was Oliver Perry Caylor. Taking over as Mets manager on June 11, Caylor left his wife and daughter Ellennora behind for the time being but brought all his talismans to New York with him in his determination to change both the Mets' luck and his own. Caylor was a big believer in luck. He believed good things followed when he saw a wagonload of empty barrels passing outside the ball park and only bad things could happen if he saw a cross-eyed man or the number "6" entered in the scorebook. To change his luck, he would wear his hat backward or move to a different seat on the bench or, if the situation was especially desperate, keep score on the back of a letter from his wife. But Caylor's mind was much more than a tangle of superstitions. It was among the first to perceive that the new overhand pitching style would be the ruin of most hurlers unless their work loads were drastically reduced. He estimated that three years was about the maximum length of time an overhand pitcher could last if he kept to a steady diet of hurling three games a week, which was the norm in the mid-1880s. Caylor's own staff bulwark in 1887, Al Mays, was never again effective, and at least some of his erosion may be traceable to his having to play under Caylor. In the bottom of the ninth inning of a game with Baltimore on August 17, Mays balked home Sam Trott from third base to give the Orioles a 2–1 win when Holbert turned to the bench as Mays was about to pitch to Matt Kilroy, causing him to pause in his delivery. Holbert had heard Caylor shouting at him to tell backup catcher Jim Donahue, subbing that day at first base for the often injured Orr, not to play so deep with the pitcher up. But even despite that demoralizing loss, the Mets, according to Caylor's calculations, went 14–5 in their August homestand and were on the upswing. Although the standings did not correspond with his figures, showing the Mets with a 12–6 home mark in July and August combined, and the fans hardly shared his view that the club had improved under him, Caylor's charges nevertheless held off Cleveland for seventh place.

Any hope of a pennant race, for all practical purposes, had been dashed way back in early June when the Browns, after getting off to a 2–3 start, won 29 of their next 31 games and roared to a nine-game lead over second-place Baltimore. In late July, the Browns' advantage shrank to seven and one-half games, still a cozy edge, but Von der Ahe grew increasingly paranoid that his fellow moguls were out to rob him of the pennant by whatever means necessary. In a game at Brooklyn on July 24, enterprising second sacker Yank Robinson scored the winning run for the Browns when he cut third base and the umpire refused to declare him out even though every player on the Brooklyn team swore he'd missed the bag. After losing the argument, Brooklyn owner-manager Charlie Byrne plopped down on the Browns' bench and lectured Robinson for cheating until Von der Ahe angrily ordered him back to his own bench. When another fracas occurred during a 4–2 Brooklyn victory the following day, Baltimore manager Billy Barnie was asked by Wheeler Wyckoff to grab a train to Brooklyn on July 26 and umpire the final game of the series to help restore sanity.

Wyckoff's intrusion spurred Von der Ahe to arrange a meeting in late July at the office of Walter Watrous before the Browns left New York. Attending were Von der Ahe, Watrous, Frank Robison of Cleveland and Zach Phelps representing Louisville. Cincinnati and Brooklyn, Von der Ahe's two biggest adversaries, had not been invited, and Barnie, who held both the Baltimore

• • •

Al Mays, the AL loss leader in 1887. Victimized by abysmal support, Mays lost two-thirds of his 51 decisions with the seventh place Mets. For the remaining three years of his career, he played with much better teams, but had so little elastic left in his arm that he was never again more than a spot starter.

THE BEER AND WHISKY LEAGUE

OLD JUDGE CIGARETTES Goodwin & Co., New York.

• • •

Long John Reilly and Hugh "Little Nick" Nicol, the extremes in height on the 1887 Reds, seem here to be on good terms, but actually they loathed each other. In 1888, Reilly was quoted as having said, "It pays to booze nowadays, for then a club will pay you extra money to keep you sober." It's hard to believe that Reilly, a contemplative man who later made his way as an artist, could have been so foolishly candid, and perhaps he wasn't. In his day many quotes from players were made up by writers to spice an otherwise bland column.

vote and the Athletics' vote by proxy, did not attend after saying he would, suggesting that he sympathized with Byrne and the Reds. The meeting was designed to oust Wyckoff as Association president, ostensibly for being a poor handler of umpires and problems in general, but really for the crime of siding against the Browns too often. Von der Ahe touted Joe Pritchard, a St. Louis writer who had been beating his own drum for the job, but the coup failed when Barnie skipped the meeting, leaving only four of the eight clubs represented, short of the majority needed to ditch Wyckoff. Afterward, a disgruntled Von der Ahe reportedly called on New York Giants owner John Day and offered to transfer his Browns to the League.

Upon learning of the meeting at Watrous's office, Byrne sprang to action. By Monday, September 5, he had set up a meeting of his own at the Fifth Avenue Hotel in New York that was billed as "the most important" in Association history. Enchambered when the door closed were Lew Simmons for Philadelphia, Byrne and Joseph Doyle for Brooklyn, Henry Von der Horst and Barnie for Baltimore, Zach Phelps and his brother J. H. Phelps for Louisville, Robison and Jimmy Williams for Cleveland, Wyckoff as a proxy for Cincinnati, Von der Ahe for St. Louis and Caylor and Watrous for the Mets. Before the gavel sounded, however, Caylor was barred from the proceeding because he was not only there as a club representative but as a working newsman. When he heatedly argued that others in attendance also wrote, his opponents countered that only he did it for a living. One suspicion was that Caylor was really dismissed because his input was unwelcome and because it was nearly certain that his report on the meeting would have been very different than the sanitized one that later appeared in *Sporting Life*. In any event, when he stalked from the room, with him went any vestige of love he still harbored for the Association.

The irony was that Caylor would probably have endorsed most of Byrne's agenda if he had been allowed to stay. With Wyckoff chairing the discussion, the eight clubs agreed to propose a new National Agreement that would include these changes: (1) A system for equalizing the playing strength of teams and ending the present unhealthy competition for players; (2) A system for grading salaries that would be fair and allow all leagues to survive; (3) A system for creating a self-sustaining reserve corps of players for all leagues; (4) A draft system for the requisition of rising players, thus keeping up a regular flow of new talent at minimum expense; and (5) A system of more equitable contracts and dealings between players and employers.

As can readily be seen, all of the proposed amendments were

Like his long-time Brooklyn teammate Darby O'Brien, third sacker George Pinkney was a native Peorian. For years, record books erroneously listed him as Pinckney. A fine base-runner and a selective hitter, Pinkney tallied 267 runs in 1887–88, though he batted under .270.

thoughtfully conceived and eventually became, if not always in the same form, governing rules for organized baseball, as did Byrne's notions for altering the division of gate receipts. After years of trying, Byrne at last pushed through a rule that gave 30 percent of the gate, or seven and a half cents on each quarter admission, to the visiting team rather than a flat $65 guarantee per game. This amount was less than Louisville, Cleveland and the Mets wanted but was passed unanimously to create a feeling of solidarity. Also passed were Byrne's desires to have one day a week, weekends and holidays excepted, designated as a day when ladies were admitted for free, and to levy an automatic $1,500 fine on any club that refused to finish a game. The primary target for this last rule was Comiskey, whose wont was to pull his team off the field if he could not get his way as had happened on July 3, when he had ordered his Browns to cease play while trailing 7–1 in the third inning of a game with Louisville. Comiskey contended that it was drizzling and he hadn't wanted to risk an injury to Boyle, which would leave the Browns without an able catcher except for Robinson, who was needed at second base. It was this incident that led the other owners to support Byrne in cracking down on teams that forfeited games they were nearly certain to lose anyway, thereby cheating fans who'd paid hard-earned money to see a full nine innings. Although his club was the leading malefactor, Von der Ahe went along with the tide, perhaps because the lead his Browns enjoyed had swelled to 19 games at the time of the meeting, rendering it absurd for him to worry about the result of any one contest. He even conceded that the Association teams needed to be made more equal, perhaps because he already had a plan that would make it appear he was doing his part to create parity.

But if Von der Ahe was not about to let anyone outside the Browns' organization break up his juggernaut, some within the family were exhibiting signs that they could bring about its disintegration. On June 10 the Athletics issued formal charges to Wyckoff regarding the foul language used at the A's Jefferson Street park by Comiskey and Curt Welch in conjunction with Welch's brutal assault on A's pitcher Gus Weyhing after a basepath collision. Six days later, at Baltimore, a game between the Orioles and the Browns was truncated by a crowd riot after Welch smashed into Baltimore second baseman Bill Greenwood on a steal attempt. Barnie and Oyster Burns, who had not dressed for the game, both rushed onto the field in streetclothes to assail Welch and several spectators exhorted a policeman to arrest the Browns star for assault.

That night Von der Ahe forked over $200 to bail Welch out

of a Baltimore jail. A *Sporting News* correspondent from St. Louis who was at the game later wrote of the incident: "The Baltimore audience displayed very little of the instincts of human beings, but on the contrary conducted themselves like idiots." Yet there were indications that the Browns players, who might have been expected to be even more partial to Welch, instead decided to police him in their own way. Several weeks later Tip O'Neill, often used by Comiskey as a kind of enforcer because of his size and stature in the club, took a wild swing at the plate and let go of his bat, which slammed Welch, who was the on-deck hitter, in the face. O'Neill claimed that the blow was an accident, but regardless, Welch's days on the Browns were numbered even though he led all Association outfielders for the third straight year in putouts. Also put on notice was shortstop Bill Gleason. Von der Ahe and Comiskey could point to the lethargic play of both against Detroit in the World's Series that fall, but O'Neill, an even bigger disappointment, escaped censure.

After leading both major leagues in runs, hits, doubles and total bases, as well as posting the highest batting and slugging averages, O'Neill was virtually invisible during the seventeen days the Browns and the Wolverines traversed the eastern half of the country in a special train of parlor cars, playing 15 games in 10 different cities ranging from St. Louis to Brooklyn. The circus-like extravaganza—the longest postseason clash in major league history—was conceived by Detroit owner Frederick Stearns as a way to milk the occasion for all it was worth. When Von der Ahe agreed to the notion, it convinced any lingering skeptics that in these matchups between the two leagues competition ran a distant second to profit. Von der Ahe further agreed to hiking ticket prices to $1 for general admission and $1.50 for reserved seats, and to employ as umpires the two most famous officiating names in the game, Honest John Gaffney and Honest John Kelly, even though both were acting as managers at the moment rather than as umpires.

Still, for all the ersatz hype, the Series got off to a good start when the Browns and the Wolves split the first two games in St. Louis and then hooked up in a pitchers' duel at Detroit in Game Three between Caruthers and Charlie Getzein, which went into the bottom of the 13th inning tied at 1–all. In an effort to help his own cause, Getzein led off the frame with a single and moved to third base on successive groundouts by Hardy Richardson and Charlie Ganzel. With two down, Getzein looked as if he would die on third when Jack Rowe hit a one-hopper to Yank Robinson. Although Robinson bobbled the hard shot, he retrieved the ball in time to retire Rowe, but Comiskey muffed Robinson's throw, allowing Getzein to cross the plate with the winning run. It was

• • •
Ed McKean signed with his hometown team after Cleveland joined the AA, but it was then revealed that he'd already signed with Rochester of the International League. A long legal wrangle ensued, before the National Commission finally allowed him to play with Cleveland. McKean then got into a similar hassle when the Players League formed. He has the stats to rank as the finest all-around performer among shortstops who spent at least two seasons in the AA.

This poster of the 1888 World's Series combatants exhibits the Dauvray Cup, originated in 1887 when popular actress Helen Dauvray, soon to be the wife of Monte Ward, offered a $500 trophy in her name to the winner of the World's Series each year. Dauvray then took it upon herself to criticize the Browns' raucous base-coaching tactics in a letter to NL president Nick Young that concluded, "There is no reason why base ball should not become to America what cricket is to England, but in order to accomplish that the players should do everything they can to *refine and improve the game.*" One might wonder if the impetus for such a letter really came from Dauvray. One might wonder, too, what happened to her trophy, which disappeared nearly a century ago.

totally unlike Comiskey to error at such a crucial juncture, and St. Louis never recovered from this very uncharacteristic loss. Already disgruntled because Von der Ahe had told them they would only get a $100 bonus for their World's Series effort, the Browns won just two of the next eight games, giving Detroit an insurmountable 8–3 lead in the 15-game Series. Nevertheless, Stearns and Von der Ahe made their charges play the last four meaningless contests.

The final count, 10–5 in favor of Detroit, made Von der Ahe so furious at his players for their humiliating trouncing that he at first kept the team's $12,500 share of the Series pot all to himself. Comiskey eventually persuaded him that he would only slit his own throat if he persisted in denying the players their cut, but a wound had opened between Von der Ahe and his stars that nothing would ever heal.

For other members of the Association, too, the year ended in shambles. No sooner had he been barred from the loop meeting in September than Caylor began railing against one of the Association's cornerstones: Sunday baseball. The public simply would not tolerate it, he said. Later in the month he held his powder for the moment when Byrne bought the Mets in the waning days of the season and vowed to pay all player salaries and keep Caylor as the club's manager. Once the season ended, however, Caylor was either given the gate or allowed to resign, depending on whose version one cared to believe. Caylor averred that he left of his own volition because it was clear he would not be given the power to make the wholesale changes needed for the club to become competitive. Be that as it may, his pen was only now about to be fully unsheathed. In late October, after Detroit bagged the World's Series, he wrote that anyone still convinced the Association was the equal of the League could "take the occasion of the Browns' disastrous defeat to turn about and fall down again at the feet of their old idol." Shortly after that, he predicted in *Sporting Life*, "It would not surprise me very much to see Chris Von der Ahe turn a flip-flop into the League's arms next week. . . . Such an idea is likely to possess him at any moment and if it comes the right time he will flop."

Nor was Caylor the only literary assailant Von der Ahe had on his tail. Other writers sank their teeth into a rumor (never proven) that the Browns had deliberately let Cincinnati sweep a four-game series at St. Louis in late September to swing second place to the Reds rather than to Baltimore. The reason proffered for Von der Ahe's having ordered his club to dump the games was so he could curry Cincinnati into becoming his badly needed ally against Byrne.

In early November, a fire destroyed the players' dressing

room at Sportsman's Park and damaged the handball court and the gymnasium. The dressing room, which was a small frame building, was a total loss. Also badly scorched was the team clubhouse and Von der Ahe's Golden Lion Saloon. Some were unkind enough to remark that all the ravaged buildings were covered by insurance and that perhaps Von der Ahe was readying himself to get whatever he could for his toppling empire. In the weeks ahead it became still more conceivable to his critics that he was planning to take the money and run. When his finances appeared to be in order, the supposition then was that the World's Series defeat must have shattered his spirit and turned his mind irrevocably against many of the same players for whom he had named his apartment buildings only the previous fall, when the Browns brought the Association its first clear-cut championship. Certainly, in November of 1887, no one could have imagined any reason other than despair or pique to cause the owner of a team that had just won its third straight pennant suddenly to begin unloading nearly half of his stars.

• • •
A collage of the 1882 NL Buffalo Bisons, with Blondie Purcell at bottom and Tom Dolan to his right. Purcell was one of the AA's more elusive figures. He and Orator Shaffer ran a bookmaking operation in 1891, a continuation of his activities during his playing days. Retrieved from the minors by Baltimore after tying for the Southern League home-run crown in 1886, Purcell hit just .250 in 1887 but tallied 101 runs and racked up 88 stolen bases.

1887 FINAL STANDINGS

	W	L	PCT	HOME	ROAD	GB
1. St. Louis Browns	95	40	.704	58–15	37–25	
2. Cincinnati Reds	81	54	.600	45–26	36–28	14
3. Baltimore Orioles	77	58	.570	42–21	35–37	18
4. Louisville Colonels	76	60	.559	46–23	30–37	19.5
5. Philadelphia Athletics	64	69	.481	41–27	23–42	30
6. Brooklyn Grays	60	74	.448	36–38	24–36	34.5
7. New York Metropolitans	44	89	.331	25–34	19–55	50
8. Cleveland Blues	39	92	.298	22–37	17–55	54

1887 SEASON LEADERS*

BATTING

BATTING AVERAGE (325 ABs)

1. O'Neill, StL	.435
2. Browning, Louis	.402
3. Orr, NY	.368
4. D. Lyons, Phila	.367
5. Caruthers, StL	.357
Foutz, StL	.357
7. O. Burns, Balt	.341
8. Comiskey, StL	.335
9. Hecker, Louis	.319
10. Latham, StL	.316

SLUGGING AVERAGE

1. O'Neill, StL	.691
2. Caruthers, StL	.547
Browning, Louis	.547
4. D. Lyons, Phila	.523
5. O. Burns, Balt	.519
6. Orr, NY	.516
7. Foutz, StL	.508
8. Davis, Balt	.485
9. Reilly, Cinci	.477
10. Kerins, Louis	.443

ON-BASE PERCENTAGE

1. O'Neill, StL	.490
2. Browning, Louis	.464
3. Caruthers, StL	.463
4. Robinson, StL	.445
5. D. Lyons, Phila	.421
6. Mack, Louis	.415
7. O. Burns, Balt	.414
8. Orr, NY	.408
9. Radford, NY	.403
10. Foutz, StL	.393

TOTAL BASES

1. O'Neill, StL	357
2. Browning, Louis	299
3. D. Lyons, Phila	298
4. O. Burns, Balt	286
5. Reilly, Cinci	263
6. Latham, StL	259
7. Davis, Balt	235
8. O'Brien, NY	228
9. Griffin, Balt	227
10. Corkhill, Cinci	224
Comiskey, StL	224

HOME RUNS

1. O'Neill, StL	14
2. Reilly, Cinci	10
3. O. Burns, Balt	9
4. Caruthers, StL	8
Davis, Balt	8
Fennelly, Cinci	8
7. Werrick, Louis	7
8. D. Lyons, Phila	6
Tucker, Balt	6
10. Kerins, Louis	5
Corkhill, Cinci	5
O'Brien, NY	5

RUNS

1. O'Neill, StL	167
2. Latham, StL	163
3. Griffin, Balt	142
4. Poorman, Phila	140
5. Comiskey, StL	139
6. McPhee, Cinci	137
7. Gleason, StL	135
8. Fennelly, Cinci	133
Pinkney, Brook	133
10. D. Lyons, Phila	128

• • •

Denny Lyons. While poring through *Sporting Life* boxscores, Bill Gottlieb recently discovered that in 1887 Lyons had a 52-game hitting streak, including two games in which he only drew a walk. Since walks counted as hits that year, it really ought to have been Lyons's skein, and not Willie Keeler's 44-game string, that Joe DiMaggio took aim at in 1941. Along with his "lost" hitting streak, Lyons in 1887 set an all-time record for the most put-outs in a season by a third baseman with 255.

*RBI leaders unavailable.

HITS			STOLEN BASES	
1. O'Neill, StL	225		1. Nicol, Cinci	138
2. Browning, Louis	220		2. Latham, StL	129
3. D. Lyons, Phila	209		3. Comiskey, StL	117
4. Latham, StL	198		4. Browning, Louis	103
5. O. Burns, Balt	188		5. McPhee, Cinci	95
6. Comiskey, StL	180		6. Griffin, Balt	94
7. Gleason, StL	172		7. Welch, StL	89
8. Reilly, Cinci	170		8. Poorman, Phila	88
9. Corkhill, Cinci	168		Purcell, Balt	88
10. Collins, Louis	162		10. Stricker, Cleve	86

PITCHING

WINS		LOSSES		INNINGS	
1. Kilroy, Balt	46	1. Mays, NY	34	1. Kilroy, Balt	589.1
2. Ramsey, Louis	37	2. Crowell, Cleve	31	2. Ramsey, Louis	561
3. E. Smith, Cinci	34	3. P. Smith, Balt	30	3. P. Smith, Balt	491.1
King, StL	34	4. Weyhing, Phila	28	4. Seward, Phila	470.2
5. Mullane, Cinci	31	5. Ramsey, Louis	27	5. Weyhing, Phila	466.1
6. Caruthers, StL	29	6. Morrison, Cleve	25	6. E. Smith, Cinci	447.1
7. Weyhing, Phila	26	Seward, Phila	25	7. Mays, NY	441.1
8. Seward, Phila	25	8. Porter, Brook	24	8. Mullane, Cinci	416.1
P. Smith, Balt	25	9. Kilroy, Balt	19	9. King, StL	390
Foutz, StL	25	10. E. Smith, Cinci	18	10. Crowell, Cleve	389.1

COMPLETE GAMES		STRIKEOUTS		WINNING PCT. (25 DECISIONS)	
1. Kilroy, Balt	66	1. Ramsey, Louis	355	1. Caruthers, StL	.763
2. Ramsey, Louis	61	2. Kilroy, Balt	217	2. King, StL	.756
3. P. Smith, Balt	54	3. P. Smith, Balt	206	3. Kilroy, Balt	.708
4. Weyhing, Phila	53	4. Weyhing, Phila	193	4. Foutz, StL	.676
5. Seward, Phila	52	5. E. Smith, Cinci	176	5. E. Smith, Cinci	.654
6. Mays, NY	50	6. Morrison, Cleve	158	6. Mullane, Cinci	.646
7. E. Smith, Cinci	49	7. Seward, Phila	155	7. Hecker, Louis	.600
8. Mullane, Cinci	47	8. King, StL	128	8. Toole, Brook	.583
9. Crowell, Cleve	45	9. Mays, NY	124	9. Ramsey, Louis	.578
10. King, StL	43	10. Chamberlain, Louis	118	10. Chamberlain, Louis	.529

ERA (140 INNINGS)		LOWEST ON-BASE PCT.	
1. E. Smith, Cinci	2.94	1. Caruthers, StL	.281
2. Kilroy, Balt	3.07	2. E. Smith, Cinci	.283
3. Mullane, Cinci	3.24	3. Seward, Phila	.294
4. Caruthers, StL	3.30	4. Kilroy, Balt	.297
5. Ramsey, Louis	3.43	5. Ramsey, Louis	.298
6. H. Daily, Cleve	3.67	6. Mullane, Cinci	.301
7. King, StL	3.78	7. King, StL	.305
8. P. Smith, Balt	3.79	8. Hecker, Louis	.306
Chamberlain, Louis	3.79	9. Mays, NY	.307
10. Foutz, StL	3.87	10. Foutz, StL	.312
		Weyhing, Phila	.312
		Terry, Brook	.312

EIGHT

1888

Jos. HALL, Photo, 111 Fulton St., Brooklyn, N. Y.

St. Louis Ball Club, 1888.
World Champions—1885, 1886, 1887.

1. Boyle.
2. O'Neil.
3. Milligan.
4. Lyon.
5. McGarr.
6. King.
7. Comisky.
8. McCarty.
9. Devlin.
10. Knouff.
11. Latham.
12. Hudson.
13. Robinson

• • • •
Chris Von der Ahe's final championship team. In 1888 his Browns won their fourth straight pennant despite not having a single lefthanded-hitting regular; the previous three flag winners had had only one lefty swinger, Bob Caruthers. Note that Tommy McCarty, though only in his first year with the team, already occupies a position of prominence beside Charlie Comiskey. Two years later McCarthy, with the "h" restored to his name, would serve most of the season as a manager "pro tem" while Comiskey was in the PL.

TIP AND SILVER PULL IT OUT

I T WAS THE BIGGEST FIRE SALE IN MAJOR league history, even more startling than the one Harry Frazee conducted some thirty years later when he peddled Babe Ruth and many more members of his championship Boston Red Sox team to bankroll his theater ventures. When it ended in November 1887, the three-time champion St. Louis Browns seemingly were decimated, and what made it all the more improbable was that the chief beneficiary was Charlie Byrne, Chris Von der Ahe's arch adversary in the Association.

The first step in the massive dismantling of the Mound City steamroller came in early November when Bob Caruthers was sold to Brooklyn for a reported $8,500. Joe Pritchard claimed that he orchestrated the sale with help from Caruthers's brother James, the head of the family's heavy hardware house in Chicago. According to Pritchard, he was given $100 by Byrne for engineering the deal and Caruthers got $1,500 up front toward the $5,000 salary that made him the highest-paid player in the Association

145

in 1888. To sweeten the pot, Von der Ahe also agreed to release Caruthers's favorite batterymate, Doc Bushong, to Brooklyn.

Far from done, Von der Ahe sold centerfielder Curt Welch to the Athletics for $3,000 and swapped shortstop Bill Gleason to the A's for catcher Jocko Milligan, outfielder Fred Mann and infielder Chippy McGarr. Finally, he auctioned Dave Foutz to Brooklyn for $6,000. His pockets bulging, Von der Ahe then sped off to Europe with his wife, leaving Charlie Comiskey to pick up the pieces.

Months later, *Sporting Life* revealed: "Very few people know that the sale of Welch, Foutz and Caruthers was made more at Comiskey's request than at Von der Ahe's desire. Comiskey wants no man on his team who would not obey him." *Sporting Life* theorized that Comiskey had lost his grip on the Browns in 1887 because of a mutinous climate emanating from the quintet of stars, but at the time the five were disposed of, many viewed it as simply a needed payroll reduction and some were even ready to credit Von der Ahe with breaking up his Browns as a show of support for the "Millennium Plan" *Sporting Life* proposed in December 1887. The hallmark of the plan was an elaborate scheme for dividing up the playing talent for the general good of baseball. Responding to those who naively lauded Von der Ahe for his fire sale, Opie Caylor assailed the notion that any club or league would ever willingly be so altruistic as to help its weaker members. Caylor's clone, Frank Brunell, fretted that if Von der Ahe had genuinely wanted to achieve competitive balance, why hadn't he steered some of his stars to lowly Cleveland?

There could be no denying, though, that the huge turnover had considerably weakened the Browns. Welch's centerfield post was expected to go to Bug Holliday, up from the minors, and Comiskey planned to move Yank Robinson to short and to install Parson Nicholson, a 6'6" rookie who came by his nickname because of his sanctimonious demeanor, at second base. But the Browns lost Holliday to Des Moines in a contract battle, and Nicholson was too green to stick. In the spring, Comiskey was forced to put Mann in center field and then to turn to rookie Harry Lyons when Mann was not up to the task. At shortstop, he eventually resorted to another rookie, Ed Herr, when Robinson was needed again at second base. To fill the enormous hole left by Caruthers and Foutz, Comiskey could only pray that Ed Knouff or Jim Devlin or Joe Murphy or some other one of the team's young hurlers would step forward. So top-heavy were the Browns with raw and untested players in the spring of 1888 that Von der Ahe formed the St. Louis Whites as a kind of farm team to play in the Western Association.

This **1888 Des Moines team cabinet** is of special interest to us because everyone here played either in the UA or the AA—including Hutchison, who was really Bill Hutchinson, the last major league hurler to win 40 games two years in a row. Centerfielder Bug Holliday would take the AA by storm in 1889, and a year later Henry Sage would set a 19th-century record for the lowest batting average by a regular catcher, when he stroked a wispy .149 as an AA rookie with Toledo.

At first it was feared that Byrne had bought the Mets to serve as a farm team in major league guise for his Brooklyn club, but Byrne really just wanted to rifle the New Yorkers of their few remaining decent players. After adding Dave Orr, Paul Radford and Al Mays to Brooklyn's roster, Byrne tried to unload the Mets, but soon after Caylor wrote that there was no one so "green that he could successfully be steered up against such a bunco game," Byrne washed his hands of the franchise. Unwilling to vacate the New York area, the Association tried for a while to move the team north of the city to Troy and then settled on Kansas City as a stopgap choice. The Missouri club was given a one-year membership in the Association in the hope that a team could be put in New York again by 1889. But if the Association believed it was entitled by the National Agreement to return to New York because it had once been there, the League felt otherwise. Even as Association president Wheeler Wyckoff began the paperwork to abandon New York temporarily, the League laid plans to fight to the death, if need be, for permanent sole possession of the most desirable location in the country for a major league franchise.

As had Cleveland the previous year, Kansas City faced a last-minute scramble to assemble a team. Overstocked with talent after he loaded up on ex-Mets and Browns, Byrne, in a parody of generosity, either sold or released aging first baseman Bill Phillips, over-the-hill third baseman Frank Hankinson, extra catcher Jim Donahue, excess centerfielder Jim McTamany and two unneeded pitchers, Henry Porter and Steve Toole, to the Cowboys. For each of the players he fobbed off on Kansas City manager Dave Rowe, Byrne was certain he had someone better, but he guessed wrong on at least one count. When former Met Radford hit just .218 in 1888, McTamany was sorely missed in center field.

But even with McTamany, Rowe and the two managers who followed him did not have a prayer in 1888. The Cowboys played most of the season in a park that was known sardonically as "The Hole" because it was located in a pit that had been dug out to create a roadbed for Kansas City's Independence Avenue. On the last day of September, the club took over Exposition Park, previously the home of the minor league Kansas City Blues of the Western Association, after the two franchises agreed to merge the following season, but by then the Cowboys had already pretty well wrapped up last place.

• • •

Movie buffs are forgiven if they thought at a glance that Fatty Arbuckle was on the 1888 Kansas City Cowboys. The Arbuckle twin is Fatty Briody. Frank Hankinson, beside Briody, is not his half brother, much as he looks it. The trend in 1888 was not to smile for team photos, but the stone-faced Cowboys carried it to an extreme. It may have been because they finished last.

Porter.   4. Allen.
Barclay.   5. Davis.
Donahue.   6. Fagan.

Jos. HALL, Pub., 111 Fulton Street, Brooklyn, N. Y.

KANSAS CITY BALL CLUB, 1888.

7. Rowe, Mgr. and Capt.   10. Kirby.
8. McTamany.   11. Esterday.
9. Briordy.   12. Hankinson.

● ● ●

Wally Andrews hit a ton in the minors and was a perennial hopeful to win the Louisville first base job. In 1884, Andrews stumbled in a 14-game trial. He returned to the Falls City in 1888 after belting 28 homers in the Southern League, but flopped again, hitting just .194 in 26 games.

Attendance in the other three second-division Association cities in 1888—Louisville, Cleveland and Baltimore—also dropped precipitously, as the separation between the haves and the have-nots was even more monstrous than it had been in the helter-skelter 1884 season. The fifth-place Orioles finished 24 and a half games behind fourth-place Cincinnati, a record for the widest gap between the first and second divisions of a major league that lasted until 1950. But the uneven quality of play was not the only reason for sagging attendance. At its sixth annual meeting in December 1887, the Association voted to institute a minimum 50¢ admission charge at each of its member parks. The fee hike meant that bleacher seats would now be priced at 50¢ and grandstand seats would go for 75¢. When the League, in late June, allowed the Philadelphia Phillies to revert to a quarter minimum, the Athletics, now under new ownership, rushed to follow suit. Once the dam broke, a flood of other clubs began to slash their prices. Surrendering to the inevitable, on August 7 in a hastily assembled meeting at the Continental Hotel in Philadelphia, the Association resolved to let clubs charge either 25¢ or 50¢ as of August 25, but, in any case, visiting teams would be guaranteed a $130 minimum per playing date. No sooner was the meeting adjourned than the second division teams scrambled to transfer games to cities that could support the 50¢ tariff. Baltimore, for one, hurriedly moved a postponed game with the Reds and an August 25 game scheduled between the two clubs to Cincinnati. Thanks to such windfalls, the Reds got to play 79 games at home in 1888 and just 58 on the road, while Baltimore was at home for a mere 56 games and away for 81. Only a year earlier, a ticket to an Orioles' game had been a scarce commodity, particularly on holidays when owner Henry Von der Horst would present each fan with a picnic lunch, a schooner of his Eagle beer and an invitation to linger after the game and dance under the stars on a platform set up on the field in Oriole Park. But the team once again had nosedived, although this time the explanation was clear. Matt Kilroy, after pitching 1,172 innings in 1886-87, was nearly arm-dead, and several other members of Barnie's youth movement, most conspicuously Mike Griffin, were plagued by the sophomore jinx in 1888.

The trouble in Cleveland was also easy to grasp. The Blues did not have enough good men, and Jimmy Williams was too lenient with those who might have been half decent under a sterner field general. In July, on the same day his father died, Williams handed over the manager's reins to Tom Loftus, a long-time journeyman minor league outfielder. Loftus's peregrinations would

1. Stricker.   5. McClelian.   JOSEPH HALL. Photo., Brooklyn, N. Y.   9. Faatz, Capt.   13. McGuire.
2. McKeon.   6. Proesser.   10. Howe.   14. Gilks.
3. O'Brien.   7. Keas.   11. Zimmer.   15. Van Sant.
4. Hogan.   8. Loftus, Mgr.   CLEVELAND BALL CLUB, 1888.   12. Albert.

• • •

Tom Loftus and his 1888 Cleveland Blues. Flanking Loftus are rookie pitcher George Proeser and club treasurer Goerge Howe. Here also are Ed Keas, Loftus's other late-season pitching addition, and popular team captain Jay Faatz. In March 1889, Faatz suffered a crushing personal setback on the eve of spring training, when he lost his wife to typhoid fever just three weeks after they were wed.

lead him to managerial jobs in a record four different major leagues before he died of throat cancer in 1910, but he never got lucky enough to pilot a team that was a pennant contender. For the 1888 Blues, the best he could attain was a sixth-place finish, not bad considering Cleveland started off 1–9 for the second year in a row and needed 11 pitchers to get through the season. The sturdiest was Jersey Bakely, who figured in 58 of the club's 132 decisions, but the most talented might have been Ed Keas. In his major league debut on August 25, Keas lost a 1–0 heartbreaker to Nat Hudson of the Browns. Six days later he gave up a mere one run again in a 2–1 win over Kansas City. By the time he made his next appearance in a September 3 victory against Louisville, Cleveland was in the midst of a nine-game winning streak. The skein ended a week later, when Brooklyn edged Bakely 2–1, and a few days after that Keas went down with a sick arm. By the time the Blues embarked on their last road trip in late September, he was still ailing and was left behind. Although Keas never pitched again in the majors, Milwaukee of the Western Association took a gamble that his arm would rebound and traded Jimmy McAleer for him over the winter. McAleer later came to be regarded as the best defensive centerfielder in the game.

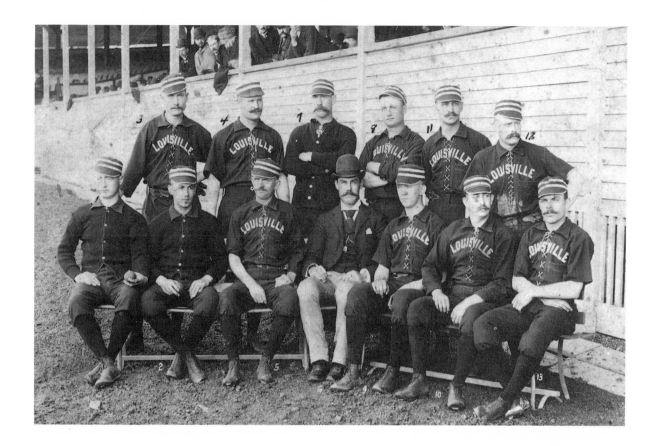

1888 Louisville Colonels. Back (left to right): Skyrocket Smith, Guy Hecker, Pete Browning, John Kerins, Paul Cook and Joe Werrick. Front (left to right): Toad Ramsey, Icebox Chamberlain, Bill White, manager Honest John Kelly, Scott Stratton, Chicken Wolf and Hub Collins. In 1888 the Colonels wore maroon pants and shirts with blue-gray stockings, belts, and caps. The entire team pledged to be temperate after a lecture to the club in mid-April by Francis Murphy, a noted temperance evangelist. Then came an Opening Day stomping in St. Louis, and the vows were soon forgotten.

Most historians now believe that in 1888 the worst defensive centerfielder played for Louisville. They are probably wrong, but there will never be any way to prove it. But if Pete Browning's fielding lapses were greatly exaggerated—why was he never put on first base if he was really such a stiff defensively?—the evidence of his personal lapses is all still on glaring display. Speaking of himself in the third person, as was his wont, Browning announced over the winter that "the Gladiator is going to brace up, and he will drink no more" but he then held out deep into the spring of 1888 before signing for around $1,800, plus another $200 conditional upon his staying on the wagon all season. Browning fell off in a big way in June, getting so soused that he bought two fishing poles and trolled all of one afternoon during a rainstorm in an overflowing gutter outside the Colonels' hotel in Kansas City. The following month he claimed he had gotten malaria and was home with his mother recuperating, which was why the team's new owner, Mordecai Davidson, had not heard from him for several days. A furniture dealer who ventured into baseball on the assumption that he could run a major league franchise much the same as he did his business, Davidson chose Charlie Byrne as his exemplar. Seeing no conflict between both owning and managing a team, he pressured John Kelly to resign the field post soon after he gained control of the Colonels and ultimately took the reins himself. Since players were no more than employees, Davidson's solution to every transgression, however minor, was to fine or suspend the offender. Browning was fined with such regularity that he seldom had any money coming to him on payday. When shortstop Bill White begged to be excused from playing on a hot afternoon because he had a fever and then made several errors when his plea was ignored, Davidson suspended him indefinitely. White was soon sold to the Browns. Later in the season, when Comiskey and Von der Ahe realized what Davidson's priorities were, St. Louis waved another handful of greenbacks to acquire Icebox Chamberlain, the lone Louisville pitcher with a winning record. Chamberlain's sale temporarily left the Colonels with only eight able-bodied players. Davidson purchased several minor leaguers to fill out the roster and reinstated Browning in late September, only to peddle leftfielder Hub Collins a few days later to Brooklyn for $4,000. Chamberlain had been let go, Davidson readily admitted, because he "made too much money" and would have been problematic to sign for 1889, but to explain the departure of Collins, the club's best all-around player in 1888, Davidson just mumbled that he had gone to the highest bidder.

When the Colonels ultimately finished seventh, barely beating out Kansas City for the cellar, several prognosticators had egg on their faces. In March 1888, Joe Pritchard had thought Cincinnati, Brooklyn and Louisville would be the cream of the Association and said it was best if the Colonels won the pennant because the League, which would leave no stone unturned to net the Brooklyn and Cincinnati franchises for its own, had no interest in Louisville. Frank Brunell also thought well of the Colonels in his preseason forecast for *Sporting Life*, rating them third behind Brooklyn and Cincinnati. Of the Reds he wrote: "Strong fielding and base-running crowd, fair hitters, well-fixed for pitchers, will win on team work." Brooklyn was the "strongest team in the Association, but unruly and unsteady," he felt, and it had "three cliques within; no captain or second baseman." Brunell was accurate in his assessment of Cincinnati. Gus Schmelz's Reds were indeed the best-looking team in the Association—on paper anyway. Along with Mullane and Elmer Smith, last year's rookie find, the Reds had a new frosh pitching star in little Leon Viau, but the club's real forte was its infield. In 1888 first baseman Long John Reilly, second baseman Bid McPhee, shortstop Frank Fennelly and third baseman Hick Carpenter were intact for the fourth year in a row, a 19th-century record for an infield unit.

Indeed, McPhee and Carpenter had been with the Reds

• • •
Hub Collins seemingly escaped hell when he was sold by Louisville to Brooklyn late in 1888. True, he played on two flag winners in Brooklyn, but in 1891 he was nearly decapitated when he collided with teammate Oyster Burns while chasing a pop fly. The following year, just as Collins was starting to return to form, he was lifted for a pinch hitter on May 14 when he felt too wobbly to take his cuts. A week later, he was dead of typhoid fever.

A rare picture of the 1888 Cincinnatis that includes the team's brass. Top (left to right): Pop Corkhill, White Wings Tebeau, Bill Hart, Bid McPhee, Bill Serad and Heinie Kappel. Middle (left to right): Tony Mullane, Long John Reilly, manger Gus Schmelz, club president Aaron Stern, club secretary Louis Hauck (whose father once owned the Reds), Jim Keenan and Leon Viau. Bottom (left to right): Elmer Smith, Frank Fennelly, Hugh Nicol and Kid Baldwin. Stern was one of the AA's most venal owners, ever ready to pull a fast one if it meant making an extra buck. In 1887 he was raked for loaning Kappel to Memphis while retaining possession of his contract. The practice, fairly common at the time, albeit illegal, was an ancient equivalent to farming out a player to the minors.

since the Association's inception, and the former would remain Cincinnati's second baseman until the century ended. After leaving the Reds for a season, McPhee returned to manage the club in 1901, finished last, and then quit in July of the following year and moved to Los Angeles, where he continued to do occasional scouting for the Reds before leaving the game altogether in 1909. Carpenter meanwhile also became a Californian, settling in San Diego. When McPhee eventually relocated there too, the two former long-time teammates lived as near neighbors, far from the madding crowd, until Carpenter's death in 1937. But whereas McPhee, Carpenter and Reilly were still going strong in 1888, that season would be the Reds' doughty interior foursome's last together, as Fennelly, after serving most of the year as team captain, was sold to Philadelphia in early October when he was unable to lift his batting average above .200 and his errors began to outnumber his hits. Like 1884, when the Reds had disappointed after a pennant was expected, the shortstop slot was the Achilles

heel of the 1888 club and was probably the most salient reason that it landed in fourth place rather than first.

But if Brunell's aim was off on Cincinnati and Louisville, he hit the bull's eye with Brooklyn. Byrne's Bridegrooms, so called now because a number of his players were newlyweds, finished second, and the keystone sack loomed large in their failure to win. Bill McGunnigle, hired to run the club on the field when Byrne finally listened to the whispers that an owner who also tried to manage his team was a fool, swiftly lost faith in holdover second baseman, Bill McClellan. McClellan's gravest flaw was that he was lefthanded, and southpaw middle infielders, common earlier in the decade, were fast going out of fashion. In early July, McGunnigle told McClellan he was now a spare outfielder and supplanted him with long-time Boston second baseman Jack Burdock, then in his seventeenth big league season.

Burdock joined the club on the eve of a four-game series in St. Louis that commenced with the Bridegrooms in second place by percentage points 41–20 (.672), but half a game up on the Browns, which stood at 37–17 (.685), and three games ahead of the third-place Athletics. That the Browns could still be in the lead, with half their 1885–87 championship team now playing elsewhere, was viewed as an aberration. On Independence Day, Opie Caylor flatly predicted the Browns would crumple like cardboard when they went head to head with Brooklyn.

Before the confrontation, Von der Ahe staged a parade and a gala reception for the Bridegrooms and invited delegates attending an Association meeting in town that had ended the previous evening to stay over an extra day and take part in the festivities. By the time the series ended, he was screaming about calling another meeting to lodge a formal complaint that Bushong, acting on Byrne's instructions, had written to his star hitter, Tip O'Neill, inviting him to play poorly against the Bridegrooms so that the Browns would release him to perform in Brooklyn. Unable to prove his charge against Byrne, Von der Ahe settled for suspending O'Neill, who testified that his lame performance in the series was caused by a bout of dysentery, and fining Silver King $1,000 for poor pitching.

King's crime was failing to protect a 4–1 St. Louis lead in a game against Brooklyn on July 10. A three-run homer by Ed Herr, playing in O'Neill's place, broke a 1–1 deadlock in the top of the ninth, but Brooklyn tied it in the bottom half on two hits and errors by Harry Lyons and Arlie Latham. Another error by Latham on a line drive right at him put George Pinkney on in the last of the tenth, and Caruthers then belted a King pitch over the low fence in right field that some three years earlier had replaced the

• • •
Old Judge sometimes made tobacco cards of players whose impact was minimal at best. Bob Gamble is an example. He pitched in just one major league game in 1888 for the A's. Another one-game A's hurler whom we can only wish there was a card of is Fred Chapman, believed by many to have been only fourteen years old at the time he made his one big league appearance on July 22, 1887, against Cleveland. Though Chapman left the game trailing 6–2, he escaped being charged with a loss when the A's won by forfeit.

beer garden once situated there. The hit was far enough for a home run, but Caruthers stopped running when he hit second base and saw that Pinkney had scored the winning tally.

Two days earlier, another Browns' scapegoat, hefty Ed Knouff, had surrendered a two-run double in the bottom of the ninth to Dave Foutz, giving Brooklyn a last-gasp 4–3 win. Both in the box and at the plate, Foutz and Caruthers between them spearheaded the Bridegrooms to a four-game sweep of the series and provided still more ammunition for those who felt their sale was tantamount to guaranteeing Brooklyn the pennant.

Up by four and a half games when they left St. Louis to fin-ish out their western swing in Kansas City, the Bridegrooms then went into a tailspin that knocked them from the lead just ten days later. Within six weeks, Brooklyn had tumbled all the way to fourth, 11 games off the pace. Rather than bringing the Bride-grooms a steady hand, Burdock stuck them with the worst offen-sive contribution ever by an infielder or outfielder who played in at least half of his team's games. In 70 contests and 246 at bats, the seventeen-year veteran hit .122 and collected just eight RBIs.

But all the fault for Brooklyn's decline could not be laid on Burdock. Some analysts would later single out a July 14 forfeit loss in Kansas City as the turning point. On that date, when regular umpire Fred Goldsmith was unavailable to work the Kansas City-Brooklyn game, two substitute players, one from each team, were designated to officiate as per the custom of the time. The Bride-grooms' nominee, spare pitcher Adonis Terry, handled the bases while Jim Donahue of the Cowboys went behind the plate. Be-hind 5–4 in the ninth inning, the Bridegrooms had Bill McClel-lan on first base with two out. As McClellan took his lead, Kansas City pitcher Red Ehret snapped the ball to first baseman Bill Phillips. Even as Donahue called McClellan out on the pickoff at-tempt, Terry ruled him safe. In 1888 there was no provision defin-ing which umpire had jurisdiction in such a situation. It more or less came down to where the game was played, and since Kansas City was the home team, Donahue and the Cowboys argued that the out call prevailed. Terry countered that he had heard Sam Barkley, the Cowboys manager, order Donahue to call McClellan out. After the wrangle had lasted for some fifteen minutes with no resolution in sight, McGunnigle pulled his team off the field. The game was then forfeited to the last-place Cowboys, and Byrne be-came the first owner to be tagged with a $1,500 fine under the amendment to the Association by-laws that he himself had pushed for the previous September.

The Bridegrooms' slide following the forfeit loss created a four-team race through the end of July, with St. Louis clinging to

• • •

In 1888, the A's discarded their 1887 "mail carrier's" uniforms and went to dark blue pants, white jerseys and belts, light blue stockings and caps. Philadelphia's two young pitchers, Gus Weyhing (8) and Ed Seward (14), also appear to sport a new look, or perhaps a couple of the vets just got at their scalps. The mislabeled "Bauer" (17) is second baseman Lou Bierbauer, the enormous bone of contention after the Players League folded.

first and Brooklyn, Cincinnati and Philadelphia hanging close. On July 28 at Philadelphia over 12,000 watched in horror as Reds rookie ace Leon Viau topped Ed Seward 2–1 when Frank Fennelly's single in the bottom of the tenth plated Pop Corkhill. The defeat seemed to crush the A's hopes of overtaking the other contenders, but by the time they journeyed to St. Louis two weeks later, Bill Sharsig had them right back in the thick of it.

On August 11, the A's missed a chance to gain when they had to settle for an 11-inning 5–5 tie at Sportsman's Park in another double-umpire fiasco involving two players. Catcher Tom Gunning of the A's, working the bases, continually clashed with plate umpire Ed Herr of the Browns. Herr, who had lost his shortstop post when St. Louis acquired Bill White from Louisville, didn't have much stomach for the job, anyway. To justify his terrible calls that provoked so many arguments the game could not be finished before darkness descended, he later said that from behind the umpire's mask he hadn't been able to see to call balls and strikes correctly.

The following day, the A's lost more precious time as they wasted Seward's sterling effort in the series closer. Seward gave the Browns just four hits, but one of them was Harry Lyons's two-run double in the fourth inning. Those two markers were all Silver King needed. After King's 2–0 triumph, a portion of the Sportsman's Park grandstand collapsed as the jubilant crowd exited, injuring several, but Von der Ahe, feeling his club now had the momentum, rushed to repair the damage in time for the opening game of a series with Cleveland the next day.

The Browns took three straight from the Blues, in keeping with their pattern all during their championship run of mauling the Association's weak sisters—in 1888 alone, they were 62–18 against the four second-division teams. Then, a week later, when Brooklyn came to town, King and Hudson led a three-game sweep of the Bridegrooms that put Byrne out of his misery for another season. On the last day of August, St. Louis stood 68–30, six and a half games ahead of the second-place A's at 61–36. Even though Brooklyn took three of four from the Browns on their last trip east, Philadelphia could never really begin to close the gap.

By the last Friday in September, the Browns' margin had grown to nine and a half games. Comiskey then allowed his men to ease off during the final two weeks of the season so they could prepare to face Jim Mutrie's New York Giants, likewise a runaway winner in the League, in their fourth straight World's Series foray. With the pressure now off, Brooklyn suddenly began playing winning ball again to surge past the A's and finish second, but the Browns were still the hottest story of the season. How had this team, which in the spring had been almost unanimously picked for the second division, won again? And not only won, but won *easily?* And not only won easily, but won with a shortstop (White) who hit .175 and a centerfielder (Lyons) who hit .194? And not only won with two regulars who hit below .200 to become the only titlist ever to achieve this unlikely feat, but won after getting just 11 wins from Jim Devlin, Ed Knouff and Joe Murphy, the trio of young pitchers expected to take up the slack when Foutz and Caruthers were sold?

The questions continue to swarm when the individual and team stats of the 1888 Browns are examined. Comiskey had one of his better years, batting .273 and knocking home 83 runs, and rightfielder Tommy McCarthy, replacing the Foutz-Caruthers tandem, joined with Latham and Comiskey to give the Browns three of the top six base thieves in the Association. Still, the Browns did not lead the loop in stolen bases—Cincinnati did. Nor did they lead in runs or batting—Philadelphia claimed both those awards. But the Browns, despite having two sub-.200 hitters, nevertheless had a balanced attack that put them only a fraction of a point off the batting lead, so close that just two more hits would have earned them the team Triple Crown, with the highest batting average and fielding average and the lowest ERA.

The player most responsible for the Browns' offensive production was once again Tip O'Neill. Although his average dropped ex-

• • •
Gus Weyhing, who teamed with Ed Seward to bag 63 of the A's 81 wins in 1888, including no-hitters by each within a six-day period in late July. The following year Weyhing had the first of the four consecutive 30-victory seasons that made him the only pitcher to post 30-win seasons in three different major leagues. Like many hurlers, he faltered when the pitching distance was lengthened in 1893.

actly 100 points from the mark he achieved in 1887 after his walks were deducted, O'Neill still claimed his second straight batting title by a comfy 14 points. In mid-July, when he was suspended after being accused of indifferent play against Brooklyn, O'Neill ranked third in batting, behind Denny Lyons of the A's and Reds first sacker Long John Reilly, who led at .359. But O'Neill went on a rampage after he returned to the lineup, and a month later he had grabbed the top rung. In September, while averages everywhere sagged toward what would eventually be an Association record low of .238, only O'Neill, Reilly and Chicken Wolf of Louisville stayed above .300. On September 17 even Browning for the first time in his career was below .300 (.297) that late in the season.

But O'Neill could have gotten a hit every time up and still not propelled the Browns to another pennant if it were not for Silver King. When Von der Ahe and Comiskey got rid of Caruthers and Foutz, some presumed they bought Caylor's axiom that pitchers then were only good for about three years. In 1887, Foutz and Caruthers had both been in their third full seasons with the Browns, and in Foutz's case it developed that he truly was pretty well spent as a pitcher by the time he went to Brooklyn. But if

• • •
Silver King (left) and Kansas City teammate Grasshopper Jim Whitney (right) in 1886, a few months before King joined the Browns. Chris Von der Ahe liked King for his German ancestry, his fondness for women, and his youth—which made him like the son Von der Ahe really wanted. In June 1887, Von der Ahe prevented prosecution of King by a St. Louis woman with whom King had two illegitimate children. But Von der Ahe turned on King when King jumped to the Players League and compounded it in 1891 by signing with Pittsburgh for $5,000, rather than returning to St. Louis, when Von der Ahe would not match the offer.

Von der Ahe and Comiskey really were influenced by Caylor, they seem, in retrospect, to have been almost sadistic in their treatment of King. In 1888, St. Louis played 132 games, and King pitched in exactly half of them. Granted, King was durable. In his adolescence he worked for his father as a bricklayer, building a powerful chest and shoulders. Yet he could not have been expected to survive long under such a pitching load. With a potential fourth straight pennant in the balance, though, King's longevity as a pitcher was not much considered. The miracle is not just that he won 45 games in 1888 and compiled an ERA (1.64) that was little more than half of the 3.06 ERA the Association's average pitcher posted that year. It is also that he had two more seasons that were nearly as phenomenal before the workload finally caught up with him. King is one of only four pitchers in big-league history who won 200 games before their 30th birthdays and none thereafter.

At the beginning of the 1888 season, Comiskey employed King and Nat Hudson about equally. The Association pitching stats through June 23 showed King with 13 wins and Hudson with 11. But after that, King compiled 32 victories and Hudson just 14. In mid-September, soon after Chamberlain was picked up from Louisville, Hudson left the team to get married. As a result, the Browns had only King and Chamberlain to combat the Giants trio of Tim Keefe, Mickey Welch and Cannonball Crane in the World's Series. Though short of pitching, Von der Ahe concurred with Giants owner John Day's proposal to play a 10-game series for the championship with an eleventh, deciding game slated for Cincinnati in the event of a 5–5 tie. The Browns owner also assented to have John Gaffney and John Kelly umpire again, although he had questioned the scruples of both the previous year.

Some two weeks later, writer Frank Brunell went on record with high praise for Kelly and Gaffney, citing their performance in the World's Series as proof that the double-umpire system touted by many Association figures over the years, most prominently Caylor, was indeed the wave of the future. Von der Ahe meanwhile was blatantly accusing both arbiters of crooked work. Although he summoned many examples of the pair's duplicity, he had a legitimate beef only in Game Five at Brooklyn, which had been called by darkness with Yank Robinson due to lead off in the top of the ninth and the Browns down just 6–4 in the count. Much of Von der Ahe's frustration came from the fact that the Browns had led the entire way before a five-run New York rally in the eighth reversed the outcome.

When the Giants won Game Six, 12–5, two days later at Philadelphia, it put the Browns down 5–1 as the Series moved to

St. Louis for the final four contests. Needing just a single victory to clinch, New York got it in Game Eight by pasting Chamberlain for 12 hits and 11 runs. But even though the Giants had nailed down the championship, Von der Ahe and Day insisted on playing two more games. The Browns saved some face by sweeping both to reduce New York's winning margin to a more respectable 6–5 score and then blasted the Giants 18–7 in a season ending exhibition contest, but Keefe, King's counterpart in 1888 who led the League in both wins and ERA, eclipsed the Browns ace in the Series with a perfect 4–0 record. It was a measure of revenge for Keefe, and also for Mutrie, a pariah in the Association ever since he had deserted the Mets and burgled Keefe off with him to the League.

Notwithstanding the shelling his Browns were handed in the Series, Von der Ahe could revel in having won an unexpected and unprecedented fourth straight pennant. Byrne, in contrast, had to endure a winter of remarks like the one flung at him by a fan spotting him on the street after he purchased Hub Collins from Louisville: "You can spend $50,000 on players and buy all the stars in the Association and put them on your team. Then next year Charlie Comiskey will come along with his gang of Job Lots and knock you out of the pennant again."

But if the Browns were indeed going to win a fifth straight pennant in 1889, they were first going to have to find at least one new weakling in whose face they could kick sand. Cleveland, after winning just five of 39 games with the Browns during its two years in the Association, defected in mid-October to the League after buying the Detroit franchise and all of its "colt" (minor league) players. The loss of Cleveland would do irreparable harm to the Association. Though not a big moneymaker, the Forest City franchise was well-run and had in Brunell a man who might, in the fullness of time, have filled the canyon left by Caylor's departure. Upon his own leave-taking, Brunell said, "There is no use for honesty, business sagacity or integrity among the Association clubs. The ball is a different kind of ball from that played in the League. And it is nearly as good. But one club cannot trust another, and it is a general chase for the spoils from January 1 to December 31. And when the latter day comes Byrne has all the spoils that he can carry without spilling. That's the way it goes."

Most found it odd that Brunell would berate the eternally frustrated Byrne rather than the colossally successful Von der Ahe. Within the year, though, they would catch his point.

••• Leon Viau launched his rookie year in 1888 with eight straight wins before suffering his first setback on June 1. Viau went on to notch 27 victories as a Cincinnati yearling. He stood just 5'4" but was stockily built and threw hard, ranking among AA strikeout leaders in both 1888 and 1889.

1888 FINAL STANDINGS

	W	L	PCT	HOME	ROAD	GB
1. St. Louis Browns	92	43	.681	60–21	55–32	
2. Brooklyn Bridegrooms	88	52	.629	53–20	35–32	6.5
3. Philadelphia Athletics	81	52	.609	54–20	27–32	10
4. Cincinnati Reds	80	54	.597	55–24	24–30	11.5
5. Baltimore Orioles	57	80	.416	30–26	27–54	36
6. Cleveland Blues	50	82	.379	34–28	16–54	40.5
7. Louisville Colonels	48	87	.356	27–30	21–57	44
8. Kansas City Cowboys	43	89	.326	23–34	20–55	47.5

1888 SEASON LEADERS

BATTING

BATTING AVERAGE (325 ABs)

1. O'Neill, StL	.335
2. Reilly, Cinci	.321
3. Browning, Louis	.313
4. Collins, Louis-Brook	.307
5. Orr, Brook	.305
6. McKean, Cleve	.299
7. D. Lyons, Phila	.296
8. O. Burns, Balt-Brook	.293
9. Stovey, Phila	.287
Tucker, Balt	.287

SLUGGING AVERAGE

1. Reilly, Cinci	.501
2. Stovey, Phila	.460
3. O'Neill, StL	.446
4. O. Burns, Balt-Brook	.440
5. Browning, Louis	.436
6. McKean, Cleve	.425
7. Collins, Louis-Brook	.423
8. D. Lyons, Phila	.406
9. Larkin, Phila	.403
10. Tucker, Balt	.400

ON-BASE PERCENTAGE

1. Robinson, StL	.400
2. O'Neill, StL	.390
3. Browning, Louis	.380
4. Collins, Louis-Brook	.373
5. Stovey, Phila	.365
6. Reilly, Cinci	.363
D. Lyons, Phila	.363
8. Pinkney, Brook	.358
9. Welch, Phila	.355
10. McTamany, KC	.345

TOTAL BASES

1. Reilly, Cinci	264
2. Stovey, Phila	244
3. O'Neill, StL	236
4. McKean, Cleve	233
O. Burns, Balt-Brook	233
6. Collins, Louis-Brook	223
7. Larkin, Phila	220
8. Foutz, Brook	211
9. Tucker, Balt	208
10. Comiskey, StL	207

HOME RUNS

1. Reilly, Cinci	13
2. Stovey, Phila	9
3. Larkin, Phila	7
4. Tucker, Balt	6
D. Lyons, Phila	6
Comiskey, StL	6
McKean, Cleve	6
8. Milligan, StL	5
O'Neill, StL	5
Caruthers, Brook	5

RUNS

1. Pinkney, Brook	134
2. Collins, Louis-Brook	133
3. Stovey, Phila	127
4. Welch, Phila	125
5. Latham, StL	119
6. Nicol, Cinci	112
Reilly, Cinci	112
8. Robinson, Balt	111
9. McCarthy, StL	107
10. D. O'Brien, Brook	105

BATTING

HITS

1. O'Neill, StL	177
2. Reilly, Cinci	169
3. McKean, Cleve	164
4. Collins, Louis-Brook	162
5. Corkhill, Cinci-Brook	160
6. Comiskey, StL	157
7. Pinkney, Brook	156
Foutz, Brook	156
9. Welch, Phila	155
O. Burns, Balt-Brook	155

RBIs

1. Reilly, Cinci	103
2. Larkin, Phila	101
3. Foutz, Brook	99
4. O'Neill, StL	98
5. Corkhill, Cinci-Brook	93
6. D. Lyons, Phila	83
Comiskey, StL	83
8. Bierbauer, Phila	80
9. Browning, Louis	72
10. McKean, Cleve	68
McCarthy, StL	68

STOLEN BASES

1. Latham, StL	109
2. Nicol, Cinci	103
3. Welch, Phila	95
4. McCarthy, StL	93
5. Stovey, Phila	87*
6. Reilly, Cinci	82
7. Comiskey, StL	72
8. Collins, Louis-Brook	71
9. Faatz, Cleve	64
10. Stricker, Cleve	60

*At one time was credited with a record 156 steals in 1888 and 143 in 1887.

PITCHING

WINS

1. King, StL	45
2. Seward, Phila	35
3. Caruthers, Brook	29
4. Weyhing, Phila	28
5. Viau, Cinci	27
6. Mullane, Cinci	26
7. Bakely, Cleve	25
Hughes, Brook	25
Hudson, StL	25
Chamberlain, Louis-StL	25

INNINGS

1. King, StL	585.2
2. Bakely, Cleve	532.2
3. Seward, Phila	518.2
4. Porter, KC	474
5. Cunningham, Balt	453.1
6. Weyhing, Phila	404
7. Caruthers, Brook	391.2
8. Viau, Cinci	387.2
9. Mullane, Cinci	380.1
10. Hughes, Brook	363

LOSSES

1. Porter, KC	37
2. Bakely, Cleve	33
3. Ramsey, Louis	30
4. Cunningham, Balt	29
5. Kilroy, Balt	21
King, StL	21
7. D. O'Brien, Cleve	19
P. Smith, Balt	19
Seward, Phila	19
10. Weyhing, Phila	18

COMPLETE GAMES

1. King, StL	64
2. Bakely, Cleve	60
3. Seward, Phila	57
4. Porter, KC	53
5. Cunningham, Balt	50
6. Weyhing, Phila	45
7. Caruthers, Brook	42
Viau, Cinci	42
9. Mullane, Cinci	41
10. Hughes, Brook	40

PITCHING

STRIKEOUTS

1. Seward, Phila	272
2. King, StL	258
3. Ramsey, Louis	228
4. Bakely, Cleve	212
5. Weyhing, Phila	204
6. Mullane, Cinci	186
Cunningham, Balt	186
8. Chamberlain, Louis-StL	176
9. P. Smith, Balt	171
10. Viau, Cinci	164

WINNING PCT. (25 DECISIONS)

1. Hudson, StL	.714
2. Chamberlain, Louis-StL	.694
3. King, StL	.682
4. Caruthers, Brook	.659
Viau, Cinci	.659
6. Hughes, Brook	.658
7. Seward, Phila	.648
8. Mullane, Cinci	.619
Terry, Brook	.619
10. Weyhing, Phila	.609

ERA (140 INNINGS)

1. King, StL	1.64
2. Seward, Phila	2.01
3. Terry, Brook	2.03
4. Hughes, Brook	2.13
5. Chamberlain, Louis-StL	2.19
6. Weyhing, Phila	2.25
7. Caruthers, Brook	2.39
8. Foutz, Brook	2.51
9. Hudson, StL	2.64
10. Viau, Cinci	2.65

LOWEST ON-BASE PCT.

1. King, StL	.227
2. Seward, Phila	.250
Caruthers, Brook	.250
4. Hudson, StL	.256
5. Foutz, Brook	.257
6. Hughes, Brook	.259
7. Weyhing, Phila	.261
Chamberlain, Louis-StL	.261
9. Terry, Brook	.267
10. Mullane, Cinci	.268
Ewing, Louis	.268

NINE

1889

• • •

The 1889 Baltimore Orioles. Matt Kilroy, 29-game winner, sits second from left, with Bert Cunningham, one of the game's first great junk-ballers, to Kilroy's left. Left of manager Billy Barnie (civvies) is batting champ Tommy Tucker; Billy Shindle stands behind Tucker, and Frank Foreman is to Shindle's left. Foreman's teammates called him "Monkey" because of the facial grimaces he made at umpires and hitters. His own pitching must have caused Foreman to grimace some, too. He had a banner year in 1889 with 23 wins, but won only 98 games in a major league career that spanned from 1884 to 1902 and saw him pitch for Baltimore teams in three different major leagues.

BROOKLYN AT LAST BREAKS THROUGH

"Nothing that the American Association may do will surprise me. I am like the parrot whose business it was to travel with his master, a famous sleight-of-hand magician, and sing out after each performance, 'That is a good trick. Wonder what he'll do next.'"

—Ople Caylor

SHORTLY AFTER THE 1888 WORLD'S SERIES ended, New York Giants shortstop Monte Ward accompanied a raft of other major league stars on a world tour organized by Chicago White Stockings owner Al Spalding to promote the still relatively new sport of baseball. The tour boat had scarcely left the dock when Indianapolis owner John "Tooth" Brush bolted into action. Ward was the president and driving force behind the Brotherhood, the first effort by players to unionize. With him now conveniently out of the country, Brush devised a meeting of all the League owners on November 21, 1888, at the Fifth Avenue Hotel in New York, where he introduced his Salary Limit and Graded Plan. Brush's program divided players into five classifications ranging from "A" to "E," depending on their skill, and established a pay scale that restricted the best players to a salary max of $2,500, while granting those at the bottom of the totem pole $1,500.

A similar kind of salary limit had been endorsed by League owners three years earlier, only to fail because too many teams disobeyed it. Now that the Brush plan was about to become law, the players hit the roof, exploding that it smacked of a civil service salary schedule in that it robbed them of initiative and paid them much less than they could obtain in a free market. On learning of the plan when he returned to the country, Ward first tried to work within the system by presenting the owners with a list of the Brotherhood's grievances. When his conciliatory effort was snubbed, he formed a war committee among the League players whose politics were closest to his own and began meeting secretly with businessmen and industrialists who pledged to help the Brotherhood form a rebel league, which would begin play in 1890.

During the winter of 1888-89, while League moguls lined up behind Brush, Association monarchs stood accused of waffling on the Salary Limit plan until they saw how the chips would fall. Finally, in a meeting on March 5, 1889, at the Neil House in Columbus, Ohio, the Association voted not to adopt the League's classification system, which meant that, for the moment anyway, Association stars were eligible to be paid more than their League counterparts.

Owing to its central location, Columbus became the new hub for the Association soon after the city's application to replace Cleveland was accepted at the loop's year-end meeting in St. Louis in December 1888. At the same session, Kansas City's membership was upgraded from temporary to permanent when Byrne abandoned all hope of reviving the Mets and no one stepped forward with a plan to resurrect a franchise in New York. The demise of the Mets not only left the League in sole command of the nation's largest city but gradually shifted the balance of power in the Association to the West. Thinking he had sufficient support, Zach Phelps, still a minority stockholder in the Louisville Colonels, lobbied for the Association presidency prior to the year-end loop meeting. But when Phelps realized that he had only the backing of his own Louisville team and the three eastern clubs—Brooklyn, Baltimore and Philadelphia—he withdrew his name from consideration even before a vote could be taken. Wheeler Wyckoff was thereupon reelected president for a fourth one-year term, and John Speas of Kansas City won the vice presidency. The two then presided while the other delegates grappled with several problems that had haunted the Association during the 1888 season. In due order, it was resolved to abolish the practice of transferring games to another team's park, to adopt a new percentage plan that would give visiting clubs 20 percent of the gate (10 percent less than in 1888), and to dispense with the "star umpire system" that had long been opposed by Opie Caylor because it authorized salaries as high as $2,500 for such esteemed arbiters

• • •

Bill McGunnigle, as he looked in the late 1870s when he played in the NL. Even though he won two pennants in a row with Brooklyn, McGunnigle was axed in 1891 when Monte Ward bid for his job. McGunnigle's 1889-90 Bridegrooms team is the only back-to-back pennant winner never to place a single cast member in the Hall of Fame.

• • •

Al Buckenberger (14) and his 1893 Pittsburgh Pirates, including Denny Lyons (1), Jack Glasscock (10), Lou Bierbauer (11), and Patsy Donovan (12). Never much of a player himself, Buckenberger knew how to put together a team. Spurring a team was another matter. Fired in 1890 when his Columbus club lagged after being touted for the AA pennant, Buckenberger suffered the same fate in 1894 when Pittsburgh failed to contend after finishing second the previous year. His replacement on the second occasion was Connie Mack (9).

as John Gaffney, a practice that, in Caylor's judgment, created prima donnas but did nothing to improve the quality of officiating. Instead, the eight Association members voted to allocate a total of $6,000 to be split among its four umpires and to find replacements if the present staff of Gaffney, Herman Doscher, Bob Ferguson and John McQuaid would not accept a pay cut. *Sporting Life* summarized the meeting thusly: "It was chiefly remarkable for the fact that almost for the first time in the history of the organization no glaring blunder was perpetrated."

This lefthanded compliment stemmed, in part, from the journal's approval of Columbus's return to the Association. During its five-year absence, the Ohio capital had nearly doubled in population, making it ambitious to vacate the Tri-State League, which it had been a member of in 1888. Ralph Lazarus and Conrad Born, the principal owners, enticed Al Buckenberger away from Wheeling, a fellow member of the Tri-State League, to act as field general once Columbus re-entered the Association and proclaimed that the club had $1,000,000 behind it. Though probably just a boast, Lazarus and Born nonetheless went to prodigious expense to remodel Recreation Park, increasing its capacity to 5,000,

and felt they had a sufficient financial cushion to forbid the sale of beer on its grounds. Their worthy intentions went awry, however, when Buckenberger assembled a team that made even the Allegheny club of the early 1880s seem like a chapter of the Temperance Union. Local sportswriters nicknamed the new Columbus entry the Senators or the Solons, but the other Association bastions called it "Lushers' Rest."

As if it was their premonition that Buckenberger's club was beyond salvation what with being the loop's "baby" and an asylum for players with alcohol problems, the Association schedule committee put Columbus in the eastern wing of the loop and slated it to play its first ten games of the season on the road in the other three eastern cities. An 0–10 start was not improbable, but to everyone's shock, the Solons opened by bombing Baltimore 13–3, and it soon grew apparent that Buckenberger had fielded a remarkably competitive team rather than the automatic doormat that Kansas City, Cleveland and virtually every other new franchise had been its first year in the Association. Whether the credit belonged to Buckenberger or to someone else in the organization —perhaps Jimmy Williams, who was instrumental in pushing for Columbus's readmission—was never established, but the Solons sized up what useful players could be acquired cheaply from other major league teams and combined them with several shrewd minor league pickups to confront Baltimore with an Opening Day batting order of Jim McTamany CF, Lefty Marr RF, Ed Daily LF, Spud Johnson 3B, Dave Orr 1B, Jack O'Connor C, Jimmy Peoples 2B, Al Mays P and Henry Easterday SS. Peoples was soon replaced by Bill Greenwood and Mays lost his status as the club's ace boxman to Mark Baldwin, but otherwise Buckenberger went with basically the same lineup for the entire season. Orr, Baldwin and McTamany formed a potent veteran nucleus, and Marr, Johnson and pitcher Hank Gastright swiftly became rookie stars.

The 1889 season was an extraordinarily fertile one for frosh players, as almost every Association team received a significant contribution from at least one yearling. Kansas City unveiled no less than four new talents: pitcher Parke Swartzel, shortstop Herman Long and outfielders Jim Burns and Billy Hamilton. Even the defending champion Browns trotted out three rookie regulars: shortstop Shorty Fuller, centerfielder Home Run Duffee and pitcher Jack Stivetts. Fuller and Duffee superseded Bill White and Harry Lyons, the club's two sub-.200-hitting regulars in 1888, and Stivetts was purchased in mid-season from York of the Middle States League when the Browns gave up on Nat Hudson, whose ambivalence about whether he wanted to continue his baseball career had left the club with just two front-line pitchers, Silver

• • •

Early in the 1889 season, Billy Hamilton almost became the first on-field fatality in major league history when a throw from Louisville catcher Farmer Weaver nailed him in the temple as he tried to steal second base. Hamilton recovered to lead the AA in thefts that year. When Kansas City withdrew from the AA prior to the 1890 campaign, Hamilton was put up for auction. He slipped off to the NL, where he posted a .344 career batting average, the highest of any player who debuted in the AA.

•••

As a KC rookie in 1889, Herman Long made a record 122 errors. However, he also led the AA in total chances per game. His range, rather than his errors, was what teams remembered when Kansas City put him on the block, too. Long went to Boston in the NL, where his play brought him more votes than all but seven other 19th-century players when the Hall of Fame conducted its initial poll in 1936. Today, Long is the only finisher among the top 12 in the first Old Timers' ballot who is not enshrined.

•••

Yet a third KC rookie find in 1889 was Jim Burns. He signed a contract for 1890 on the condition that the club would remain in the AA. When Kansas City opted to play in the Western Association instead, Burns wanted out but didn't fight hard enough for his freedom. Except for a short stay with Washington in 1891, he served out his days in the minors.

King and Icebox Chamberlain. The Athletics also had a new budding pitching star in Sadie McMahon, and Billy Barnie, good for at least one surprise each season, got 23 wins from Frank Foreman, a bust with the Orioles a few years earlier. But, in terms of productivity, Cincinnati had the largest rookie windfall. Bug Holliday, Jesse Duryea and Ollie Beard, all minor league stars in 1888, blossomed still more against major league competition. Taking over for Pop Corkhill in center field, Holliday led the Association in batting for much of the season before ceding the crown to Baltimore's Tommy Tucker. Duryea gave the Reds their third frosh pitching sensation in three seasons when he nailed 32 wins. By the end of the season, Beard had succeeded Bid McPhee as team captain and nosed out fellow rookie Herman Long for the shortstop station on the loop all-star team.

But while most of the other Association teams were striving to build through youth, Brooklyn went a very different route. Apart from second-string catcher Joe Visner, who had been acquired for 1889 delivery from Hamilton of the International Association, every member of the club was either a returning Bridegroom or an experienced major leaguer purchased from another team. At first base, manager Bill McGunnigle planted Dave Foutz, finished as a pitcher but still a capable hitter and certainly more agile around the bag then Dave Orr, whose booming bat was so vastly negated in McGunnigle's estimation by his enormous girth that he was sold to Columbus. Hub Collins, snared from Louisville late in the 1888 season, was switched from the outfield to fill the club's sore spot at second base. Another 1888 late-season gift, former Oriole Oyster Burns, took over in right field when Foutz went to first base. Pop Corkhill, yet a third late purchase in 1888, fell heir to the centerfield slot after Paul Radford was released, and Tom Lovett, at one time with the Athletics, had been garnered from Omaha to join Adonis Terry, Bob Caruthers and 1888 rookie whiz Mickey Hughes in giving McGunnigle a four-man pitching staff. The third base, shortstop, leftfield and catching positions were manned by incumbents George Pinkney, Germany Smith, Darby O'Brien and Bob Clark, respectively.

Taken individually, none of the Bridegrooms outside of Caruthers was the best in the Association at his position in 1889, but collectively, McGunnigle had a smoothly meshed, durable unit that was reminiscent of the 1884 Mets. Corkhill, Foutz, Collins and Pinkney participated in every one of the club's 138 contests—Pinkney, in fact, was in the midst of playing in a 19th-century record 577 straight games. O'Brien missed only two games all season, Burns sat out just seven contests, and Smith, the lone Bridegroom who was injured for any appreciable length of time during

CINCINNATI NATIONAL LEAGUE 1895.

Bug Holliday, the AA's top rookie in 1889, sits at far left in the middle row in this picture of the 1895 Reds. After ranking among the game's elite for six seasons, he was idled for most of 1895 by an appendectomy. For a while, it was even doubtful whether Holliday would live, and he never really bounced back.

the regular season, still got into 121 frays. Burns was the club's jack-of-all-trades, filling in at short when Smith was out, while Visner took over in right field. On the rare occasions when Foutz went into the box, Terry played first base. Clark, a fine defensive catcher with a tendency to be brittle, worked 53 games behind the bat, exactly the same number as Visner. Nearing retirement, Doc Bushong served as a combination coach and utility catcher, and rookie backstopper Charlie Reynolds, who split the season between Brooklyn and Kansas City and took part in just 13 games, completed the squad.

From the original cast of 1884, when Brooklyn first entered the Association, only Terry remained, and Smith and Pinkney were the last holdovers from the Cleveland crew that had been combined with the team a year later. Clark, who had come to Brooklyn in 1886 from Atlanta, the 1885 Southern League champion, was the only other Bridegroom with more than one year of service with the club when the 1889 campaign began. The twin prizes from the Browns, Caruthers and Foutz, were seemingly the most important recent additions. In 1889, Caruthers's winning percentage of .784 established an Association record, and Foutz led the club in RBIs. But three other newcomers—Burns, Collins and Corkhill—also contributed so heavily to the Bridegrooms' success that picking the club's most valuable everyday player in 1889 is a particularly difficult task. The leading candidate is Darby O'Brien, if only because he was the captain of the team and the player Byrne coveted most when he purchased the Mets. Byrne

• • •

Rookie Jesse "Cyclone Jim" Duryea became Cincinnati's ace when he rang up 32 wins in 1889. The following year, Duryea got the blame when the Reds, by then in the NL, slumped after leading the loop by five games on July 4. A teammate explained Duryea's sudden decline this way: "The 'Cyclone' doesn't eat enough to keep a cat alive. If his appetite was as strong as his arm, he would still continue to play hob with his opponents."

had watched how the Browns had pieced together their championship teams by seeking heads-up fielders and base runners and meshing them with pitchers who likewise relied on their brains as much as their arms. O'Brien fit perfectly. He was cast from the same mold as Yank Robinson, but unlike Robinson he could hit. In 1889, O'Brien paced the Bridegrooms in runs, hits, thefts and total bases. Not far behind him were Burns and Collins, both of whom had been constrained by their former teams. In his four-year tour with Baltimore, Burns had continually been in Barnie's doghouse, and Collins, despite being a Louisville native and the Colonels' best all-around player, was speedily dispatched by Mordecai Davidson when he bought the club. Corkhill similarly had fallen out of favor in Cincinnati after the last of a long string of acrimonious contract disputes. In all, the Bridegrooms were, for the most part, a compound of players who had either been too recalcitrant or too expensive for their former clubs to keep.

Whether Byrne had at last found the formula, though, to break the Browns' chokehold on the Association title seemed extremely doubtful when St. Louis once again burst from the starting gate to a huge early-season lead. By June 7, Comiskey's club was already five games up on the second-place Athletics and six and a half in front of Brooklyn. But Von der Ahe, still writhing under the two straight embarrassing World's Series defeats, was jeopardizing the team's chemistry with his constant interference. On May 2, he fined Yank Robinson $25 when the second baseman walked away during one of his harangues. After Robinson jumped the team, grumbling that he'd already paid Von der Ahe enough in fines "to build a stone front house," the rest of the club forced Von der Ahe to cancel the fine by threatening to stage a sympathy strike. Still, morale was tenuous after that. In July, Von der Ahe charged Arlie Latham and Silver King with throwing games after a rumor reached him that gamblers were making a boodle betting against the Browns. When the whole team once again poised to rebel, Von der Ahe retracted the accusations, claiming that he'd found no truth in them after carefully sifting through the evidence. With all that, the Browns still led the Association as August began, albeit Brooklyn had replaced Philadelphia as their closest pursuer.

Far back in last place, already some 40 games behind the Browns after little more than half the schedule had been played, was Louisville, still reeling from an even more debilitating morale problem under owner-manager Mordecai Davidson. In January 1889, Davidson appointed former Association star Dude Esterbrook manager of the club and then fired him 10 games into the season for "losing his temper quickly and confusing the players by his scolding." Within days after Esterbook's departure the Louisville players were begging for his return as Davidson put the team under the nominal command of leftfielder Chicken Wolf, while he resumed running it himself. The result was an unmitigated disaster. On May 22, the Colonels embarked on an all-time record 26-game losing streak that was made all the more mortifying when six team members went on strike in Baltimore to protest Davidson's incessant, niggling $25 fines for missing signals and general boneheaded play. The delinquents were the core of the team: centerfielder Pete Browning, second baseman Dan Shannon, third baseman Harry Raymond, first baseman-pitcher Guy Hecker, catcher Paul Cook and pitcher Red Ehret. When the six refused to take the field on June 15, for a game with the Orioles, Davidson threw up his hands in disgust and went to New York, leaving the team in Wolf's charge. All six strikers were subsequently fined $100 by Davidson for the missed game, as was pitcher John Ewing, who had been sent home to Cincinnati to heal a sore arm expecting to draw full pay during his recuperation. The incident came to a head while the Browns were in Louisville and led to the formation of an Association chapter of the Brotherhood of Base Ball Players, patterned after the League organization, when most of the players on both teams enrolled and a charter was drawn up.

But even though the Colonels terminated their losing skein during the Browns' visit, winning 7–3 on June 23, behind Toad Ramsey, morale continued to plummet. Before a road trip to Kansas City in late June, Davidson as a last resort installed Buck McKinney, a bull-necked 225-pound theater doorkeeper, as his new manager in an effort to promote discipline, but when the team laughed at McKinney's lack of baseball acumen, Davidson turned over the franchise to the Association. In an emergency meeting on July 5 in Louisville, the club was sold to a welter of new owners who went along with the Association's entreaty to return almost all the money the team's players had been fined by Davidson except the $100 levy imposed on each of the Baltimore strikers.

Davidson's exit from baseball brought this jot of relief from the Louisville press: "At last the National game here is rid of its incubus." Lawrence Parsons eventually emerged from the miasma to seize the club presidency, and Dan Shannon was named player-manager, but if the Colonels were the better in 1889 for having gotten rid of Davidson, they never manifested it on the playing field. Louisville won only eight of its last 53 contests to finish at 27–111 and become the first major league team ever to lose 100 games.

The Falls City entry also shared with seventh-place Kansas

•••
Tom Lovett was given a trial by Providence, his hometown team, in 1885 and caught on with the A's later that year. After spending the following three seasons in the minors, he then won 70 games for Brooklyn over the next three years, including 30 games in 1890 when he led the NL in winning percentage. Remarkably, it is still not known for certain with which arm Lovett threw.

Only nine Louisville players dared to show their faces on picture day in 1889. Top (left to right): Dan Shannon, Farmer Vaughn, someone named Brown (who was serving as one of the team's many interim managers on this particular day), John Galligan and Chicken Wolf. Bottom (left to right): John Ewing, Farmer Weaver, Scott Stratton, Red Ehret and Ed Flanagan. Camera shy were Pete Browning, Guy Hecker, Harry Raymond, Paul Cook and Phil Tomney, as well as owner Mordecai Davidson. Hounded out of baseball in 1889, Davidson later did well in business and was feted for being one of Kentucky's last surviving Civil War veterans. His obituary in 1940 mentioned everything but the fact that he had once been a major league owner.

City the unpleasant honor of being the first two teams to give up more than 1,000 runs. The Cowboys tallied over six runs per game, however, making for reasonably close contests, whereas the Colonels were outscored on the average by three runs each time they took the field. For Columbus, which surrendered 924 runs, high-scoring games were also the norm. Run totals and batting averages were up nearly 20 percent from 1888 mainly because of a new rule in 1889 that pared the number of balls needed to walk from five to four "on the basis of obliging a pitcher to be more accurate in his delivery, and that to accomplish this he would have to reduce his speed."

Another important rule change in 1889 permitted a team to make one substitution per game, for any reason, at the end of an inning. This amendment enabled a manager to bring a fresh pitcher off the bench to relieve a starter who was getting battered rather than having to make his beleaguered starter switch positions with another player in the lineup. It had the further advan-

OLD JUDGE
CIGARETTE FACTORY.
GOODWIN & CO. New York.

• • •
Early in the 1880s, Bill Watkins was a promising young player. He then came up against Gus Shallix, a "terror" at hitting batters before the hit batsman rule was introduced, and was all but killed. Turning to managing, Watkins built Detroit into a power in 1887, only to be fired when the Wolves sagged the next year. He was in the process of doing a similar rebuilding job in Kansas City; had the Cowboys stayed in the AA in 1890, they almost certainly would have been a strong contender.

tage of absolving an umpire of the responsibility of having to decide whether a player was genuinely injured or only faking so that a substitute could be inserted in his place. Any rule that lightened an umpire's burden was welcomed except the one that might have reduced his load more than any other, namely the double-umpire system. Although tried at times during the 1889 season, mostly in St. Louis where John Kerins, a former Louisville player, was paired with experienced arbiters like John Gaffney and Bob Ferguson, the experiment was eventually judged a failure, at least for the time being. With each game again in the hands of only one man, even the best in the profession were ripe for criticism, and it was quick in coming. At one point in the 1889 season, Cincinnati manager Gus Schmelz contended that the Reds had won just four of 18 games when John Gaffney officiated, and Columbus begged Wyckoff not to assign Will Holland to work any more of its games. Holland and Fred Goldsmith had replaced McQuaid and Doscher, two of the four original regular umpires for the 1889 season, after they resigned rather than submit to the salary reduction the Association adopted at its March meeting.

The umpiring situation reached a crisis point on June 24 in Brooklyn when Goldsmith failed to appear for a game with Columbus and the Bridegrooms chose Bill Paasch to substitute. The Solons refused to accept Paasch and stayed on their bench when he called for play to begin, whereupon he forfeited the game to Brooklyn. A furious argument then began as to whether Paasch had the authority to declare a forfeit. Finally Columbus agreed to play and beat Brooklyn 13–7. Only then did Buckenberger learn that Brooklyn meant to count the game as a makeup for an earlier rain-out rather than as the contest that had been scheduled for that day. According to the report Brooklyn submitted to Wyckoff, Columbus had, in essence, split a doubleheader that afternoon, losing the first game by forfeit. Weeks later, the Board of Directors upheld the forfeit, giving the Bridegrooms a much-disputed win that would become crucial as the last weeks of the season unfolded.

In early September, St. Louis journeyed to Brooklyn for a three-game series that was expected to decide the pennant. Instead, only one game took place, on Saturday, September 7, and even *it* was not played to completion. With over 15,000 on hand at Washington Park, the Browns scored two runs in the sixth inning to take a 3–2 lead and then began pressuring Goldsmith that it was too dark to continue. When Goldsmith dissented, Comiskey had the Browns huddle endlessly in conferences over nothing, while Von der Ahe bought candles from a nearby grocer and then lit and arranged them around the Browns' bench like footlights. The crowd threw beer steins at the candles, knocking them over and igniting a pile of papers near the grandstand. Before a stampede could occur, the fire was extinguished, but another riot nearly erupted when Browns outfielder Tommy McCarthy was seen ducking the game ball in a water bucket to make it waterlogged just before the Bridegrooms, trailing 4–2, took their last turn at bat. Bob Clark led off the ninth inning by fanning but reached first safely when the third strike escaped Browns catcher Jocko Milligan. While Milligan muttered to Goldsmith that he hadn't been able to see the pitch in time to catch it, Clark tried to steal second. Comiskey contended that Milligan's throw beat Clark to the bag. When he lost that argument, he began pleading anew for Goldsmith to stop the game. Goldsmith again disagreed that it was too dark to continue, so Comiskey ordered his team to the sidelines and Goldsmith then forfeited the game to Brooklyn. Enraged, the crowd fired beer steins at the Browns as they left the field. McCarthy was made a particular target. Later the Browns needed a police escort to get out of the park safely.

The following day, an even larger crowd of 17,000 came out to Ridgewood Park, the Bridegrooms' Sunday home site, but Von der Ahe refused to play unless Byrne would either concede the previous day's game or play it over on Monday, a scheduled off day. Byrne would not consent to either condition and further

• • •
Seen here in this imaginative litho of the 1884 A's is rookie backstopper Jocko Milligan (center, second row from top). Milligan was an electrifying hitter but barely adequate defensively. In 1889 he collected 100 hits in just 273 at bats for the Browns. Milligan belonged at first base, but Charlie Comiskey wasn't about to give up his job. The Browns got Milligan from the A's prior to the 1888 season because Philadelphia also had no place for him to play.

Jack Stivetts, the pitcher for whom the phrase "helping his own cause" may have been coined. On June 10, 1890, he won his own game for the Browns, 9-8, with two home runs, one a ninth-inning grand slam. One of four pitchers who won 200 games before they were thirty and none thereafter, Stivetts stands alone among late 19th-century moundsmen as a hitter.

fanned the flames by denying the Browns their cut of Saturday's gate, claiming they owed the Association coffers a $1,500 forfeit penalty. Sunday's game was thus also forfeited to Brooklyn when the Browns did not show up.

On Tuesday, for the scheduled final game of the series, Comiskey brought the Browns by buggy to Washington Park in full uniform on orders from Von der Ahe. But a heavy rainstorm, which held off until the 4:00 PM starting time, caused the game to be postponed. The Browns were immensely relieved, for they had feared another crowd assault and had gouged Byrne for extra police protection though he insisted it was unnecessary.

An intense and convoluted dispute ensued over whether Brooklyn's two forfeit wins should be allowed. Von der Ahe contended that a League game on September 7 at the Polo Grounds between Indianapolis and New York was halted at 5:55 PM because of darkness, whereas his game at Brooklyn that same day, just a few miles away, had gone past 6:30. Byrne argued that the League game had been one-sided, with New York up 12–4, and besides, the Polo Grounds was set in kind of a bowl where it got darker quicker. Caught in the tug-of-war between the two, Wyckoff called a special meeting for September 14 to hash out the issue and then changed the date to September 23 because the 14th was on too short notice. In the interim, he ordered all clubs to withhold gate money from the Browns until they paid a fine for the two forfeited games. The Athletics ignored the directive in the Browns' next scheduled game on September 13 and gave Comiskey a $100 cut of the gate while blanking his men, 11–0. The drubbing put the Browns five games behind Brooklyn, seemingly so far out of the chase that the meeting to settle the forfeited games was superfluous. But St. Louis then put on a tremendous finishing kick, winning 12 straight games at one point.

When the Association owners gathered, as ordered, in Cincinnati on September 23, it was to learn that they were only there to rubber-stamp a decision that had already been made by the Board of Directors. In an inane moment of compromise, the Board decided Comiskey had been within his rights to pull his team off the field when Goldsmith would not stop the game on September 7 but was wrong in refusing to play the following day. As a result, the Sunday forfeit stood, but St. Louis was awarded the September 7 contest by a 4–2 score. Not only did the Board psychologically undermine the Association's umpiring staff by overruling Goldsmith's judgment that it was still light enough to play, but they went a step further, dismissing Goldsmith. The clumsy compromise appeased no one but the Browns. All of Brooklyn was indignant with the verdict, and Henry Chadwick, the game's leading commentator, who had attended the "candlelight" contest, condemned it, warning that it would license managers and players to kick unmercifully, now that they were aware they could sometimes get their way.

Once the two disputed games had been split down the middle, with each contender getting one win and one loss, the controversy turned to the postponed game of September 10 between the Browns and Brooklyn, as well as to several other contests with potential bearing on the pennant race that had been lost to the weather. The Board of Directors left it up to each individual club to decide whether to make up missing games by October 17, the absolute closing date that had been set prior to the season. St. Louis then arranged to play three postponed contests with the A's after the regular season closed. When the Bridegrooms went into a late tailspin that nearly put the Browns back on top, Byrne had to decide if he too should make up postponements. The danger was that if he did and his Bridegrooms ended the season in the lead, they could be overtaken if they lost the makeup games. On the other hand, he'd be caught short if he didn't make arrangements to play the missing games and the race ended in a near tie. This would open the door for the Browns to snare a fifth straight pennant by posting a higher winning percentage if they were victorious in all their makeup games with the A's.

In the end, Byrne gambled that Brooklyn would finish the regular season with an insurmountable lead, and it proved to be the right decision. But first, the Bridegrooms had to beat the Solons two straight games at Columbus after losing the opener of a season-ending three-game series on October 12, and then they had to sweat all during the long train-ride home to Brooklyn, while the Browns played a morning-afternoon doubleheader at Cincinnati on October 15. If the Browns swept the twinbill, it meant they would win the pennant by taking all three makeup games with the A's and the margin of victory would be the disputed game of September 7 that had been awarded to St. Louis.

A huge throng greeted the Bridegrooms' train at the Brooklyn depot. Not until Byrne had alit, though, was he apprised that

SHINDLE, 3d B., Baltimores
OLD JUDGE
CIGARETTE FACTORY
GOODWIN & CO., New York

• • •

Billy Shindle was among the best players the AA produced and later became one of the game's top third basemen when the AA and NL merged. Put at shortstop by the Philadelphia Quakers after he jumped from Baltimore to the PL in 1890, he tied Herman Long's all-time record for the most errors in a season when he committed 122 miscues.

Ollie Beard, whose family invented "burgoo," a famous Kentucky dish. Two good years at Syracuse earned him a big league shot in 1889, and he made the most of it initially. But even though he was Oliver Perry Beard, he was not fancied by Oliver Perry Caylor, who, after seeing Beard play just one game in 1889, said that Beard would never be nearly the shortstop Frank Fennelly had been for Cincinnati. Once again, Caylor was right—Beard lasted less than three seasons in the majors.

Brooklyn had won the flag when St. Louis was beaten 8–3 by Duryea in the morning game at Cincinnati. The loss meant it was pointless to make up the three games with the Athletics, as the Browns would still finish half a game behind Brooklyn even if they won them all. But the games with the A's would still have been meaningful, interestingly enough, if Brooklyn had agreed to make up its own postponed game of September 10 with the Browns. A sweep of the A's could have brought the Browns from Philadelphia to Brooklyn on the afternoon of October 17—say after beating the A's a twinbill on the 16th and a single game on the morning of the 17th—for a single do-or-die clash that could have spelled the greatest finish to a pennant race in the last century.

Instead, Byrne wimped out, and the season's most critical moment, rather than being the "Candlelight" game of September 7, or even the compromise Brooklyn forfeit win of the following day, might well have come on June 24 when substitute umpire Paasch awarded the Bridegrooms a forfeit victory over Columbus. For the moment, though, Byrne could not have cared less how he had at long last ascended to the Association crown. It was only fitting, too, that the Reds, his chief ally in the loop, had enthroned him by knocking off the Browns. For Byrne, the season had been an unqualified success. Nearly all the money he had shelled out to build a winning team came back to him in gate receipts, as the Bridegrooms shattered all previous attendance records by drawing 353,000 fans in 1889. Moreover, he could count on a hefty World's Series cut, for his opponents would be none other than the New York Giants, in the first ever postseason clash between two teams from the same urban sector.

To repeat as League champions, Jim Mutrie's Giants had fought off an even more arduous challenge than the Bridegrooms. A scant two percentage points ahead of Boston on the last morning of the season, the Giants had won the pennant by beating Cleveland that afternoon, while Boston ace John Clarkson lost to Pittsburgh. Unlike the Bridegrooms, though, Mutrie's men had a lengthy rest before the Series commenced, as the League campaign ended on October 5, a full ten days before the Association race was finally settled. The extra recovery time appeared to give the Giants' stellar pitching duo of Tim Keefe and Mickey Welch a vital edge over Caruthers and Terry, who had been worked hard by McGunnigle down the stretch, but the poolsellers in the Big Apple still considered the teams evenly matched.

Byrne and Giants owner John Day agreed upon a best six-of-eleven fray, but they had learned enough from the 1887 and 1888 Series fiascos to stipulate that play would be terminated once the outcome had been decided. New York won the honor of hosting

• • •

If you'd gone to a World's Series game in 1889, this smashing array of stars was on the cover of the scorecard you could have had for a dime. The 1889 Series should have been the best postseason affair in the last century. Not only were the combatants evenly matched, but the entire fray was played in New York. And indeed it began as if it would be a classic, drawing big crowds in the first two games. But the audience soured when Charlie Byrne had his Bridegrooms behave as they had all year whenever they played the Browns.

the first game on October 18 and chose League umpire Tom Lynch to officiate, while the Bridegrooms nominated Association arbiter John Gaffney. The opening pitch was then delayed when Lynch held out at the last minute for an $800 Series appearance fee. Rather than give in to the demand, Day called Bob Ferguson out of the stands to substitute for Lynch. The game finally began at 3:05, with Keefe opposing Terry in the box, as McGunnigle elected to save Caruthers for the second contest at Brooklyn the following day. With Ferguson and Gaffney alternating plate and base duties each inning, the Giants staggered to a 10–8 lead entering the bottom of the eighth. After Brooklyn pushed across four runs to go ahead 12–10, Ferguson and Gaffney called the game because of darkness as the Giants raced off the field expecting to take their last turn at bat. Mutrie was livid, shouting that the two Association umpires could just as easily have halted the game an inning earlier with the Giants up 10–8, since it had been so deep into dusk even then that the lights were on in the elevated trains passing the park. Although his manager's choler could not change the outcome, it did induce Day to pony up enough money to buy Lynch's services for the remainder of the Series.

The next afternoon, in front of a postseason record audience of 16,172, Mutrie, as if conceding the game, pitted Cannonball Crane (14–10 during the season) rather than Welch (27–12) against Caruthers. To his pleasant surprise, the Giants hammered Caruthers for six runs and 10 hits, while Crane shut down Brooklyn with just two tallies. In Game Three, though, Mutrie's wrath was aroused again when Brooklyn began stalling as early as the sixth inning while holding a narrow 8–7 edge. In the top of the ninth, with the Bridegrooms still up by just one run, the Giants loaded the bases against Caruthers, working in relief of Mickey Hughes. With Hank O'Day, who had relieved Welch in the sixth inning, at bat, Brooklyn launched another protest that it was too dark to continue. Suddenly, Gaffney, umpiring the plate, threw up his hands and stopped the game, sending Mutrie into a tantrum.

Game Four only worsened his disposition. The Giants overcame a 7–2 Brooklyn lead by scoring five runs in the top of the sixth, but with two men on base in the bottom of the frame Oyster Burns slapped a sinking liner to left field off Crane that eluded Jim O'Rourke in the gloaming. The ball rolled all the way to the wall for an inside-the-park three-run homer that put Brooklyn back in the lead, 10–7. Burns had scarcely crossed the plate before the Giants stalked off the field in protest, again prompting the umpires to call the game and give the Bridegrooms their third darkness-abbreviated victory in the four contests thus far.

The following morning, Day and Buck Ewing, the Giants' field captain, informed Byrne that they didn't "care to run any chance of losing another game on account of darkness or intentional delays" and would compete no more "against a club that insists on playing dirty ball." Realizing they were serious, Byrne buckled under the threat and agreed to move up the starting time for Game Five and all future Series games to 2:30. The extra half hour of light assured that the remaining contest would go the full nine innings. More importantly, however, in the scheme of things, Game Five marked the last appearance of Clark, Brooklyn's best catcher.

Clark began the game also leading the Bridegrooms in hitting, but after he twisted his ankle in the sixth inning trying to take an extra base on a single, the tide abruptly turned. On a brutally cold afternoon, Crane, pitching for the second day in a row,

beat Caruthers 11–3 at Washington Park, with a mere 2,901 on hand. The next afternoon, Terry held a 1–0 lead over O'Day with two out and the bases empty in the bottom of the ninth. Monte Ward then singled for the Giants and proceeded to steal both second and third on Visner, subbing for Clark. Moments later, Ward scored the tying run when Jumbo Davis, filling in at short for Germany Smith, fumbled Roger Connor's grounder that would have ended the game if it had been smoothly handled. In the 11th inning, Foutz held the ball a fraction of a second too long after Ward beat out an infield hit, allowing Mike Slattery to speed all the way home from second and slide in under Visner's tag to give the Giants a 2–1 win and knot the Series at 3–all.

The weather for the final three games continued to be cold, dank and disagreeable, but Mutrie's mood had gone all sunny and cheerful as the Giants rattled off three more wins in a row to bag their second straight World's Series by a 6–3 count. McGunnigle could find excuses in Clark's wrenched ankle and Caruthers's weary arm, but it was probably more the unforeseen brilliance of Crane and O'Day that cut down the Bridegrooms just when they looked to be headed for the Association's first Series victory since 1886. Between them, the two second-line pitchers won all six of the Giants' triumphs, while Keefe, Welch and Caruthers, responsible for 95 victories during the season, were an aggregate 0–4 in the Series. O'Day's performance was especially dazzling. In his two starts, he was given just five runs to work with but won both, as Brooklyn could reach him for only 10 hits and three runs in the 23 innings he labored.

The Series, with its snatches of luster knifing through the grisly weather and flaring tempers, capped a season that ought to have been the Association's most exciting to date but was more often ragged and neurotic. Though Byrne might feel he had overcome Von der Ahe's political clout and the Browns' skullduggery to win the pennant, he could not squelch the many observers like Caylor, who were unkind enough to notice that his Bridegrooms had stooped to Comiskey's stalling and wheedling tactics in the World's Series to gain all three of their victories. The allusion that he was at bottom no better than Von der Ahe and Comiskey spoiled what ought to have been his finest hour and made him all the more vindictive.

While every other potentate in baseball was wringing his hands at the prospect of the looming war with the players, Byrne eliminated the specter by signing all of his key team members to contracts for the 1890 season before they left Brooklyn for the winter. That freed him to think only about how he would take his final revenge on the Browns.

In 1889, Tommy Tucker hit .372 to set a record for switch-hitters that still endures. Tucker was the Mickey Vernon of his day, but Vernon at least had two exceptional seasons, whereas Tucker never again had a year even remotely like 1889. In 1895, when the NL as a whole hit .296, he batted .249.

1889 FINAL STANDINGS

	W	L	PCT	HOME	ROAD	GB
1. Brooklyn Bridegrooms	93	44	.679	50–18	43–26	
2. St. Louis Browns	90	45	.667	51–18	39–27	2
3. Philadelphia Athletics	75	58	.564	46–22	29–36	16
4. Cincinnati Reds	76	63	.547	47–26	29–37	18
5. Baltimore Orioles	70	65	.519	41–23	29–42	22
6. Columbus Solons	60	78	.435	36–33	24–45	33.5
7. Kansas City Cowboys	55	82	.401	33–35	20–47	38
8. Louisville Colonels	27	111	.196	18–47	9–64	66.5

1889 SEASON LEADERS

BATTING

BATTING AVERAGE (325 ABs)

1. Tucker, Balt	.372
2. Holliday, Cinci	.343
3. O'Neill, StL	.335
4. D. Lyons, Phila	.329
5. Orr, Colum	.327
6. Larkin, Phila	.318
7. Purcell, Phila	.316
8. Shindle, Balt	.314
9. Stovey, Phila	.308
10. Marr, Colum	.306

SLUGGING AVERAGE

1. Stovey, Phila	.527
2. Holliday, Cinci	.519
3. Tucker, Balt	.484
4. O'Neill, StL	.478
5. D. Lyons, Phila	.469
6. Orr, Colum	.446
7. Larkin, Phila	.426
8. O. Burns, Brook	.423
9. Bierbauer, Phila	.417
10. Marr, Colum	.414

ON-BASE PERCENTAGE

1. Tucker, Balt	.450
2. Larkin, Phila	.428
3. D. Lyons, Phila	.426
4. O'Neill, StL	.419
5. Hamilton, KC	.413
6. McTamany, Colum	.407
Marr, Colum	.407
8. Stovey, Phila	.393
9. O. Burns, Brook	.391
10. Griffin, Balt	.387

TOTAL BASES

1. Stovey, Phila	293
2. Holliday, Cinci	292
3. Tucker, Balt	255
O'Neill, StL	255
5. Orr, Colum	250
6. D. Lyons, Phila	239
7. D. O'Brien, Brook	237
8. J. Burns, KC	236
9. Bierbauer, Phila	229
10. Marr, Colum	226

HOME RUNS

1. Stovey, Phila	19
Holliday, Cinci	19
3. Duffee, StL	15
4. Milligan, StL	12
5. D. Lyons, Phila	9
O'Neill, StL	9
7. Corkhill, Brook	8
Visner, Brook	8
9. Foutz, Brook	7
Bierbauer, Phila	7
G. Tebeau, Cinci	7

RUNS

1. Stovey, Phila	152
Griffin, Balt	152
3. D. O'Brien, Brook	146
4. Hamilton, KC	144
5. Collins, Brook	139
6. Long, KC	137
7. McCarthy, StL	136
8. D. Lyons, Phila	135
9. Welch, Phila	134
10. O'Neill, StL	123

HITS			STOLEN BASES			RBIs	
1. Tucker, Balt	196		1. Hamilton, KC	117		1. Stovey, Phila	119
2. Holliday, Cinci	193		2. O'Brien, Brook	91		2. Foutz, Brook	113
3. Orr, Colum	183		3. Long, KC	89		3. O'Neill, StL	110
4. O'Neill, StL	179		4. Nicol, Cinci	80		4. Bierbauer, Phila	105
5. Shindle, Balt	178		5. Latham, StL	69		5. Holliday, Cinci	104
6. J. Burns, KC	176		6. Stearns, KC	67		6. Comiskey, StL	102
McCarthy, StL	176		7. Welch, Phila	66		7. O. Burns, Brook	100
8. Stovey, Phila	171		8. Collins, Brook	65		8. Tucker, Balt	99
9. D. O'Brien, Brook	170		Comiskey, StL	65		9. J. Burns, KC	97
10. D. Lyons, Phila	168		10. McPhee, Cinci	63		10. R. Mack, Balt	87
Comiskey, StL	168		Tucker, Balt	63		Orr, Colum	87
			Stovey, Phila	63		Stearns, KC	87

PITCHING

WINS			LOSSES			INNINGS	
1. Caruthers, Brook	40		1. M. Baldwin, Colum	34		1. Baldwin, Colum	513.2
2. King, StL	33		2. Ewing, Louis	30		2. Kilroy, Balt	480.2
3. Duryea, Cinci	32		3. Ehret, Louis	29		3. King, StL	458
Chamberlain, StL	32		4. Swartzel, KC	27		4. Weyhing, Phila	449
5. Weyhing, Phila	30		5. Kilroy, Balt	25		5. Caruthers, Brook	445
6. Kilroy, Balt	29		6. Weyhing, Phila	21		6. Chamberlain, StL	421.2
7. M. Baldwin, Colum	27		Foreman, Balt	21		7. Foreman, Balt	414
8. Foreman, Balt	23		8. Widner, Colum	20		8. Swartzel, KC	410.1
9. Viau, Cinci	22		Viau, Cinci	20		9. Duryea, Cinci	401
Terry, Brook	22		10. Cunningham, Balt	19		10. Viau, Cinci	373
			Conway, KC	19			

COMPLETE GAMES			STRIKEOUTS			WINNING PCT. (25 DECISIONS)	
1. Kilroy, Balt	55		1. Baldwin, Colum	368		1. Caruthers, Brook	.784
2. Baldwin, Colum	54		2. Kilroy, Balt	217		2. Chamberlain, StL	.681
3. Weyhing, Phila	50		3. Weyhing, Phila	213		3. King, StL	.660
4. King, StL	47		4. Chamberlain, StL	202		4. Lovett, Brook	.630
5. Caruthers, Brook	46		5. King, StL	188		5. Duryea, Cinci	.627
6. Swartzel, KC	45		6. Terry, Brook	186		6. Terry, Brook	.619
7. Chamberlain, StL	44		7. Duryea, Cinci	183		7. Weyhing, Phila	.588
8. Foreman, Balt	43		8. Foreman, Balt	180		8. Seward, Phila	.583
9. Duryea, Cinci	38		9. Viau, Cinci	164		9. McMahon, Phila	.571
Viau, Cinci	38		10. Ewing, Louis	155		10. Kilroy, Balt	.537

ERA (140 INNINGS)			LOWEST ON-BASE PCT.	
1. Stivetts, StL	2.25		1. Stivetts, StL	.280
2. Duryea, Cinci	2.56		2. Foreman, Balt	.290
3. Kilroy, Balt	2.85		3. Caruthers, Brook	.294
4. Weyhing, Phila	2.95		4. Duryea, Cinci	.296
5. Chamberlain, StL	2.97		5. Terry, Brook	.298
6. Mullane, Cinci	2.99		6. Conway, KC	.299
7. Caruthers, Brook	3.13		7. King, StL	.302
8. King, StL	3.14		Chamberlain, StL	.302
9. Conway, KC	3.25		9. Kilroy, Balt	.303
10. Terry, Brook	3.29		10. Lovett, Brook	.306

TEN

1890

• • •

Jack Chapman (civvies) and his 1889 Syracuse Stars, which included several members of the 1890 Syracuse AA club. Top row, far right, is Moses Walker, then playing in his last professional season before the unwritten color ban forced him out of the minors, too. Chapman was a manager much like Bill Sharsig. Masterful when he had a team with which he could maneuver, Chapman was even good when he had very little talent. Chapman's achievement with Louisville in 1890, when he piloted the club from worst to first, appears to have stunned everyone but him. He seemed to know almost from the outset of the season that he was going to win.

O N NOVEMBER 4, 1889, JUST SIX DAYS AFTER
his shortstop play had sparked the Giants to their
second straight World's Series triumph, Brotherhood president Monte Ward convened his war committee at the Fifth Avenue Hotel in New York.
Within minutes after the door had closed, Ward
flung it open and announced to the reporters milling about outside that the Brotherhood had severed all ties with the National
League and would form a new federation, owned and operated by
League players. Undetermined as yet was the status of players in
the American Association. Although they had endeavored to organize a Brotherhood chapter of their own several months earlier,
Ward was curiously noncommittal when he was asked whether
they would be included in his new "Players League." Long John
Reilly later faulted Arlie Latham for the Association players not
being on the cutting edge of the players' revolt, claiming that
Latham, after being put in charge of gathering signatures for the
Brotherhood, had lost the list.

• • •
In this gorgeous cabinet card of the 1889 Toledo Maumees (a.k.a. Black Pirates) are many of the principals on the 1890 AA club. At upper left is owner Valentino H. Ketcham. His star first baseman Perry Werden is perched at the apex of the diamond. Werden set a 19th-century record when he slammed 45 homers for Minneapolis of the Western League in 1895. Minneapolis's tiny park had a lot to do with his feat. During Werden's AA sojourn in Toledo and Baltimore, which had bigger parks, most of his long blasts were only good for triples. He had 38 in 1890–91.

In any event, Association magnates felt they could put other matters ahead of the impending Brotherhood war when they assembled at the same New York hostelry a week later, on November 12. Topping the agenda was the selection of a new loop president. A cabal comprised of Von der Ahe, William Whittaker of the Athletics and delegates from the Columbus and Louisville clubs had already caucused prior to the general meeting to handpick a successor to Wheeler Wyckoff. Their choice was Louis Krauthoff, an officer of the Kansas City club, but Krauthoff spurned the invitation upon learning that he would have to agree to meet a certain condition—namely to exclude Brooklyn and Cincinnati from all important Association committees—before the cabal would push for his election. Von der Ahe's bloc then cast its weight with Zach Phelps, by this time the loop's attorney.

Hostilities opened when ex-Missouri congressman John O'Neill, there at Von der Ahe's invitation, nominated Phelps, and Byrne proffered Krauthoff's name. The two aspirants tied 4–4 on the first ballot. For all of the first day of the meeting and deep into the second day, the deadlock continued with Von der Ahe's coalition of St. Louis, Philadelphia, Columbus and Louisville lined up stubbornly against Byrne's foursome of Brooklyn, Cincinnati, Kansas City and Baltimore. Late on the afternoon of November 13, Byrne and Cincinnati president Aaron Stern were called out of the room by a messenger from the League, which was conferencing simultaneously and receiving periodic reports from a spy at the Association meeting. League titans were hopeful that the battle over the Association presidency would tip Brooklyn and Cincinnati over the edge. In addition to their loathing of Von der Ahe and Comiskey and the way they had bullied the Board of Directors into awarding the Browns the "Candlelight" game, both clubs could no longer benefit from the Association's major attraction to them. For Brooklyn, Sunday games at Ridgewood Park were certain to be problematic in 1890, and the Reds had definitely lost Sunday ball to the Sabbatarians. What made a new home in the League still more appealing to Byrne and Stern was knowing that Ward's insurrection would decimate the other League clubs while leaving their own relatively unscathed. Perhaps at Byrne's urging, the Cincinnati owner had also hastened to sign most of his key players to contracts for the 1890 season as soon as he saw the Brotherhood trouble brewing.

Half an hour after they had left the Association meeting, Byrne and Stern returned and dropped a bombshell on the assembly by tendering the formal resignation of their clubs from the Association. When they exited, with them went the delegates from Baltimore and Kansas City. The next morning Billy Barnie announced that Krauthoff had withdrawn from the presidential duel. Later that day, Kansas City resigned from the Association and joined the minor Western League, taking its players who were either already under contract or else preferred to stay with the club and auctioning off those who wanted to stay in the majors. Barnie was mum on Baltimore's intentions, but it was presumed that the Orioles would also try to join the National League, perhaps by purchasing the Washington franchise. Sure enough, on November 30, Baltimore added its resignation to the mass exodus from the Association.

Though the loop was now down to just four teams, not even a quorum according to its constitution, the shell-shocked survivors went about the business of electing Phelps president and Conrad Born of Columbus vice president and then began searching through the rubble for material with which to rebuild. In contrast, the League was now a 10-club enterprise, if only temporarily, while its wealthier franchises connived to dispose of Washington and Indianapolis, two perennial losers both at the

Lyons, L. F. with Taylor Trainer, Philadelphia.

SMOKE KALAMAZOO BATS

• • •

Ed Daily, being attended to in 1887 by a Phillies trainer. He caught a break in 1890, ending up on first-place Louisville after starting the year with last-place Brooklyn. Daily's luck seemed destined to hold when he got the Opening Day starting assignment for Louisville in 1891. But that summer his lungs started to decline. Joining Washington to see if he could rebound in different air, he died there in October of consumption. Among the pallbearers at Daily's funeral was his Washington teammate, the shadowy rookie Larry Murphy. Despite a fine debut in 1890, Murphy was mysteriously released soon after the sad event. He drifted off from Washington as unknown as when he arrived and was never heard from again.

gate and on the field. It took much of the winter, but eventually the pair were ousted in favor of Brooklyn and Cincinnati, freezing Indianapolis owner John Brush out of the majors scarcely a year after he had tried to save his fellow moguls from bankruptcy with his Salary Limitation plan. In March, a sensational story broke that Brush was in Columbus orchestrating a labryinthine series of deals that would enable the Association to start the 1890 season with a radically altered alignment consisting of Brooklyn, Washington, Philadelphia, Baltimore, St. Louis, Columbus, Detroit and Brush's own Indianapolis club. Many suspected that Brush himself leaked the story, but whatever its source, the Association already had commitments by then from four new franchises, leaving no room for Indianapolis.

Three of the four newcomers were the Syracuse Stars, Rochester and the Toledo Maumees, all refugees from the troubled minor leagues. Syracuse had been the first to bid for a franchise, rushing representatives to the Association meeting in New York the instant that club director R. C. Morse heard the news that Brooklyn and Cincinnati had defected, and the last to put up the cash. After weeks of dithering, the Stars reorganized under twenty-nine-year-old George Kasson Frazier and at an emergency Association meeting in mid-January produced the $10,000 bond that assured their membership.

Frazier then declared that he would manage the team, but if he seemed young and inexperienced to the veteran Association owners at the table, what must they have thought of Jim Kennedy? Still just twenty-two years old, the roly-poly former semi-pro infielder was called the "Napolean" of sports promoters by the Brooklyn press. He came to the meeting with William Wallace, president of the Ridgewood Exhibition Company, which owned the park where Byrne's Bridegrooms had played their Sunday games. Kennedy was there as an emissary for a team of his own creation called the Brooklyn Gladiators, and when he too posted a $10,000 bond with Wallace's help, the Association again had eight members in good standing.

Von der Ahe, the lone club owner whose roots reached back to the Association's inception, remembered the invidious result when the Baltimore team had been started from scratch on the eve of the 1882 season and made a plea for the new Brooklyn entry. At his behest, each of the other seven Association clubs pledged to supply Kennedy's Gladiators with at least one experienced player. The only teams that lived up to the spirit of the bargain were Columbus, which turned over pitcher-outfielder Ed Daily, and Rochester, which presented the Gladiators with four useful players—outfielders Hank Simon and Jack Peltz, first baseman Billy O'Brien and pitcher Steve Toole. To fill out their roster, the Gladiators had to hire such antiques as Joe Gerhardt, Candy Nelson and Jim Toy, the first American Indian player in major league history. Nevertheless, when Kennedy announced he would pilot the Gladiators, and writers learned his age, the team was labeled "Kennedy's Kids."

Against the likes of Kennedy's Kids, the three minor league parvenus, and a Louisville team that had lost more than 80 percent of its games the previous year, Von der Ahe was supremely confident his Browns would regain the Association pennant in 1890. True, he had lost Comiskey, his right-hand man, plus Silver King, Tip O'Neill, Arlie Latham, Jocko Milligan, Yank Robinson and Jack Boyle to Players League raiders once the Brotherhood made up its mind to enlist Association players in its cause, but his only two likely competitors, Columbus and Philadelphia, had also suffered gaping losses to the Brotherhood. The A's were minus 30-game winner Gus Weyhing and Harry Stovey, probably the Association's top player in 1889, along with first baseman Henry Larkin and second baseman Lou Bierbauer, the right half of an infield that was among the best in the majors. Gone from the Solons were Dave Orr, Mark Baldwin and Lefty Marr. What gave Von der Ahe pause was that in Jack Crooks, Charlie Reilly, Frank Knauss, "Dirty" Jack Doyle and Mike Lehane, Columbus had unearthed a batch of rookies who promised to be skilled replacements for the lost trio. Actually, the longer Von der Ahe reflected, the more convinced he grew that the Solons were his only serious challenger. But what his Browns had that Columbus lacked was a solid pitching staff built around rookie wonder Jack Stivetts, Icebox Chamberlain and Toad Ramsey, bought late in the 1889 season from the floundering Louisville franchise.

So certain was Von der Ahe that his Browns would breeze home first in the temporary absence of most of the Association's top players that his war-time replacements at the start of the season were: at first base, Pat Hartnett, a rookie notable only for "shaking his hoof" until all hours; at second base, career minor leaguer Billy Klusman; at third base Pete Sweeney, a good-hit, no-field type who in 1890 lost the knack for hitting too; in centerfield, Chief Roseman, whose "rotund form" had been out of the majors since 1887; and behind the plate, Frank Meek, long the club's batting-practice catcher and destined to return to that chore after just four games. The Browns' opposition in the 1890 curtain-raiser was Louisville, now under the helm of Jack Chapman who had returned to the club late in the previous campaign after twelve years in exile following the 1877 game-dumping scandal that cost the Falls City its League franchise. Chapman had

• • •

By 1894, ex-Browns star Shorty Fuller was in his third season with the New York Giants. In 1890, Fuller enjoyed his best year, hitting .278 and scoring 118 runs. Fuller's nickname suggests his probable physical dimensions, but his exact height is unknown. For a while, the Browns hoped he and his brother, Harry, would give them a replica of the Gleason brothers at shortstop and third base, but Harry played only one game in the majors. Shorty, on the other hand, lasted nine years.

added first baseman Harry Taylor, who really aspired to be a lawyer
and in time became a judge; pitcher Herb Goodall, who talked all
year of quitting to practice medicine and eventually did; leftfielder Charlie Hamburg, a career minor leaguer who had played under
Chapman at Buffalo in 1889; and second baseman Tim Shinnick,
who boasted, with utter truth, that he had never played on anything but championship teams since his days at Philips Exeter
Academy in the mid-1880s. But from a club that had lost 111
games, Chapman was missing Pete Browning, Guy Hecker, John
Ewing and Paul Cook, to say nothing of Ramsey, so everyone
knew Shinnick's lucky streak was about to end.

When Ramsey knocked off the Colonels' Scott Stratton
11–8 on Opening Day in a sluggish, error-filled game, the Browns'
unpolished performance was of far more concern to observers
than Louisville's. The Colonels figured to be raw. In early March,
while most major league clubs had long since begun doing their
spring conditioning in the South, Louisville club president Lawrence Parsons vetoed the expense and kept the Colonels home to
train, reasoning that it would not only save money, but that "the
soft climate of the South weakens the muscles and tendons and
unfits them for the long and arduous work in the severe climate of
the North." Execrable weather throughout the spring then confined the Colonels to working out most of the time in the gym. In
March, a terrible cyclone in Louisville killed over 100 and did
massive property damage. When Chapman arranged a benefit
game for the disaster victims, it was snowed out. The Colonels at
last began to seem so thoroughly jinxed that locals began calling
them the Cyclones. It was typical of the Falls City luck when the
opening game was postponed by rain until the following day and
then the team lost anyway. Nor was it a surprise that, on April 20,
the first Sunday game of the season sent an overflow crowd of
10,000 away in an ugly mood. In the third inning, with the
Colonels new catcher John Ryan on first base, Chicken Wolf
socked a ball into the standees ringing the outfield, scoring Ryan
while Wolf wound up at third. Abiding by a pregame agreement
that a ball hit into the crowd on the field was a ground-ruled double, umpire Terence Connell sent Wolf back to second but refused
to return Ryan to third, contending that the rule pertained only
to the batter. Browns captain Tommy McCarthy would not continue play unless Ryan's run was nullified, driving Connell to forfeit the game to Louisville. The decision so infuriated the capacity
crowd, which had sacrificed its Sunday expecting a full afternoon's entertainment, that to soothe matters the two clubs played
an exhibition contest that ended in an unrewarding 13–13 tie. To
further stoke tempers in Louisville, for a while it appeared that the

• • •

Tommy McCarthy had his greatest season in 1890 against depleted AA pitching staffs. Later, he was an outfield companion of Hugh Duffy's in Boston, where the two Irishmen were dubbed the "Heavenly Twins" by the Hub's multitude of Irish fans. McCarthy was a fine player, but it nevertheless seems highly ironic that of all the performers who spent more than two seasons in the AA, he alone made the Hall of Fame entirely on the basis of his playing accomplishments even though he was never one of the game's top stars.

Colonels would not even get a forfeit win out of the incident. Several weeks later, however, when the Browns' protest received a formal hearing, Connell's verdict was upheld.

In other action on the first Sunday of the season, Toledo bested Columbus before a discouragingly small audience of less than 500 at the Solons' Recreation Park, but Kennedy's Kids pulled nearly 4,000 to watch Toole outduel Syracuse's Dan Casey 9–8 at Ridgewood Park. There was a good reason for the "flash" crowd. Two days earlier, the Gladiators and the Stars had played probably the wildest and most exciting game in Association history, with Brooklyn prevailing 22–21. Jim Powers, a local boy making his initial major league appearance, got the win in relief. It was a rocky outing and proved to be Powers's only big-league victory, but his catcher that day, another Brooklynite named Herman Pitz, staged one of the most sensational debuts of all time. Pitz went 2-for-2, walked four times, scored three runs and showed himself to be exceedingly "spry and quick" behind the bat and on the bases. The Gladiators' rookie backstopper ought to have quit right there. Though he played 89 more games, Pitz never again distinguished himself. Indeed, he batted just .165 and set an unsought record for the most career at bats (284) without an extra base hit by a player other than a pitcher.

One who did quit when he was ahead was Billy Price. On April 27, for his club's first Sunday home game of the season, Philadelphia manager Bill Sharsig borrowed Price from the Frankfurt club to pitch against Syracuse. After topping the Stars 5–3, Price never appeared again in the majors and so claimed the odd distinction of playing his entire big league career in the state of New Jersey, which only once since 1876 (in 1915, when Newark was part of the rebel Federal League) has harbored a major league team.

The Pennsylvania Blue Laws prevented the Athletics from playing on the Sabbath in Philadelphia, but on occasion, ever since 1888, they had experimented with using Gloucester City, New Jersey, as their Sunday home, and that was where Price was king for a day. But this sanctuary was toppled after the 1890 season by the Sabbatarians. With Sunday ball growing in popularity and threatening to invade even the nation's capital, everywhere its opponents worked all the harder to cut its lifeline.

Syracuse was made one of the prime target areas. The Stars had anticipated strong opposition from local Sabbatarians even before the police halted a preseason game at Star Park, their home ground. Their fallback plan was to move their Sunday dates to a field at Three Rivers Point, located about an hour's buggy ride north of Syracuse, where the Seneca and Oneida Rivers converge to form the Oswego River. Syracuse's sister team in upper

New York State, Rochester, tried to dodge the Sabatarians by playing on Sunday at the nearby Windsor Beach resort in the town of Irondequoit. For several weeks, a kind of unstated truce existed, but on July 20 members of the Irondequoit Law and Order Society, most of them local farmers, broke up a game when they drove their horses and buggies onto the field and tried to arrest everyone present. Rochester manager Pat Powers pointed out that the invaders were lacking a certain amenity, namely a warrant, and the confrontation swiftly exploded into a near riot. After the players from both teams were hauled before an Irondequoit JP, Powers made one last try, on August 3 at Buffalo, while the Browns were visiting Rochester. But he despaired of instituting Sunday ball anywhere in upper New York State after a patrol wagon pulled up during pregame practice and cops came pouring out. Syracuse ran into a similar problem at Three Rivers Point on July 27 and switched its Sunday dates to Iron Pier. When the police vowed to stop games from being played there too, Louisville did not come to Iron Pier for a scheduled Sunday date on August 3, assuming it had been canceled. But the Stars appeared on the field with a local umpire in the stead of regular umpire Wesley Curry, who had stayed away fearing arrest, and got an easy forfeit win, over Chapman's incensed objections.

In June the Brooklyn Gladiators also were stripped of their Sunday home at Ridgewood Park when Wallace caught the club playing some of its weekday home games at the Polo Grounds in violation of its agreement with the Ridgewood Exhibition Company. By then Wallace was looking for any excuse to sever ties with a team that had become a blight on the market, but Kennedy scouted up new lodgings, and the Gladiators began playing on Sundays at the Long Island Grounds in Maspeth, New York. The other Association czars wished he hadn't bothered. Forced to vie for patrons with Byrne's Bridegrooms and also with a strong Brooklyn entry in the Players League, Kennedy's Kids, after a promising start, had become the odd man out in the City of the Churches once the team settled down to its true level and the money well began to run dry.

The Athletics, which also had stiff competition in Philadelphia from both League and Players League teams, by July found themselves in even worse financial straits. Long notorious for their front office squabbling, the A's had become the most ineptly run club in the Association, barring only Louisville, after the original ownership had sold out two years earlier to a group headed by William Whittaker and H. C. Pennypacker. The pair let Bill Sharsig remain as manager because he still had a piece of the club, but ordered him to cut costs to the bone in an effort to ride out the

OLD JUDGE
CIGARETTES
GOODWIN & CO., New York.

• • •

Aided by Charlie Mason, Bill Sharsig reorganized the Athletics in 1880 as a semi-pro team. Ten years later, Sharsig's Athletics were called the Troubadours because they were felt to be masquerading as a big league team. Distraught, Sharsig sold his portion of the club. After a long absence from the majors, in 1901 Sharsig became business manager of the new Philadelphia AL entry, also called the Athletics, under Ben Shibe, who had owned a piece of the AA Athletics in 1890. A very underappreciated contributor to the game, Sharsig died in 1902 on the eve of the A's dash to their first AL pennant.

Players League menace. Anyone else would probably have given up hope after the A's were blown out by the Yale collegians 19–6 in their first preseason game, but Sharsig saw a ray of promise in his rookie keystone combination of shortstop Tommy Corcoran and second baseman Dennis Fitzgerald. Unfortunately, the Pittsburgh Players League club also caught Corcoran's act and snatched him on the eve of the 1890 season. Sharsig forged ahead as best he could, moving Fitzgerald to short and taking on another rookie second baseman, Taylor Shaffer, the younger brother of Orator Shaffer. The elder Shaffer meanwhile was penciled in to man right field for the A's at age thirty-eight after four years in the minors. But Sharsig's other two outfielders were Curt Welch and Blondie Purcell, and at third base he had Denny Lyons. The three, although among the top players of their time, had been eschewed by Players League raiders, who viewed them as more trouble than they were worth. Purcell, a gambling addict, ran a bookmaking operation on the side, and Welch and Lyons both had an alcohol problem. For his pitching mainstay, Sharsig had Sadie McMahon, a rough-and-tumble carouser who had narrowly escaped a prison sentence in 1888 for manslaughter. To play first base, the A's manager retrieved Jack O'Brien from the scrap heap nearly four years after O'Brien had

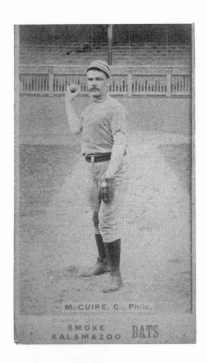

An 1887 Kalamazoo Bat Card of Deacon McGuire. Nearing age twenty-seven, McGuire finally reached the majors to stay with Rochester in 1890. His nickname stemmed from his splendid habits. Reportedly he was never fined or ejected from a game. McGuire was among the first catchers to put a raw steak inside his glove to protect his battered left hand. It helped him to work 1,611 games back of the bat, a major league record prior to 1944.

been canned for engaging in one too many shouting matches with previous owner Lew Simmons, and Sharsig's catcher was Wilbert Robinson, soon to rank among the best in the 19th century but in 1890 still a weak hitter and a poor base runner. It was not an inspiring lineup, but Sharsig was accustomed to getting mileage from teams that would have confounded most managers.

On Opening Day, the A's, behind McMahon, beat Rochester 11–8. The next day they took Rochester again 12–9 in another shabbily played game that was further marred when Fitzgerald wrecked his ankle so badly that his major league career was finished almost before it started. Fitzgerald's injury made it matter all the less that the A's two triumphs over Rochester left them alone for the moment in first place. Who were these Rochesters, anyway? Practically all that was known of them was that their followers liked to call them the Hop Bitters after an early-day barnstorming team based in Rochester that had taken its quixotic nickname from a popular patent medicine.

But by May 9 the Hop Bitters, of all teams, held the top rung in the Association, a game ahead of the Browns and a game and a half up on the A's in the third spot. A week later, the A's had grabbed the lead, with Rochester second, Louisville moving up to third, and the Browns dropping to fourth. Von der Ahe still saw no grounds for alarm. Columbus was wallowing well below .500. Louisville and the rumdum Hop Bitters would soon be joining them. As for the A's, they had only two decent pitchers and one of them, Ed Seward, had an arm about as lively these days as a wet noodle. They were certain to self-destruct.

Some six weeks later, on June 27, the A's had expanded their lead to a full four games, and Rochester was still running second, four and a half games in front of third-place Louisville. Von der Ahe remained unconcerned because Columbus continued to struggle, but others had started to notice the A's and the Hop Bitters. Could they be for real? If anyone could get a silk purse out of a sow's ear, it was Sharsig, and Powers must have been an even bigger magician. Rochester was hanging tough with a team that had just three players with significant major league experience—second baseman Bill Greenwood, leftfielder Harry Lyons and pitcher Bob Barr. It could only mean that the level of play was so far down in 1890 that perhaps the A's really could sneak off with the pennant.

On the afternoon of July 2, the A's did not learn until they arrived at Toledo's Speranza Park that Bob Emslie, the scheduled umpire, had been called out of town suddenly. As per the custom of the time, two players, one from each team, were chosen to fill in for Emslie. Sharsig's pick was McMahon, who was not slated to pitch that day, and Maumees manager Charlie Morton selected

• • •

Dan Casey. In the 1930s, he pushed a claim that either he or his older brother Dennis was the real "Casey at the Bat." The younger Casey had some good years in the NL and was the southpaw ace of the Syracuse pitching staff in 1890 but never appeared in the majors again.

one of his own extra pitchers, Fred Smith. Down 5–2 in the ninth, Toledo put Frank Scheibeck on second base and Perry Werden on first with two out. White Wings Tebeau then singled off Seward to score Scheibeck and chase Werden to third. A moment later, when Werden tried to score on a wild pitch, McMahon, working the bases, called him out to end the game, but Smith, who was behind the plate, ruled his teammate safe. During the argument no one thought to call time, so Tebeau scampered home with the tying run. The A's at that point stalked off the field, and Smith declared his Toledo mates the winners by forfeit. For several weeks, it seemed like a reprise of the July 1888 forfeit game between Brooklyn and Kansas City that had knocked the Bridegrooms into an irreversible slump. Then, on August 13, in a split decision, Phelps and George Frazier outvoted Von der Ahe and awarded the game to the A's, bringing a rightful howl from Toledo that there was "a conspiracy to give new clubs the worst of it."

Yet the gift win came too late for Philadelphia. On July 12, the A's lost the lead for the first time since early in the season, when George Meakim beat Seward 8–4 at Louisville. The win, Louisville's fourth straight over the A's, vaulted the Colonels temporarily into the Association penthouse. A day later, the A's were back on top after squeezing by the Browns 8–7 at St. Louis while the Colonels were losing to Syracuse, but after that the going was swiftly downhill for Sharsig's crew. Denny Lyons was out much of the time with real or imagined injuries; the secondary pitchers were so awful that Sharsig turned in desperation to Jim Whitney, a great pitcher in the early 1880s who by July 1890 was riddled with consumption and had less than a year to live; Taylor Shaffer had been released when he could not get his batting average out of the low .170s; and Ben Conroy, the replacement for Fitzgerald at shortstop, was hitting in the .160s. To boot, Louisville won 18 of 20 games during a June-July homestand. Traditionally strong at home, the Colonels had done the same thing in June-July 1884 to seize first place, only to fold, as was also their custom, when they went back on the road. But although 1884 had also been a war year, with three major leagues vying for a public that had not yet proven it could support two, the Unions had plainly been the weakest of the three. By July 1890 even the Association acknowledged that, between losing Brooklyn and Cincinnati to the League and many of its remaining leading lights to the Brotherhood, it was the cripple. Awful as the Colonels had been the previous year, they looked like a reasonably decent unit now, and in 1890, a reasonably decent team could be good enough.

But as late as August 1, Von der Ahe exuded confidence that his Browns were bound for an easy pennant. On that morning,

CATCHER RYAN, PITCHER JONES, LEFT FIELDER HAMBURG, MANAGER CHAPMAN, PITCHER GOODALL, CATCHER BLIGH, SHORT STOP TOMNEY, FIRST BASEMAN O'CONNOR, SECOND BASEMAN SHINNICK, PITCHER EHRET, CENTRE FIELDER WEAVER, PITCHER STRATTON. RIGHT FIELDER WOLF, PITCHER MEAKIM, THIRD BASEMAN RAYMOND, FIRST BASEMAN TAYLOR.

THE TEAM OF THE LOUISVILLE BASE BALL CLUB.

• • •

Louisville held a five-game lead on the Browns when this illustration appeared. Scott Stratton had eloped prior to the season, spiriting his bride away from her parents' home by stage. Conjugal life seemed to revitalize him. After going 3-13 in 1889, Stratton clicked for 34 wins in 1890 and hit .323, making his bat so valuable that Chapman used him in the outfield part-time. Dan O'Connor and Mickey Jones were no longer with the club by the time the 1890 World's Series rolled around. The following spring, just about everyone else was gone, too. On October 4, 1891, when the Colonels played their last game in the AA, Wolf, Shinnick, Weaver, and Taylor were the only members of the 1890 champs in the lineup.

Louisville was at 49-29, three and a half games ahead of St. Louis and five up on the A's, which were still 10 games above .500. From that point on, however, Philadelphia went 8–42 and tumbled all the way to seventh place. It proved to be the worst collapse in history by a team that had been in first place on July 4, the proverbial date that separates the contenders from the pretenders. The Colonels meanwhile won 39 of their last 54 decisions to extend their lead over St. Louis to 12 games when the curtain fell on October 14. In the finale, Red Ehret trimmed the Browns 13–1 to bag his 25th win. With Stratton contributing 34 victories and rookies Meakim and Goodall chipping in another 20 between them, Louisville became the only major league team prior to 1991 that leaped to the pennant after suffering a basement finish the previous year.

Yet Von der Ahe had not been entirely wrong. In August, when the Solons were still languishing in the second division, Buckenberger was fired. His seat at the Columbus helm went to Gus Schmelz, who had been axed by Cincinnati when the Reds defected to the League. Schmelz parlayed Spud Johnson's hot bat and Hank Gastright's steady pitching to lead the Solons on a furious 37–13 finishing kick that aced the Browns out of second

• • •
Spud Johnson (above) and rookie Mike Lehane, the 1889 International League bat king, were expected to provide most of Columbus's punch in 1890. Near the close of the 1890 campaign, a Columbus observer wrote, "At no time this season has Lehane been hitting the ball with anything like the record he had in the Internationals." Later it was discovered that Lehane had begun to go blind in 1890. Johnson contended that everyone in the AA was blind. He swore he'd been cheated out of the 1890 batting crown and a thorough investigation would prove he won. When no investigation was made, he jumped to the NL.

place. Toledo, which put on a mini surge of its own in the closing days, claimed the fourth spot when Rochester fell back to fifth after its money-strapped owners suspended several key players to chop their payroll.

Brooklyn, even deeper in the red, became the first Association team since Washington in 1884 to fail to complete the season. In their final game on August 25, the Gladiators demonstrated that even though they might be outmanned and out-bankrolled, they would not go quietly. Trailing Syracuse 5–2 in the bottom of the ninth, Kennedy's Kids rallied for two runs and nearly pulled out the game despite knowing it would be their last for Brooklyn. The following day the Baltimore Orioles deserted the Atlantic Association and took the Gladiators' place. Since Baltimore was the class of the minor league loop with a 77–24 record, its departure created tremendous ill will, but Barnie and Von der Horst had only been biding their time once they realized they had been mistaken to leave the Association without a guarantee of another major league perch. Before he would cede his spot to the Orioles, however, Kennedy had to be dragged off the stage kicking and hollering that he knew now why Byrne had quit the Association, for its owners were all scoundrels.

Brooklyn's forced exit only momentarily relieved Phelps's financial headaches. In early September all of the Athletics players threatened to strike when the team could not pay their salaries. Whittaker, who functioned as the club's treasurer, responded by releasing most of them. Sharsig was sent on the club's last western road trip with $245 and a cast of nonentities who were paid per diem rather than signed to regular contracts. The money got him to Louisville, where he was dependent on the A's receiving enough in visitors' gate receipts to keep afloat. Fortunately the weather cooperated and allowed all five games with the Colonels to be played, supplying him with sufficient funds to pay his players after each game in cash. Louisville swept the entire series that only a month earlier had seemed as if it would decide the pennant but now meant nothing. On his return to Philadelphia, Sharsig discovered the A's no longer had a home, as the sheriff had sold the seats and stands at Jefferson Street Grounds to obtain the money to pay back rent to the city and to meet a local company's $1,435 claim for lumber. The sale brought only $600, and Sharsig and Johnny Ryan, the park's groundskeeper for all seven years it existed, were the only club representatives on hand to witness its tawdry demise. Sharsig's patchwork club nevertheless managed to complete its schedule, which was no mean feat. After assembling for the first time in Louisville, his reconstructed A's lost every game they played, finishing the season with a 22-game losing streak.

By 1890, Billy Earle, though just twenty-two, was already known as "The Little Globetrotter." When he uttered his standard threat to bolt as soon as things in St. Louis began to displease him, he was released by the Browns and ended the season with Tacoma in the Pacific Northwest League. That December, Earle studied hypnotism so he could mesmerize a girl who had heretofore resisted his charms, but many of his teammates thought it was overkill. If he didn't already have the "evil eye," there was something weird going on around him anyway. For all that, Earle was so good a player that teams, no matter how unnerving they found his presence, were constantly putting a uniform on him.

Some two months later, the Athletics stockholders disclosed that the club was over $18,000 in debt. When everything was sorted out, Whittaker appeared to be the chief culprit, responsible for a $26,000 deficit at final accounting despite the club having turned a profit in 1888 and again in 1889, and then in 1890 taking in $42,000 while paying out only $24,000 in salaries. The *Ohio State Journal* reported the following losses in 1890 throughout the Association: Rochester $18,000, St. Louis $15,000, Philadelphia $13,000, Columbus $12,700, Toledo $16,000, Brooklyn-Baltimore $9,000 and Syracuse $10,000. But many thought these figures were way too optimistic—Stars' owner George Frazier later admitted Syracuse had lost closer to $21,000. At any rate, only Louisville had turned a profit in 1890, and that a mere $3,000. The major reason the Colonels finished in the black was their modest payroll. Wolf, Stratton and Ehret were the only team members who were paid much above the minimum. Meakim, Goodall, Ryan, Taylor, Shinnick and Hamburg all earned rookie wages, and shortstop Phil Tomney, third baseman Harry Raymond and centerfielder Farmer Weaver were only in their second full seasons in the majors.

Shinnick's record for playing exclusively on championship teams, though it had been miraculously maintained during the regular season, seemed certain to end when the Colonels clashed with the Brooklyn Bridegrooms in the seventh annual World's Series. Following a four-club League dogfight, the Bridegrooms had pulled away in the last fortnight of the season to become the only team ever to win consecutive pennants in two different major leagues.* But battle-weary as McGunnigle's men were, his lineup was essentially the same as the one that had finished 66 and a half games ahead of the Colonels the previous year. Missing was only 23-game winner Bob Caruthers, who had sprained his ankle in an exhibition game with the Browns a few days earlier, and even he would be available to take a turn in the outfield later in the Series. Never was a postseason encounter viewed with so little appetite by the major league community as the 1890 fall frolic.

Parsons and Byrne contracted for a best-five-of-nine affair, but few expected it to go much more than the minimum number of games. The opener, scheduled for October 16 in Louisville, was rained out, but the following afternoon was warm and sunny. As in 1889, the League and the Association selected one umpire each. Wesley Curry was the Association's nominee, and former Association ump John McQuaid represented the senior loop. In

*The 1891 Boston Reds, though the same franchise as the 1890 Players League champion, had only a handful of the same players who had been on the 1890 club.

• • •

Strapped for a shortstop after Phil Tomney (above) badly bruised his shoulder in a base path collision, Jack Chapman had first sacker Harry Taylor play shortstop at one point in 1890. Tomney reinjured the shoulder several more times during the season. Sharps thought he was an industrious and scientific player, but Chapman felt he was "too light" for the AA. He never played again after hurting his shoulder a final time in the 1890 World's Series.

front of some 5,600 faithful, the Colonels collected just two hits in a 9–0 loss to Adonis Terry and fielded dreadfully. The following afternoon, Louisville's defensive lapses again conspired to hand the Bridegrooms a 5–3 win, although Brooklyn managed just five hits against Ed Daily. In Game Three, Tomney was struck in the right shoulder by a bad-hop grounder. It was the last of a multitude of injuries Tomney suffered in the closing weeks of the 1890 season, and it sidelined him not only for the rest of the Series but, as it turned out, forever. He never played another inning in the majors and died less than two years later.

Tomney's departure forced Chapman to juggle his already thin roster, moving Raymond to short, bringing Wolf in from the outfield to play third, and sending Daily, a late-season acquisition from the defunct Gladiators, to right field. Despite the makeshift lineup, the Colonels pulled out a 7–7 tie that might have been a victory had Wolf not cost his team a chance for a big inning when he was thrown out trying to stretch a leadoff double into a triple in the sixth frame.

But the tie failed to excite the Falls City faithful. Game Four continued a depressing pattern that would hold for the entire Series, as the crowd for each contest dwindled. Before just 1,050 onlookers, Louisville's Red Ehret beat Tom Lovett 5–4 on a run in the seventh inning manufactured by Shinnick's triple and John Ryan's RBI groundout to first base. The Series then moved to Brooklyn, where Lovett returned, after a four-day hiatus caused by rain, to shut down the Colonels 7–2 in the cold and mud. Two days later, Stratton and Ehret combined for a 9–8 Louisville win that drew just 600. The following afternoon only about 300 braved the icy air to watch Ehret cruise to a 6–2 victory over Lovett that knotted the Series at 3-all.

With November fast approaching and the weather unlikely to improve, the combatants agreed, at that point, to call the Series a draw. There was talk of finishing it the following spring, prior to the start of the 1891 season, but by then the two loops were at each other's throats, annulling even inter-league exhibition games. Byrne's decision to postpone the Series was governed as much by his fear of losing to the lightly regarded Colonels as by the nearly nonexistent gate receipts, and Louisville was just thankful to gain a tie. Still, the draw left an unpleasant taste. Since it seemed inconceivable that the Colonels could be the equal of the Bridegrooms, the inconclusive result was taken as proof that McGunnigle's charges had approached the Series lackadaisically. That was probably close enough to the truth. Indeed, the evidence strongly suggests that the players were never highly motivated for any of the postseason affairs in the last century. Hard as the Asso-

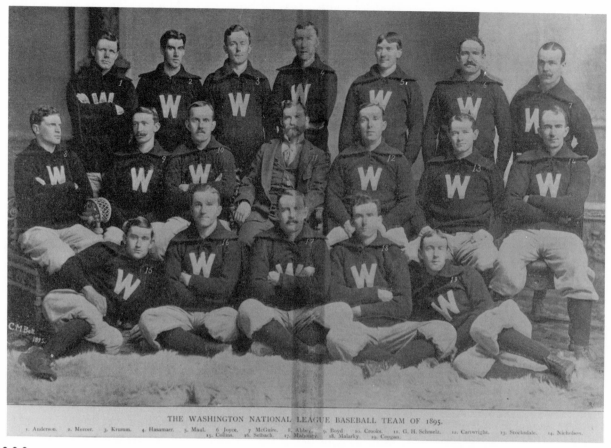

THE WASHINGTON NATIONAL LEAGUE BASEBALL TEAM OF 1895.

1. Anderson. 2. Mercer. 3. Krumm. 4. Hasamaer. 5. Maul. 6. Joyce. 7. McGuire. 8. Abbey. 9. Boyd 10. Crooks. 11. G. H. Schmelz. 12. Cartwright. 13. Stockdale. 14. Nicholson.
15. Collins. 16. Selbach. 17. Mahoney. 18. Malarky. 19. Coogan.

• • •

The 1895 Washington Nationals were peppered with AA grads, including manager Gus Schmelz, Deacon McGuire, Ed Cartwright, Bill Joyce, Parson Nicholson and Jack Crooks. As a Columbus rookie in 1890, Crooks hit just .221 but had a .357 on-base percentage. The following year he posted a .957 fielding average to set a new record for second basemen. Crooks, a deft fielder with a great eye, was basically the same sort of player as Jim McTamany and, like McTamany, he always had trouble holding a job. He died in 1918 in a St. Louis mental hospital.

ciation tried to assert that the 1886 clash, its lone undisputed Series win, had been played by both sides to the hilt, the games were haphazardly staged and condensed into too brief a period, indicating that the desire for a quick financial killing ruled rather than a zest to establish athletic superiority. Much the same can be said of all the fall matches between the two leagues. Certainly it would be absurd to contend that the 1890 Series demonstrated that the Association held its own against the League during the Brotherhood war. Nor can it be argued that the League was superior in the late 1880s because it won the three previous Series. The most that can be said is that the League had a stronger and wiser executive body, but even that conjecture would have produced a lively debate in the fall of 1890.

It was the League, after all, that had incited the Brotherhood revolt with its thickheaded Salary Limitation plan. And it was the League that, in 1890, allowed its Pittsburgh franchise to deteriorate to the point where it was in even worse shape than Louisville had been the previous year. Even as the Colonels were rising from the ruins to tie for the world's championship, the Pittsburgh

League team reached a new nadir with a record-low winning percentage of .169 and just 23 victories in 136 games. Ever since leaving the Association in 1886, Pittsburgh had struggled to establish an identity. Prior to 1890, the local media, for the lack of anything better, had continued to call the team the Alleghenys. By the end of that ragtag season, however, Pittsburgh's callow performance had caused its players to be dubbed the Innocents.

Before the 1891 campaign began, the club received another nickname, and one that it carries to this day. The newly bestowed handle came at the expense of the Association, and the stimulus for it provoked an all-out war between the two major leagues just as they were reaching an armistice with the Brotherhood. The renewed hostilities swiftly grew into the fight to the death that the League had been girding itself for all along.

1890 FINAL STANDINGS

	W	L	PCT	HOME	ROAD	GB
1. Louisville Colonels	88	44	.667	57–13	31–31	
2. Columbus Solons	79	55	.590	47–22	32–33	10
3. St. Louis Browns	78	58	.574	45–25	33–33	12
4. Toledo Maumees	68	64	.515	40–27	28–37	20
5. Rochester Hop Bitters	63	63	.500	40–22	23–41	22
6. Baltimore Orioles	15	19	.441	8–11	7–8	24
7. Syracuse Stars	55	72	.433	30–30	25–42	30.5
8. Philadelphia Athletics	54	78	.409	36–36	18–42	34
9. Brooklyn Gladiators	26	73	.263	15–22	11–51	45.5

• • •
A Columbus writer said of Cupid Childs in the winter of 1890-91: "The fat little second baseman of last year's Syracuse team is in great demand and will be given a chance to become a star of the first magnitude." Childs signed with Cleveland, where he teamed for nine years with another AA-developed keystoner, Ed McKean. There are only four middle infielders not in the Hall of Fame who posted .300 career batting averages while achieving over 1,500 hits, and two of them are Childs and McKean.

BATTING

BATTING AVERAGE (325 ABs)

1. Wolf, Louis	.363
2. D. Lyons, Phila	.354
3. McCarthy, StL	.350
4. S. Johnson, Colum	.346
5. Childs, Syracuse	.345
6. Swartwood, Tol	.327
7. O'Connor, Colum	.324
8. McQuery, Syracuse	.308
9. S. Griffin, Roch	.307
10. Taylor, Louis	.306

SLUGGING AVERAGE

1. D. Lyons, Phila	.531
2. Childs, Syracuse	.481
3. Wolf, Louis	.479
4. McCarthy, StL	.467
5. S. Johnson, Colum	.461
6. Werden, Tol	.456
7. Swartwood, Tol	.444
8. S. Griffin, Roch	.432
9. B. O'Brien, Brook	.415
10. O'Connor, Colum	.411

ON-BASE PERCENTAGE

1. D. Lyons, Phila	.458
2. Swartwood, Tol	.442
3. Childs, Syracuse	.434
4. McCarthy, StL	.430
5. Wright, Syracuse	.427
6. Wolf, Louis	.419
7. S. Johnson, Colum	.409
8. McTamany, Colum	.405
9. Werden, Tol	.403
10. S. Griffin, Roch	.388

TOTAL BASES

1. Wolf, Louis	260
2. McCarthy, StL	256
3. S. Johnson, Colum	248
4. Childs, Syracuse	237
5. Werden, Tol	227
6. Weaver, Louis	215
7. Swartwood, Tol	205
8. Simon, Brook-Syracuse	199
9. Sneed, Colum	196
10. H. Lyons, Roch	195

HOME RUNS

1. Campau, StL	10
2. Cartwright, StL	8
3. Stivetts, StL	7
D. Lyons, Phila	7
5. Werden, Tol	6
McCarthy, StL	6
7. S. Griffin, Roch	5
Knowles, Roch	5
9. Six with four	

RUNS

1. McTamany, Colum	140
2. McCarthy, StL	137
3. Fuller, StL	118
4. Sneed, Tol-Colum	117
5. Welch, Phila-Balt	116
6. Taylor, Louis	115
7. Werden, Tol	113
8. Scheffler, Roch	111
9. Purcell, Phila	110
10. Childs, Syracuse	109

HITS

1. Wolf, Louis	197
2. McCarthy, StL	192
3. S. Johnson, Colum	186
4. Childs, Syracuse	170
5. Taylor, Louis	169
6. Weaver, Louis	161
H. Lyons, Roch	152
8. Swartwood, Tol	151
9. O'Connor, Colum	148
10. Sneed, Colum	147
Werden, Tol	147

STOLEN BASES

1. McCarthy, StL	83
2. Scheffler, Roch	77
3. Van Dyke, Tol	73
4. Welch, Phila-Balt	72
5. Daily, Brook-Louis	62
Shinnick, Louis	62
7. Fuller, StL	60
8. Crooks, Colum	57
Scheibeck, Tol	57
10. Childs, Syracuse	56

*RBI leaders unavailable.

PITCHING

WINS

1. McMahon, Phila-Balt	36
2. Stratton, Louis	34
3. Gastright, Colum	30
4. Stivetts, StL	29
5. Barr, Roch	28
6. Ehret, Louis	25
7. Ramsey, StL	24
8. Healy, Tol	22
9. F. Smith, Tol	19
Casey, Syracuse	19

LOSSES

1. Barr, Roch	24
J. Keefe, Syracuse	24
3. Casey, Syracuse	22
4. Healy, Tol	21
Cushman, Tol	21
McCullough, Brook	21
McMahon, Phila-Balt	21
8. Stivetts, StL	20
9. E. Daily, Brook-Louis	18
10. Ramsey, StL	17

INNINGS

1. McMahon, Phila-Balt	509
2. Barr, Roch	493.1
3. Stratton, Louis	431
4. Stivetts, StL	419.1
5. Gastright, Colum	401.1
6. Healy, Tol	389
7. Casey, Syracuse	360.2
8. Ehret, Louis	359
9. J. Keefe, Syracuse	352.1
10. Ramsey, StL	348.2

COMPLETE GAMES

1. McMahon, Phila-Balt	55
2. Barr, Roch	52
3. Stratton, Louis	44
Healy, Tol	44
5. Gastright, Colum	41
Stivetts, StL	41
7. Casey, Syracuse	40
8. E. Daily, Brook-Louis	37
9. J. Keefe, Syracuse	36
Ehret, Louis	35

STRIKEOUTS

1. McMahon, Phila-Balt	291
2. Stivetts, StL	289
3. Ramsey, StL	257
4. Healy, Tol	225
5. Barr, Roch	209
6. Gastright, Colum	199
7. Ehret, Louis	174
8. Casey, Syracuse	169
9. Knauss, Colum	148
10. Easton, Colum	147

WINNING PCT. (25 DECISIONS)

1. Stratton, Louis	.708
2. Gastright, Colum	.682
3. Ehret, Louis	.641
4. McMahon, Phila-Balt	.632
5. F. Smith, Tol	.594
6. Knauss, Colum	.586
7. Ramsey, StL	.585
8. Stivetts, StL	.563
9. Calihan, Roch	.545
10. Easton, Colum	.517

ERA (140 INNINGS)

1. Stratton, Louis	2.36
2. Ehret, Louis	2.53
3. Knauss, Colum	2.81
4. Chamberlain, StL-Colum	2.83
5. Healy, Tol	2.89
6. Meakim, Louis	2.91
7. Gastright, Colum	2.94
8. Barr, Roch	3.25
9. McMahon, Phila-Balt	3.27
10. Calihan, Roch	3.28

LOWEST ON-BASE PCT.

1. Stratton, Louis	.265
2. Gastright, Colum	.274
3. Knauss, Colum	.277
4. Healy, Tol	.282
5. Ehret, Louis	.288
6. Meakim, Louis	.293
Ramsey, StL	.293
8. Hart, StL	.299
9. F. Smith, Tol	.300
10. Chamberlain, StL-Colum	.303

ELEVEN

• • •

The PL champion Boston Reds may have been the strongest nine in the last century. King Kelly's crew was mediocre at second base, where Joe Quinn worked, and shortstop Arthur Irwin was slipping, but the rest of the team was rock solid. Matt Kilroy (top, second from left) was the lone disappointment. In 1890 the former Baltimore star became the first pitcher to figure in as many as 20 decisions on a pennant winner and lose more often than he won.

THE PLAYERS LEAGUE: THE ASSOCIATION STARS PROVE THEIR METTLE

❝ The Players League officials, after winning the best fight in the history of the game, threw up the sponge and cried quit. . . . They had the League in the same position you have a drowning man when he has gone down for the third and last time. But when they had him down they let him get up and kick the life out of them. ❞

—Charlie Comiskey

MANY OBSERVERS FELT THE 1890 WORLD'S Series should properly have been a three-way affair, involving not only Louisville and Brooklyn, the Association and League champions, but also the Boston Reds, the champion of the rebel Players League. In fact, some thought the Players League had put on the best display of ball up to that moment in history, thanks largely to Monte Ward.

In 1884, the only other interlude during the 19th century when three major leagues battled to coexist, Ward had been little more than another sore-armed former pitching star who looked to be an early burnout at age twenty-four unless he could find a new position. The following year, after the Union Association collapsed, Billy Voltz, manager of Chattanooga in the Southern League, formed the Brotherhood of Professional Base Ball Players to provide players with a voice in how the game was run and to help protect them against the tyranny of the reserve clause. Voltz

... An early picture of Monte Ward, who started the Brotherhood war and founded the Players League. He was on the frontlines throughout the battle but still contrived to hit .337 in 1890. Among the handful of NL stars who never played, managed, or umpired in the AA, Ward was still one of its strongest boosters. He knew what the competition it provided meant to players and forever regretted that the AA became a casualty when the PL failed.

had no clout among major league performers, however, and the leadership of the Brotherhood movement was soon usurped by Ward, who in 1885 developed an on-field future for himself at shortstop, and an off-field passion for player-related labor problems that would last him for life.

After doing undergraduate work at Penn State, Ward later obtained a law degree from Columbia. Unlike Tony La Russa, a much more recent law school graduate who has said he would rather drive a bus in the minor leagues than be an attorney, Ward made instant use of his diploma by practicing law in the off-season. He finally quit the game to set up a full-time practice in New York when he resigned from his managerial post with the Giants at the close of the 1894 season rather than continue to battle with the club's volatile owner, Andrew Freedman. His background in baseball labor problems made Ward the natural choice of players seeking legal counsel in suits against owners, and many of his cases involved former teammates and opponents. Late in 1911, Ward returned to the game when he, John Carroll and James Gaffney bought the moribund Boston Braves for $187,000. Three years later, owing in part to Ward's player selection, the Braves claimed their first pennant since 1898, but by then Ward had sold his holdings to Gaffney and resumed his law career. He remained close to baseball, however, working on the rules committee and also, ironically, on legal briefs that supported the reserve clause. Nevertheless, his early activities as a unionizer and rebel league founder continued to weigh against him long after his death in 1925. It was not until 1964 that Ward, arguably the most influential baseball figure in the last century, was forgiven his transgressions by the game's establishment and voted into the Hall of Fame.

In an era when many players spent their leisure time in saloons and brothels, Ward, a member of an old and prominent Pennsylvania family, was urbane, articulate and at home in even the most exalted social and business circles. Within a year after he assumed command of the Brotherhood movement from Voltz, it numbered 107 members among major league players and had earned the sympathetic ear of such leading baseball writers as Ren Mulford in Cincinnati, Tim Murnane in Boston, and Francis Richter, the editor of *Sporting Life*. The reserve clause was the Brotherhood's foremost target, but priorities shifted when League owners worked deviously to install John Brush's Salary Limitation plan prior to the 1889 season while Ward was abroad.

Ward's response was to begin conspiring with Albert Johnson, a fast-talking young streetcar baron who owned the Brooklyn and South Side lines in Cleveland with his brother Tom, then the mayor of the Forest City. Although League owners heard rumors that Johnson was helping Ward to finance a new league run by the players, they regarded the scheme as a pipe dream until they discovered early in 1890, to their dismay, that Ward and Johnson had sowed franchises in every League city except Cincinnati and had captured many of the League's elite players.

The Brotherhood's "Manifesto" required each of the eight Players League franchises to contribute $25,000 to a central fund designed to cover the expenses of the weaker or less fortunate clubs. Any individual club profits above $20,000 were to be pooled and divided equally among all eight members. Of the allowable $20,000 profit, half would go to the club's backers and the rest would be divided among its playing personnel. All players enlisting in the Players League were guaranteed salaries at least equal to their 1889 salaries in addition to equal representation with team owners on the PL's Board of Directors. Yet, for all the players' complaints about the reserve clause and the way it often denied them any say in what team owned their services, the Brotherhood made compulsory player assignments in an attempt to equalize the eight club rosters. And despite his desire to break away from the League's tyranny, Ward abided by its minimum 50¢ admission charge, as well as its rules against playing on Sunday and selling alcohol in its parks.

Monetary and competitive inequities were not the only flaws in baseball's structure that the Brotherhood sought to remedy. Ward and his executive officers, vice president Dan Brouthers and secretary Tim Keefe, also tried to improve the game itself. The two most important changes the PL introduced were to move the pitcher a foot and a half farther from the plate when he started his delivery and to legislate that each game would be officiated by two umpires attired in all-white uniforms and treated accordingly as paragons of infallibility.

The eight original PL umpires were: John Gaffney, Bob Ferguson, Lon Knight, Bobby Mathews, Tom Gunning, Charley Jones, Bill Holbert and Ross Barnes. All except Gaffney were former major league players. For several years prior to 1890, Gaffney and Ferguson had been the Association's two most honored umpires and were as big a loss to the loop as any of its star players who jumped to the PL.

If the goal in putting each game into the hands of two umpires who commanded respect was to curb the ruthless haggling that produced the many forfeits that littered the yearly summary sheets during the last century, it could not have been more successful. In 1890 there were three forfeit games in the League, six in the Association, and none in the PL. If the intent in lengthening the distance between the pitcher and home plate was to in-

Bill Joyce. As a rookie with the Brooklyn Wonders, he led the PL in walks by a wide margin, posting 123. Injured much of the next season, he nevertheless was among the AA's premier performers in its coda. Joyce later emerged as one of the game's top sluggers during the 1890s.

crease offense, it too could not have been more successful. In 1890 the average League player batted .254, the average Association player batted .253 and the average PL player batted .274. Another reason that the PL generated more offense may have been the Keefe ball it used. Devised by pitcher Tim Keefe, it reportedly was much livelier than the balls used by the NL and the AA. Consequently, there were nearly two a half more runs scored in each PL game than in games played in either of the other loops. But the lesson still was not absorbed by the League and the Association. Not until dignitaries like Cap Anson and King Kelly hit .272 and .189, respectively, in 1892 would the pitching length be increased to its present 60'6" distance, and it would another full decade before two umpires became the norm in each major league game.

The PL did not altogether deliver, however, on its promised improvements. Despite the Brotherhood's pledge to achieve competitive balance, the Buffalo team, a late addition when a franchise planned for Cincinnati fell through, came out of the common player pool with by far the least talent. Still, manager-shortstop Jack Rowe for the most part had proven major leaguers, including forty-two-year-old first baseman Deacon White, who had played in the first major league game back in 1871, deaf-mute centerfielder Dummy Hoy, destined to be the last surviving PL player when he died in 1961 at ninety-nine, and catcher Connie Mack, whose death in 1956 at ninety-four left the field to Hoy.

Long before the eight PL teams took the field in mid-April for their first championship games, everything was in place—their players, their owners, their nicknames, their parks and their uniforms. The uniform issue was one of the first to be resolved. By 1890, uniforms had become highly important, and considerable thought went into their selection. All of the PL clubs wore white at home—which was customary by then but not mandatory—and gray on the road, except Chicago and Cleveland, which played their away games in black unis, and Philadelphia, which chose navy blue at home and dark maroon outfits with seal brown socks, belts and caps for the road.

The complete cast and their home sites were:

Boston Reds, Congress Street Grounds
Brooklyn Ward's Wonders, Eastern Park
Buffalo Bisons, Olympic Park
Chicago Pirates, South Side Park
Cleveland Infants, Brotherhood Park
New York Giants, Polo Grounds IV (which lay next to Polo
    Grounds III, used by the League New York Giants, and lat-
    er became the League team's home)

• • •

A collage of the Pittsburgh Burghers. Rookie flash Tommy Corcoran (10) bypassed the Athletics in 1890 to play in the PL, but he returned to Philadelphia the following spring for the last AA campaign. Though he compiled 1,135 RBIs and 2,252 hits, Corcoran was still regarded as a light hitter. On defense, there have been few better. Below Corcoran is Joe Visner (9), Brooklyn's backup catcher in 1889, who replaced injured Bob Clark at a crucial juncture in the World's Series.

Philadelphia Quakers, Forepaugh's Park (called Brotherhood Park in 1890)

Pittsburgh Burghers, Exposition Park (destined to become the Pittsburgh League club's home until 1909)

Seasoned observers expected Chicago and New York to be the PL's two strongest teams. New York was comprised mainly of disgruntled members of the defending League champion New York Giants and was managed by catcher Buck Ewing. The Pirates were a mix of Chicago White Stockings and St. Louis Browns, guided by Comiskey. From the Browns came Comiskey, Silver King, Tip O'Neill, Jack Boyle and Arlie Latham. To rotate with King, Comiskey had Mark Baldwin, Columbus's top hurler in 1889, but he lacked a reliable third pitcher. The Pirates also had a huge problem at shortstop, where roamed Charlie Bastian, a career .189 hitter. Comiskey was something of a problem himself, batting just .244 in 1890, but the biggest calamity of all was Latham, who hit .229 and fielded atrociously. Two months into the season, Pirates second baseman Fred Pfeffer said for the record: "Latham has been a disappointment to the Chicago team. He has not played his position up to the standard he sets himself, nor the standard of any ball player in any association or league." Old team ties notwithstanding, Comiskey released Latham soon after that, but it was too late to salvage the season. The Pirates ultimately finished fourth despite having in King and Baldwin the two top winners in the PL. Ewing's Giants fooled prognosticators too, staggering home third when Keefe, who had figured to be the PL's most dominant pitcher, won just 17 games.

Buffalo, in contrast, wound up as predicted—dead last. But even the Bisons gave their followers a flurry of optimism in the first week of the season by sweeping all four games of their open-

Buck Ewing. The 19th century's greatest catcher might have altered baseball history if he'd jumped to the AA as promised in the spring of 1883. By 1890, though Ewing led the PL in slugging averages, his career was on the wane. Never especially durable, he played in 100 games just once during the dozen years when he was primarily a catcher.

ing series with Cleveland. The intoxicating 4–0 start briefly put the Bisons in first place, but they soon sank to the rear by winning just one of their next nine games. As for the Cleveland team, its lone highlight was that it led the majors with a .286 batting average, thanks to Pete Browning, the game's top batsman in 1890. But the Infants allowed enemy hitters to bat .287 and outscore them by 178 runs to make for a drab seventh-place result. Starved for pitching, Cleveland manager Jay Faatz gave the ball to a sixteen-year-old southpaw named Willie McGill on May 8. McGill proceeded to chalk up 11 victories and was the only regular pitcher on the Infants to win more often than he lost, but one of the team's bit players, Charlie Dewald, posted a perfect 2–0 record in a most remarkable fashion. On September 20, Dewald, just up from Jamestown of the New York-Penn League, beat second-place Brooklyn 4–3 in his major league debut. Five days later, he victimized first-place Boston 10–4 in his second and last big league game, making him probably the sole pitcher ever to polish off the top two teams in his only two appearances.

Of the 124 players who participated in 10 or more PL games, 81 were former League players, 28 had been recruited from the Association and the others were garnered from minor leagues. Much of the reason there were relatively few Association players in the PL was because they came late to the Brotherhood's cause. But even though it contributed less than a quarter of the talent pool, the Association had an enormous impact on the quality of play in the PL. For every Latham or Comiskey who delivered less than expected, there were five players whose accomplishments were entirely in keeping with their previous performances in the Association. Browning, Orr, Stovey, King and Baldwin were the obvious stars who shone just as brilliantly when they were sprinkled among their League counterparts, even going so far as to lead the PL in most of the major batting and pitching departments. But O'Neill, Lou Bierbauer, Gus Weyhing, Billy Shindle, Mike Griffin, Henry Larkin and Buck Ewing's younger brother John also excelled in the PL.

With the sole exception of Comiskey, however, the managers' posts and the captaincies of the PL teams rested in the hands of League players, and it was the League that the Brotherhood regarded as its implacable enemy. In late February 1890, John Day received a mysterious offer of $1,000,000 for every franchise in the League (which at the time consisted of ten teams) from a syndicate of wealthy men, reportedly acting anonymously through a Wall Street law firm. The immediate speculation was that the offer was bogus, and that the PL had authored it just to prove, when it was refused, that the League owners had more money than they admitted. Former Mets owner Erastus Wiman was thought to be

OLD JUDGE CIGARETTES Goodwin & Co., New York.

• • •

George Van Haltren first gained stardom by hitting .300 three years in a row in three different major leagues. He followed his .335 PL season in 1890 with a stellar year for Baltimore of the AA and then was traded in 1892 to Pittsburgh for Joe Kelley in what should have been a swap of two future Hall of Famers. Van Haltren missed out on the Hall of Fame when a broken leg cost him the mobility to add to career stolen base and hitting stats that were already top caliber.

the brains behind the scheme, but he denied it and the real instigator was never uncovered. Had the offer been revealed to be legitimate, some League owners would have been all for taking it several weeks later, when an injunction against Ewing playing in the PL was thrown out of a New York court.

The Ewing decision was the League's second major legal setback. On January 28, Judge Morgan O'Brien denied the suit of the Metropolitan Exhibition Company and Day for a temporary injunction against Ward, ruling that the reserve clause in player contracts made the contract in its entirety unequal in its conditions, and therefore unenforceable in a court of law. After this victory (whose full import would not be understood and utilized by player representatives until the 1970s), PL leaders gave loop secretary Frank Brunell the green light to draft a schedule. Brunell, long a stanchion of Cleveland's various major league teams, was just one of the front-office luminaries the PL cornered to assist with operational matters. On putting together the PL's schedule for 1890, he proclaimed it the best in history, but then miscalculated by allowing it to be released before the League committed to a schedule. Thus, League owners were able to engineer box-office showdowns by scheduling games in League cities on dates when PL teams were also at home. It then became more important that club executives be creative mathematicians than accurate in their crowd count. When the PL claimed to be winning at the box office, spies sent by League teams to PL games reported the PL's attendance figures were grossly exaggerated. Meanwhile, League loyalists followed the example of the Chicago White Stockings secretary who, when asked by a reporter what the attendance was at that day's game, promptly said, "Twenty-four eighteen." Asked later by Al Spalding how he could reconcile his conscience to such a lie, the secretary replied there had been 24 on one side of the park and 18 on the other, and if the reporter published the attendance as 2,418, that was a matter for *his* conscience, not the secretary's.

In late May, the PL debated changing its schedule to avoid conflicts with League games in the same cities, and then decided against it since most PL clubs were more than holding their own in head-to-head confrontations. By mid-season, though, teams in all three major leagues had begun leaving passes for games in barber shops, saloons and other public places, free for the taking in an effort to pad attendance figures, only to go on lying about them on top of it. The League Giants drew just 60,667 all season and averted financial ruin only because Spalding, Brush, Boston owner Arthur Soden and Philadelphia owner Al Reach bought $80,000 worth of stock in Day's club, making them part owners (a situation that eventually led to Day's being shorn of the franchise). The Phillies, by remaining in contention all year for the pennant, led the League in attendance with 186,000, but last-place Pittsburgh drew a paltry 16,064. The true League attendance was estimated to be 813,678, while the PL's was some 165,000 higher, or close to a million. Guesstimates were that the League lost $300,000 altogether, the PL around $340,000 (largely because of its higher payrolls), and the Association, which never made public its 1890 attendance figures, dropped nearly as much as the two other circuits combined.

On September 2, 1890, three representatives from the Association, Chris Von der Ahe, Zach Phelps and William Whittaker, and three from the PL, Brunell, Ward and Albert Johnson, conferred in secret at the Colonnade Hotel in Philadelphia. What evolved from the meeting was never made public, but later events suggested that it may have been a final attempt by the Association to join forces with the PL. All during the summer, the sports pages of every major journal had been rife with rumors that the Association and the PL would consolidate the following year to form one league. The August 9 issue of *Sporting Life* reported that Von der Ahe still firmly believed his Browns and the Chicago PL club would win their respective pennants and was working to arrange a postseason series, after seeing "in prospect a rich harvest of shekels in the contests which will occur between the team represented by his former manager and the architect of his baseball reputation and prowess and his own team. . . . The combine implies a leaving out in the cold of the National League and a subsequent amalgamation of the two friendly base ball organizations for mutual protection." But soon after that, Louisville took charge of the Association pennant race, the Brooklyn franchise folded, and the Athletics disgraced themselves. By early September the PL could hardly be blamed for having changed its mind about forming an alliance with the Association. Besides, the course its own pennant race had taken in the past month had eliminated any hope of a postseason collision between Von der Ahe and Comiskey. After holding first place briefly in mid-May, Comiskey's Pirates had nearly retaken the top spot in early July, but since then had gradually fallen farther and farther off the pace set by the Boston Reds.

In fact, once they seized the lead from the Pirates in May, the Reds would relinquish it again just once, and at that only for a single day, on July 8. Under the relaxed leadership of King Kelly, the Boston players were given free rein both on and off the field and utilized the permissive atmosphere to run wild on the base paths. Nearing the end of a superlative if sometimes erratic career, Stovey,

DOGS HEAD &
OLD JUDGE CIGARETTES Goodwin & Co., New York.

• • •

When asked if he drank while playing baseball, King Kelly replied, "It depends on the length of the game." Kelly was begged by Al Spalding not to join the Players League and offered a signed blank check to remain loyal to the NL. After heavy soul-searching, the game's most renowned performer of his day resisted the enormous blandishment. An NL'er at heart, the following year Kelly made amends with Spalding when he bolted the AA to rejoin the Boston Beaneaters.

although approaching thirty-four, led the PL in stolen bases and averaged over a run a game. So did centerfielder Tom Brown, another former Association stalwart before he followed the Pittsburgh franchise to the League in 1887. Between them, the pair scored 288 runs and swiped 176 bases on just 293 hits.

Excluded from postseason activity, the Reds still lost money even though they pulled around 200,000 fans to lead all three major leagues in attendance.* Indeed, every Brotherhood team finished in the red. By the close of the PL campaign on October 4, Buffalo and Ewing's Giants were in so grave a plight that they could no longer meet their payrolls, and PL president Edward McAlpin, one of the owners of the New York club, had resigned. Yet the loop remained viable, a force to be feared by League owners even while the players themselves began to realize that the PL was a vision whose time had not yet come.

Meanwhile, the League feigned that it held all the trump cards. So convincing was its act that the PL franchises began to topple, one by one. Sniping attacks in the press between Ward and Eddie Talcott, another owner of the New York PL club, did not help. Nor did Comiskey's publicly dickering, in November 1890, to return to the Browns, saying he believed the PL was "a thing of the past."

But the PL had one last trump card of its own to play. It purchased the Cincinnati League club from Aaron Stern just after the 1890 season ended, elected Charles Prince, a lawyer for the New York and New England Railroad Company, its new president and had Prince aver on November 14 that the PL would do battle again in 1891 as a six-team circuit, with clubs in Cincinnati, Cleveland, Boston, Brooklyn, Philadelphia and Washington.

League owners, though inwardly panicked, continued to radiate an external confidence that victory would soon be theirs. On January 14, 1891, after two more of its teams knuckled under to the League and folded, the PL officially gave up the fight. Prince was of a mind to combine forces with the Association, which looked about ready to throw in the towel itself. The League nipped that plan in the bud by voting to allow new Association franchises in Boston and Chicago in 1891, conditional upon the return of all reserved players on ex-PL clubs to their former teams. Instead of following the League's bidding, the Association took on the Boston Reds virtually intact, plus the core of the Philadelphia PL franchise, and then elected to hold in abeyance a deci-

---

*The Louisville Courier-Journal credited the Cyclones with a total attendance of 206,000 in 1890, but its figures were highly suspect, particularly in light of the fact that the team later claimed it lost money that year despite having one of the smallest payrolls in the majors.

Al Spalding appropriately occupies the center in this woodcut of the first NL champions, the 1876 Chicago White Stockings. A 41-game winner that year, he quit soon after that to devote more time to his fledgling sporting goods empire. Some think, though, that he really retired prematurely because he could learn neither to throw a curveball nor to hit one. In any event, Spalding was masterful in his new role as White Stockings president at curveballing rival major leagues to death. He was by far the NL's most powerful weapon in its war against the Players League. Within another year he had also helped bring the American Association to its knees.

sion about whether to put a team in Chicago. The bold move meant that although the PL was dead after just one year, at least two remnants of it would survive into the 1891 season.

Before the Brotherhood was given a symbolic burial, several of its members and sympathizers held a wake for it at the Home Plate saloon near the Polo Grounds. Ward raised his glass and said, "Pass the wine around, the League is dead, long live the League." After taking a moment to absorb the irony in the fallen leader's toast, Richter rejoined, "Base ball will live on forever. Here's to the game and its glorious future." But if Richter was to be correct, little evidence of it lay ahead. By the dawn of the 1891 season, both the Salary Limitation plan and the reserve clause were once again in force. The Brotherhood revolt, for all its impact, seemed to have had only one lasting effect. It had sapped the Association of strength that it would have taken years to regain, and the League, now that one rival had been knocked out of the ring, was not about to allow the other to get off the ropes. To restore its monopoly, all that was needed was one killer blow. The Association saw it coming but was too proud to duck. Though warned repeatedly by Richter all through the winter of 1890-91 that the League would manipulate and hoodwink it in any peace settlement, the Association lay there on the ropes and took the League's best shot squarely on the chin.

PL FINAL STANDINGS

	W	L	PCT	HOME	ROAD	GB
1. Boston Reds	81	48	.628	48–21	42–38	
2. Brooklyn Ward's Wonders	76	56	.576	46–19	30–37	6.5
3. New York Giants	74	57	.565	47–19	27–38	8
4. Chicago Pirates	75	62	.547	46–23	29–39	10
5. Philadelphia Quakers	68	63	.519	35–30	33–33	14
6. Pittsburgh Burghers	60	68	.469	37–28	23–40	20.5
7. Cleveland Infants	55	75	.423	31–30	24–45	26.5
8. Buffalo Bisons	36	96	.273	23–42	13–54	46.5

PL SEASON LEADERS*

BATTING

BATTING AVERAGE (325 ABs)

1. *Browning*, Cleve	.3732
2. *Orr*, Brook	.3728
3. O'Rourke, NY	.360
4. Connor, NY	.349
5. Ryan, Chic	.340
6. Ewing, NY	.338
7. Ward, Brook	.337
8. Van Haltren, Brook	.335
9. *Larkin*, Cleve	.332
10. Brouthers, Boston	.330

SLUGGING AVERAGE

1. Ewing, NY	.545
2. Connor, NY	.541
Beckley, Pitts	.541
4. *Orr*, Brook	.537
5. *Browning*, Cleve	.517
6. O'Rourke, NY	.515
7. Gore, NY	.499
8. H. Richardson, Boston	.494
9. *Larkin*, Cleve	.484
10. *Shindle*, Phila	.481

ON-BASE PERCENTAGE

1. Brouthers, Boston	.466
2. *Browning*, Cleve	.459
3. Connor, NY	.450
4. *Y. Robinson*, Pitts	.434
5. Gore, NY	.432
6. *Larkin*, Cleve	.420
7. Kelly, Boston	.419
8. Hoy, Buff	.418
F. Carroll, Pitts	.418
10. *Orr*, Brook	.416
Ryan, Chic	.416

TOTAL BASES

1. *Shindle*, Phila	281
2. Duffy, Chic	280
3. Beckley, Pitts	279
4. H. Richardson, Boston	268
5. Connor, NY	262
6. *Orr*, Brook	249
7. O'Rourke, NY	246
8. *Larkin*, Cleve	245
Browning, Cleve	245
10. *Bierbauer*, Brook	243

HOME RUNS

1. Connor, NY	13
2. *Stovey*, Boston	11
Richardson, Boston	11
4. *Shindle*, Phila	10
Gore, NY	10
Beckley, Pitts	10
7. Fields, Pitts	9
O'Rourke, NY	9
Wood, Phila	9
10. Ewing, NY	8

RUNS

1. Duffy, Chic	161
2. T. Brown, Boston	146
3. *Stovey*, Boston	142
4. Ward, Brook	134
5. Gore, NY	132
6. *Bierbauer*, Brook	128
7. *Griffin*, Phila	127
Shindle, Phila-Boston	127
9. H. Richardson, Boston	126
10. Joyce, Brook	121

*PL leaders who were in the AA in 1889 are in italics.

• • •

Dave Orr suffered two broken ribs when he was hit by a pitch on July 12, 1890. Otherwise he might have won both the PL batting and RBI crowns, as he was having his finest year. Shortly after the season ended, Orr had a stroke in an exhibition game at Renova, PA, and never played again.

HITS			STOLEN BASES			RBIs	
1. Duffy, Chic	191		1. *Stovey*, Boston	97		1. H. Richardson, Boston	143
2. Ward, Brook	189		2. T. Brown, Boston	79		2. *Orr*, Brook	124
3. *Shindle*, Phila	188		3. Duffy, Chic	78		3. Beckley, Pitts	120
4. *Browning*, Cleve	184		4. Hanlon, Pitts	65		4. O'Rourke, NY	115
5. H. Richardson, Boston	181		5. Ward, Brook	63		5. *Larkin*, Cleve	112
6. *Bierbauer*, Brook	180		6. *Shindle*, Phila	51		6. Connor, NY	103
7. O'Neill, Chic	174		Kelly, Boston	51		7. Wood, Phila	102
8. Orr, Brook	173		8. Seery, Brook	44		Wise, Buff	102
9. O'Rourke, NY	172		9. Joyce, Brook	43		9. *Bierbauer*, Brook	99
10. *Larkin*, Cleve	168		Corcoran, Pitts	43		10. Brouthers, Boston	97

PITCHING

WINS			LOSSES			INNINGS	
1. *King*, Chic	32		1. Haddock, Buff	26		1. *Baldwin*, Chic	501
M. *Baldwin*, Chic	32		2. Staley, Pitts	25		2. *King*, Chic	461
3. *Weyhing*, Brook	30		Bakely, Cleve	25		3. *Weyhing*, Brook	390
4. Radbourn, Boston	27		4. *Baldwin*, Chic	24		4. Staley, Pitts	387.2
5. Knell, Phila	22		*Cunningham*, Phila-Buff	24		5. Gruber, Cleve	383.1
O'Day, NY	22		6. Gruber, Cleve	23		6. Sanders, Phila	346.2
Gumbert, Boston	22		7. *King*, Chic	22		7. Radbourn, Boston	343
8. Staley, Pitts	21		8. Crane, NY	19		8. Crane, NY	330.1
Gruber, Cleve	21		9. Sanders, Phila	17		9. O'Day, NY	329
10. Sanders, Phila	20		10. D. O'Brien, Cleve	16		10. Bakely, Cleve	326.1
			Weyhing, Brook	16			
			Sowders, Brook	16			
			G. Keefe, Buff	16			

COMPLETE GAMES			STRIKEOUTS			WINNING PCT. (25 DECISIONS)	
1. *Baldwin*, Chic	54		1. *Baldwin*, Chic	211		1. B. Daley, Boston	.720
2. *King*, Chic	48		2. *King*, Chic	185		2. Radbourn, Boston	.692
3. Staley, Pitts	44		3. *Weyhing*, Brook	177		3. Knell, Phila	.667
4. Gruber, Cleve	39		4. *Ewing*, NY	145		4. *Weyhing*, Brook	.652
5. *Weyhing*, Brook	38		Staley, Pitts	145		5. Gumbert, Boston	.647
6. Sanders, Phila	37		6. Haddock, Buff	123		6. O'Day, NY	.629
7. Radbourn, Boston	36		7. Crane, NY	117		7. T. Keefe, NY	.607
8. *Cunningham*, Phila-Buff	35		8. *Cunningham*, Phila-Buff	111		8. *Ewing*, NY	.600
9. O'Day, NY	32		9. Daley, Boston	110		Van Haltren, Brook	.600
Bakely, Cleve	32		Gruber, Cleve	110		10. *King*, Chic	.593

ERA (140 INNINGS)			LOWEST ON-BASE PCT.	
1. *King*, Chic	2.69		1. Staley, Pitts	.285
2. Staley, Pitts	3.23		2. *King*, Chic	.296
3. *Baldwin*, Chic	3.31		3. Radbourn, Boston	.304
Radbourn, Boston	3.31		4. T. Keefe, NY	.312
5. T. Keefe, NY	3.38		5. Sanders, Phila	.315
6. D. O'Brien, Cleve	3.40		6. Maul, Pitts	.327
7. *Weyhing*, Brook	3.60		7. Morris, Pitts	.329
Daley, Boston	3.60		8. *Ewing*, NY	.330
9. Sanders, Phila	3.76		9. *Baldwin*, Chic	.331
10. Maul, Pitts	3.79		Galvin, Pitts	.331

• • •

The 1896 Cincinnati Reds with William Ellsworth Hoy in the front row, far left. No one in the brutally frank atmosphere of Hoy's day was shy about calling him "Dummy." After all, he was a deaf mute. In 1890 umpire Jack Sheridan cast some doubt on that by claiming he heard Hoy say, "Why did he hit me?" when he was tagged hard in a Players League game, making it appear that Hoy could speak "under intense excitement, but was unaware he did so." The story is almost undoubtedly apocryphal. Though Hoy lived to be ninety-nine, no one ever boasted of hearing him speak again. By any name, Hoy was a fine player for 15 seasons in the majors. When he died on December 15, 1961, so passed the last surviving AA participant.

THE LAST HURRAH

❝*Resolved, That the American Association withdraws from the National Agreement, said action to take effect this date.*❞

—From the wire sent to National League president Nick Young by American Association vice president Billy Barnie on February 18, 1891

**HEN CHRIS VON DER AHE PRANCED INTO** the room at the Louisville Hotel for the Association's annual winter meeting on November 22, 1890, much to the delight of the other magnates, he was trailed by Charlie Comiskey, his old manager and captain. With the Players League in disarray, Comiskey's return to the Association had been predicted, but his presence was still a welcome surprise. It began the proceeding on an upbeat note, which was heightened when Tim Murnane, a former player turned sportswriter, rose and announced he was there to represent the Boston Reds and that the Players League champion wished to apply for Association membership. A while later ex-Orioles catcher Sam Trott arrived and filed a membership application on behalf of several Washington businessmen.

The prospect of having Comiskey back in the fold and franchises in Boston and Washington partially mitigated the staggering financial losses the Association had sustained in the season just past and the precarious situation in Philadelphia where sever-

In 1891, Baltimore bought John McGraw from Cedar Rapids on a tip from Bill Gleason, a friend of Billy Barnie's. Then an eighteen-year-old shortstop, McGraw did not move to third base until 1894, when the Orioles won their first of three straight NL flags. Like Frank Foreman, he played on Baltimore teams in three different major leagues, but the difference was that McGraw played on all of Baltimore's good ones.

• • •
No, nothing's wrong with this picture of Hughie Jennings. While it's true he wasn't a southpaw, he had to play first lefthanded for a spell, owing to an arm injury. Jennings also cut his teeth in the AA, meaning that he, McGraw, Sadie McMahon and Wilbert Robinson— the heart of the great Orioles' teams in the 1890s—all were AA alums. In 1891, Jennings took the Louisville shortstop job away from Phil Tomney and hit .292.

al of the Athletics' minority stockholders had filed a bill of equity the previous week, demanding that a receiver be appointed to protect their claims to the insolvent club. Riding a wave of optimism, the assemblage re-elected Zach Phelps loop president and named Billy Barnie vice president. Barnie then asked Allan W. Thurman, a recent addition to the front office of the Columbus club, to join them on a three-man committee to determine the Association's composition for 1891. Before the trio sat down to the task, however, Phelps unexpectedly resigned the presidency, claiming he had too heavy a legal workload, and recommended that Thurman replace him. Von der Ahe then went through the formality of nominating Thurman for the post, and he was routinely elected.

An inconsequential figure prior to the meeting, Thurman would soon play a devastatingly prominent hand in the Association's downfall; but for the moment he worked constructively to redesign the loop. In early December, he and Barnie awarded J. Earle Wagner and his brother George, co-owners of the Philadelphia Players League club, the Athletics franchise. With the backers of two Players League outfits now in tow, plus what appeared to be a sound organization in Washington, Thurman and Barnie turned their attention to paring the weaker franchises from the Association. Syracuse, Rochester and Toledo, known as "The Little Three," were the obvious candidates. On December 11, Thurman and Barnie met with George Frazier of Syracuse and Rochester owner General Henry Brinker and offered each around $5,000 to leave the Association. The two New York State clubs grudgingly agreed to exit after bargaining to retain their players, but Toledo owner Valentino Ketcham dug in his heels, securing an injunction to avert his club's expulsion. Inspired by Ketcham's fiber, Frazier and Brinker retracted their pledge to depart, and the three clubs united to fight their joint ouster at another meeting in early January, before finally conceding for a higher price than the Association had hoped to pay. Syracuse received $7,000, Rochester got $10,000, spread over three payments, and Ketcham, the ringleader of the resistance action, was handed $8,500 in cash, on the spot, to surrender Toledo's franchise deed.

Thurman and Barnie had no more than put the finishing touches on this delicate reconstruction project when the Players League collapsed, creating an even thornier problem. The National Agreement obliged renegade players to return to their former teams, and the Wagner brothers, as owners of the reconstituted Athletics franchise, rightfully expected to regain all of the club's stars who had been swept away in the Brotherhood rebellion. Instead, they learned that the Pittsburgh League entry aimed to filch second baseman Lou Bierbauer, and that Harry Stovey meant to sign with the League's Boston Beaneaters when it emerged that the previous Athletics' management had neglected to reserve them again for the forthcoming season. Bill Sharsig, who had been retained by the Wagners to pilot the A's, claimed that the club was not at fault because he had reminded Phelps the previous October, even while the franchise was disintegrating, to reserve all of its Players League participants. To defend himself, Phelps belatedly produced a wire he'd been sent collect on October 14, 1890, by William Whittaker, stating: "Name the players as reserved that finished the schedule, though nearly a new nine will be got for next season."

Even though the wire seemed to prove the A's were remiss, the Wagners contended they were being had on a cruel technicality, and a Board of Control comprised of Thurman, Louis Krauthoff (who was now president of the Western Association) and Philadelphia Phillies owner Colonel John I. Rogers convened to settle the dispute. Inasmuch as Krauthoff was known to be sympathetic to the Athletics' grievance, Association monarchs expected Thurman to tip the vote their way. Instead, Thurman stunned his colleagues and sided with Rogers, awarding Bierbauer to Pittsburgh and allowing Stovey to sign with Boston. In his defense, the new Association president averred that he had decided the Bierbauer and Stovey cases without regard to his personal feelings. But to most of the baseball world his motives remained a deep puzzle. It was widely known that Thurman had helped settle the Players League war and had been nicknamed "The White-winged Angel of Peace" for his work. Less well known was that Thurman had been touted for the Association top spot by none

• • •

Hugh Duffy. When the PL collapsed, he jumped to the AA rather than return to the Chicago White Stockings, because he liked playing in Boston near his Rhode Island home. He then joined the Boston NL entry, once the AA folded, and became one of the game's brightest stars during the 1890s.

• • •

Paul Radford was famed for emitting bloodcurdling war whoops from the open windows of trains passing at night through sleeping towns. As a player, he could do everything but hit. Like Yank Robinson and Jack Crooks, Radford compiled huge walk totals despite seeming to pose a minimal threat at the plate. Normally an outfielder, Radford plugged the Boston Reds' shortstop hole when Arthur Irwin decided to quit as a player. Radford did so well that it is puzzling why 1891 was his only full season at the position.

other than Al Spalding, who felt that its president "ought to be someone in whom the National League had confidence." But apart from that knowledge and from the seemingly trifling facts that he had a son who was a second baseman on the University of Virginia team, and that he had once played ball himself at Trinity College, he was a cipher. Not even Thurman's Columbus peers knew how he had so swiftly ingratiated himself among the members of the Association's inner circle and assumed a leadership role. To some it almost seemed that he was a mole the League had insinuated at this crucial juncture to undermine the very group he was pledged to serve.

In any case, the Association scheduled an emergency meeting at New York's Murray Hill Hotel on February 18, 1891. Negotiations were delayed until late in the day when Von der Ahe, Gus Schmelz, Henry Von der Horst and the Wagners were all detained in Johnstown by one of the area's frequent floods of that era. But once the opening gavel finally sounded, Boston Reds owner Charles Prince moved instantly to depose Thurman. The motion carried unanimously, and the president's office was declared vacant. As the vice president and the Association's highest-ranking officer, Barnie then seized the reins, shouting, "It was bad enough to have Spalding's fingers on our throats for nine long years. Spalding says he wants war and we will give it to him." Following this declaration, all the delegates present voted to withdraw from the National Agreement. Minutes later, a wire was fired off to League president Nick Young, notifying him of the Association's intention to operate as an outlaw loop.

The Association then sprang another nasty surprise on its former confrere. Earlier that winter the Cincinnati League franchise, verging on bankruptcy, had been captured by Frank Brunell and Albert Johnson, who planned to transfer it to the Players League. When the Players League quit the fight, Prince and his newly appointed manager Arthur Irwin began courting Brunell and Johnson. Both Ohioans were at the Association meeting on February 18, and once the momentous wire had been sent to Young, Cincinnati was accepted as the loop's eighth and final member for 1891.

Johnson boasted that he would have most of the 1890 Cincinnati Reds on his club, including such former Association stars as Bid McPhee, Long John Reilly, Bug Holliday and Tony Mullane. In addition, he was given a present by Prince in the person of King Kelly. The Boston owner was not so much trying to help out Johnson as bowing to Kelly's threat to retire unless he could play in Cincinnati, where he had begun his major league career thirteen years earlier. Kelly, who had belonged to the Boston Beaneaters prior to the Brotherhood revolt, thus became the first

League star to break the reserve rule and join the Association after the National Agreement was rescinded.

The League replied by hiring former Association pitching bellwethers Mark Baldwin and Guy Hecker to tempt Association players to bolt their contracts. In March, Baldwin was jailed in St. Louis on Von der Ahe's charge that he had bribed Silver King to sign with Pittsburgh. Von der Ahe then pulled strings to have the case delayed so that Baldwin would be detained indefinitely in St. Louis and would be unable to continue his poaching for the League.

Pittsburgh, which already had Baldwin under its wing, retaliated by suing Von der Ahe for false imprisonment. For the way it had so brassily snatched Bierbauer and now looked to steal King, arguably the best pitcher in the game at the time, the Pennsylvania club's tactics were branded piracy and it, at long last, gained an enduring nickname. But if the Pittsburgh "Pirates" were making hay from the furious bidding war for players that followed the dissolution of the National Agreement, the other League clubs were worried. Not only were salaries again threatening to spiral out of control, but the Association, rather than caving in after Thurman's act of treachery, was showing itself still to be astonishingly resilient. By trimming Syracuse, Rochester and Toledo, and then adding Boston, Washington and now Cincinnati, the Beer

• • •
Lave Cross followed his older brother, Amos, to the majors. The two shared the Louisville catching job until Amos took ill and died, but then the younger Cross couldn't win a full-time position anywhere. Beginning in 1890, he played with Philadelphia teams in three different major leagues in a three-year span. However, once Cross found his proper niche at the hot corner, he lasted there until 1907 and set a new mark for the most career hits by a third sacker.

Dan Brouthers won five batting crowns and is the only player to cop a hitting title in both the NL and the AA. On flag-winning teams in three different major leagues, he is also one of the few 19th-century stars who played in both an AA vs. NL World's Series and a Temple Cup Series. By a slender one-point margin—.342 to .341—Brouthers beat out Pete Browning for the honor of the highest career batting average among players who were active primarily before 1893.

and Whisky loop seemed actually to be stronger, at least on paper, than it had been at any time since the glorious 1886 season.

In self-defense, the League opted in early March to put a new team in Cincinnati headed by John Brush. For reasons that still remain veiled, Albert Johnson wilted almost immediately under the challenge. By mid-March he had sold his Cincinnati franchise to the League for $30,000 (after reportedly paying $40,000 for it just a few months earlier), on the condition that he stay out of baseball for ten years and not let his Brotherhood Park in Cleveland be used for anything but League games.

Johnson's defection was a crushing blow to the Association, though it battled to install a new franchise in Cincinnati and retained Kelly to manage it. Ed Renau, a partner in the outfit that made the Reds' scorecards, was elected president of the novitiate club, Charles Kauffman, the son of a prominent Queen City brewer, assumed the vice presidency and a young sportswriter named Ban Johnson, who was destined to lead the next great revolt against the League, joined the front office and served as the club's *Sporting Life* correspondent. Kelly was given carte blanche to sign players, and a new park was hurriedly built in the Pendleton district in the East End of Cincinnati. The club was christened Kelly's Klippers, but members of the local press espoused another nickname once they saw the caliber of the veteran players Kelly had landed. With heavy irony they dubbed the team Kelly's Killers and mentally consigned it to last place.

Favored for the flag in the preseason were Boston and the Browns, with Columbus given an outside shot despite rumors of internal disorder. Over the winter, the Ohio club had lost pitcher Frank Knauss, third baseman Charlie Reilly and leftfielder Spud Johnson to League raiders, along with pitcher Icebox Chamberlain, who was sold to the Athletics after he was implicated in a prizefight-fixing scam. Some thought the trouble was that Schmelz was too harsh a taskmaster, while others argued that a team with as many problem children as the Solons needed someone even tougher.

But at any rate, Columbus's disharmony was kept within the house for the moment, whereas the turmoil in Louisville had become public knowledge. Though believed to have made a profit in 1890, the Falls City club bafflingly was put up for sale in January 1891 to satisfy a mortgage held by a local bank. Lawrence Parsons, still the principal owner and president, contended that the team had really lost money in 1890, but stockholders accused him of careless business practices at the very least, and perhaps even of criminal behavior in bilking them of their holdings. The financial maze was never unraveled. There was speculation that Parsons,

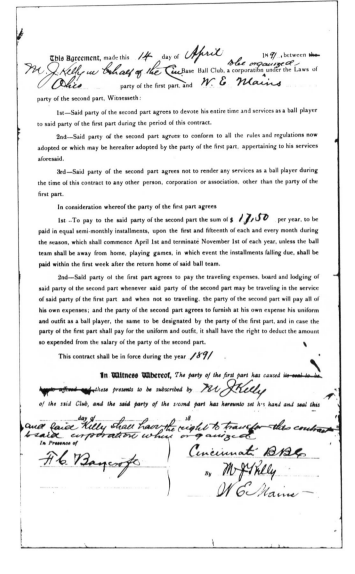

An 1891 AA contract between Kelly's Killers and rookie pitcher Willard Mains. The ownership issue of the fledgling Cincinnati club had yet to be resolved when the document was drawn up, requiring manager King Kelly to act as agent for the team and Frank Bancroft, one of the club's advisors, to be the witness. All the internal havoc probably amused Mains, a non-conformist who changed teams nearly as often and as quixotically as Billy Earle. The 1891 season was Mains's only full year in the majors, but he was the first hurler to bag 300 wins in the minors.

noting what the old Athletics owners had gotten away with, had been inspired to emulate them. Nevertheless, he successfully ran for the presidency of the club again when it was reorganized, only to turn the franchise over to Phelps in May and flee the scene.

This rash of episodes of front-office misconduct further pointed up the Association's desperate need for a strong leader. Instead, the loop allowed the vacant president's job to fall, almost by default, to Louis Kramer, a businessman who had been an official of the Cincinnati club off and on ever since its inception in 1882. Kramer took the presidency for a salary of $3,000 on the agreement that he would not have to travel much and that his duties would not interfere with the demands of his business. *Sporting Life* warned that he was a poor choice for the job. What it demanded was someone who would be both savvy and indefatigable in protecting the Association from being, in Brunell's word, "dinky-dinked" at every turn by the League.

Kramer's most daring act while in office was to steal a march on the League by opening the Association season on April 8, two full weeks ahead of the senior circuit's scheduled starting date. The day was marred, however, when Kelly's Killers, acting on their manager's complaint that it was too dark to continue, went into a stall at the top of the tenth inning of a 7–7 tie with St. Louis, bidding rookie umpire Bill Gleason, once the Browns shortstop, to forfeit the contest to his old team. Each of the other three lid-lifters was also remarkable, though in a positive way. Over 5,800 turned out in Baltimore despite raw, mucky weather and thrilled as the Orioles bopped the highly regarded Boston Reds, 11–7. Washington's first game in the Association since 1884 drew only some 2,250 to Forepaugh Park, the Athletics' new home, but all got their money's worth in thrills as the Nationals plated five runs in the top of the ninth to lead 9–3, and then stifled a furious five-run rally by Philadelphia in the bottom of the frame that fell a hair short when rookie hurler Kid Carsey kept George Wood and Jack McGeachy, the meat of the A's batting order, from delivering the tying marker. At Louisville, the band played "Dixie" and 4,277 cheered as the 1890 pennant was hoisted prior to the game. The crowd had no more occasion to rejoice until the ninth inning, when the Colonels fought back from a 6–2 deficit to beat Columbus 7–6 on infield errors by Jack Crooks and Elmer Cleveland.

On April 9, the Falls City faithful roared harder as the Colonels won again, 13–6, and ended the day alone in first place at 2–0. A week later Louisville still held the top perch with a 5–1 record, trailed by St. Louis at 4–2, Baltimore and Boston at 3–2, Philadelphia and Washington at 2–3, Columbus at 2–4, and Cincinnati in the cellar with just one win in six outings. Kelly blamed his Killers' poor start on lousy umpiring and an epidemic of the grippe that felled most of his starting nine. Columbus had no good excuse. One writer following the club muttered, "There is a woeful lack of ginger in its work."

Louisville, in contrast, seemed to have plenty of snap. Falls City writers now called the team the Cyclones because "they [were] sweeping everything before them," and credited the fast start to Jack Chapman, who had his men on a strict 10:00 PM road curfew. In truth, the Louisville manager probably was largely responsible. Even with all the front-office highjinks going on around

• • •

Longtime NL outfielder George Wood was made the A's player-manager in 1891, after Bill Sharsig was axed. He held the title, if not the job, until Billy Barnie left Baltimore in late September. Wood followed a good year in the PL by hitting .309 for the 1891 A's.

• • •

In September 1891, even though he was Louisville's leading hitter, Patsy Donovan was given his walking papers when he tried to turn the team against manager Jack Chapman. Minus Donovan's .321 batting average, the Colonels ended the season in a rush, winning 13 straight games at one point. Donovan meanwhile hooked on with Washington, which finished last. He then stayed in the majors another 15 years, usually hitting his .300, but he never played on a pennant winner.

him, he whipped his team into peak condition, enabling it to get out of the starting gate quickly, while most of the other clubs had yet to round into shape.

By the end of April, however, the Colonels had surrendered the lead to Baltimore and begun a swift descent through the standings that eventually entangled them in a summer-long struggle with Washington to avoid the cellar. But while Barnie finally seemed to have a team that could make a serious pennant bid, another long-time Association stalwart, Bill Sharsig, became the first managerial casualty of the season. In early May, after the A's bumbled to a 6–11 start, Sharsig was fired by J. Earle Wagner. The situation turned ugly when Sharsig, rather than exit gracefully, tried to sue Wagner for breach of contract, claiming that the A's owner really wanted to manage the team himself, and that the club's new skipper, leftfielder George Wood, had been installed only as a figurehead. But regardless of who was really piloting the A's, they overcame their internal disunity to reach the .500 mark before the month was out. Louisville, on the other hand, continued its horrendous skid, plummeting all the way down to seventh place on Decoration Day, when Columbus took a doubleheader from Boston to move ahead of the Colonels.

The Reds' twin defeat at the hands of the Solons allowed the Browns to creep to within percentage points of the top spot, which Boston had wrested from Baltimore some two weeks earlier. On June 6, the Reds arrived in St. Louis for a key four-game series. A seesaw 11–10 victory in the opener briefly catapulted the Browns into first place, but the Reds had regained the lead before they left town and held it by a narrow margin for all but one day throughout the rest of the month.

Heading into July, Boston remained in front at 40–22 for a .645 winning percentage, St. Louis was seven percentage points behind at 44–25, Baltimore stood third at 35–26 and Cincinnati rounded out the first division. The surprisingly strong early showing by Kelly's Killers was largely due to Kelly himself. Not only was he leading the team in hitting but he had also become, quite literally, a "hands-on" manager. In April he decked Cannonball Crane, his top pitcher, outside a Louisville hotel for overimbibing and fished another hurler, Willie McGill, out of a Louisville drunk tank. Kelly eventually gave up hope of reforming the seventeen-year-old McGill and peddled the "infant phenom" to St. Louis, where he sobered enough to become the youngest 20-game winner in history. A few weeks later, Kelly released Yank Robinson for being drunk once too often, only to have to reinstate the former Browns star when his replacement at second base, Billy Clingman, a local amateur, was unready for the majors. But all of Kelly's

Frank Dwyer was the only pitcher on Kelly's Killers who was coveted by Milwaukee when the Brewers took Cincinnati's spot in the AA. He returned to Cincinnati in 1892 after the AA and NL merged and was the Reds' most reliable pitcher until late in the decade.

Ted Breitenstein warmed the bench for St. Louis until the last day of the 1891 season. Making his first major league start, he fired a no-hitter against Louisville that was marred only by a walk to Harry Taylor. The lone player of consequence to be retained by the Browns when the AA and NL merged, Breitenstein was the last of the long string of outstanding pitchers to be discovered by the Von der Ahe–Comiskey pairing.

lineup juggling could not prevent the inevitable from occurring. His Killers had the most wretched hitting attack in the majors, numbering five regulars who batted under .230, and drew meagerly at home as a result. Compounding their attendance problem was a new war in Cincinnati over Sunday ball. In mid-May, a Sunday game with the A's at Pendleton Park was halted by police colonel Phil Deitsch, and club president Ed Renau had to honor his guarantee to give every ticketholder a refund in the event the Sabbatarians got their will. When Cincinnati began to lose on the field as well as at the box office, Von der Ahe, who had gradually taken much of the club's financial burden upon himself in an effort to keep it afloat, was persuaded to throw in the towel. On August 17, after an apathetic 8–0 loss to the Browns at St. Louis, Kelly's Killers were disbanded and the franchise was awarded to Milwaukee, which had been the class of the Western Association before that minor league loop had begun to crumble earlier in the month. Stepping right into action the following day with most of its Western Association cast, including manager Charlie Cushman, Milwaukee assumed Cincinnati's schedule and got off to a flying start by belting the Browns' Jack Stivetts, 7–2, behind George Davies. The loss dumped St. Louis five and a half games behind Boston and virtually annihilated any lingering hopes Comiskey's crew had of overtaking the Reds. To ensure the pennant, Boston president Charles Prince offered Kelly the Reds' captaincy after the Killers folded, and was exultant when he accepted. Kelly's return to the Reds seemed certain to decide the battle with the Beaneaters for the hearts of the Hub populace.

But Prince's jubilation was soon dashed. A week after Kelly joined the Reds, League and Association leaders met in Washington with an eye toward drafting a new National Agreement and seemed ready to mend their differences. But even as the delegates were talking of a reconciliation, the news that Kelly had jumped from the Reds to the Beaneaters "came like a flash of lightning from a clear sky" and ended any prospect of an amicable settlement, when the League would not accede to the Association's command that Kelly be returned to the Reds. Association titans at first drew up a "dignified" letter of appeal, which the League rebuffed. An angrier letter was then drafted that caused Charlie Byrne to wring his hands and claim the League was anxious for peace, but his agony may only have been feigned for the media's sake. Certainly the chain of events during that week made it seem that League moguls could not really have wanted peace at that juncture and may even have engineered Kelly's defection on the eve of the conference to kill any possibility of it.

But although Kramer resigned the Association presidency in

disgust, forcing Phelps again to take on the job for the lack of any other qualified volunteers, the Beer and Whisky loop was still very much alive. In September, the Association landed a rabbit punch when the League learned that it meant to put a team in Chicago in 1892, bankrolled by several prominent Windy City investors who claimed also to have the backing of E. H. R. Green, son of the eccentric millionairess Hettie Green. To add to the League's torment, the Reds continued to charge just 25¢, outdraw the Beaneaters, and win. By mid-September, Irwin's club had a prohibitive six-and-a-half-game lead over the Browns. When Cap Anson hinted that his Chicago White Stockings, which seemed nearly as certain to win the League flag, would be willing to meet the Reds in a World's Series, the crisis came to a head. Knowing that another postseason clash could only benefit the Association, particularly if the Reds were to win it, several League officials held a secret strategy session. What they decided will always be food for controversy, but subsequent events tend to support Anson's angry wail that his club was robbed of the pennant.

On September 15, in their final series of the season with the League leaders, the Beaneaters suffered a second straight loss to Chicago that prompted *The Sporting News* to proclaim they "might as well give up all hope of flying the flag." The following afternoon, however, with just 20 games left on the schedule, Kid Nichols beat Chicago for the first time in 1891, to launch an 18-game winning streak that enabled the Beaneaters to overtake the White Stockings in the season's final week and capture the pennant. Five of the victories came at the expense of the New York Giants, while Giants manager Jim Mutrie kept star catcher Buck Ewing on the bench for the entire series, played slugging first baseman Roger Connor in just one of the five games, and refused to pit his two best hurlers, Amos Rusie and Ewing's brother John, against the Beaneaters. Mutrie claimed Buck Ewing's arm was shot and the others simply needed a rest, but Anson and former Louisville manager Jim Hart, who had ascended to the Chicago presidency upon Spalding's retirement, so unremittingly accused the Giants of lying down against Boston that the League was compelled to appoint a committee to investigate the charge. *The Sporting News* mused, "It would be strange if the National League, after withstanding an outbreak like that of the Players League last year, and after successfully resisting the attempt to disrupt it made by the American Association, should go to pieces on account of dissension in its own ranks." But to no one's surprise the investigating committee, which was comprised entirely of League minions, whitewashed the Giants of any wrongdoing. The League flag nonetheless was not officially awarded to Boston until early November.

The controversial 1891 NL champion Boston Beaneaters exuded a pungent Beer and Whisky League aroma. Boston fleeced the AA of Herman Long in 1890, Billy Nash was an AA rookie in 1884, Harry Stovey was hijacked from the AA prior to the 1891 season and King Kelly stabbed the AA in the back when he jumped to the Beaneaters in August 1891.

Some historians have attributed the Beaneaters' torrid stretch drive to Kelly, claiming his acquisition ignited the team, but the facts indicate otherwise. The 18-game winning streak did not begin until nearly three weeks after Kelly arrived. Moreover, he seldom played, participating in just 16 games with the Beaneaters after joining them on August 27. But whatever the truth of the Beaneaters' last-gasp charge to the pennant, Kelly dealt the Beer and Whisky loop a mortal blow when he absconded. A World's Series between the Beaneaters and the Reds would have helped restore the Association's credibility, since the Reds almost certainly would have given an excellent account of themselves. Irwin boasted a solid veteran nine that revolved around first baseman Dan Brouthers, catcher-third baseman Duke Farrell, rightfielder Hugh Duffy, centerfielder Tom Brown and pitchers Charlie Buffinton and George Haddock, who posted 62 wins between them to go with just 20 losses. Brouthers won the loop batting title, Farrell grabbed the RBI and home-run crowns and Duffy ranked second in several major hitting departments. But if there had been a Most Valuable Player Award in 1891, Brown almost certainly would have won it. Although serving as the Reds' leadoff hitter, he nevertheless topped the Association in total bases, doubles and triples, while tallying an amazing 177 runs in just 137 games. With Brown, Duffy, Brouthers and Farrell the first four hitters in their batting order and strong defensive work by second baseman Cub Stricker and shortstop Paul Radford, the Reds easily survived severe injuries to two key regulars, leftfielder Hardy Richardson and third baseman Bill Joyce, to romp home first by an eight-and-a-half-game margin. On clinching the flag, Prince and Irwin received this cable from Phelps: "Gentlemen—It is my very pleasant duty to formally present to you the 'association pennant.' You have, after a most interesting fight, fairly won it, and the association club members 'doff their caps' to you as 'the champions.' "

Several days later, on October 1, the city of Boston staged a huge parade for the champions that began at the corner of Boylston and Charles Streets and wormed its way slowly to the team's Congress Street Grounds. As a preamble to the regularly scheduled Association game between the Reds and Washington, the Thompson-Houston Electrics of Lynn played Murray & Irwins for the local amateur championship, with Murray & Irwins winning 4–1. The Reds then edged Washington 2–1 behind Buffinton for their 16th straight win over the Nationals. As each Boston starter came to the plate for his first at bat of the game, he was serenaded by the crowd. The song chosen for leadoff hitter Brown was "Home Again." Pitching ace Buffinton was greeted with "Hail to the Chief" as he stepped to the dish. When Duffy and Brouthers both scored in the first inning on a trio of Washington errors, the band struck up "Oh, Dear, What Can the Matter Be?"

On Monday, October 5, the Reds closed out their regular-season schedule by splitting a doubleheader with the Athletics. The following day, the Reds and the A's played an exhibition game at Trenton, New Jersey, while last-place Washington hosted Baltimore in a twinbill. On that Tuesday afternoon, the endeavors in both cities were plagued by rain and cold. In New Jersey the exhibition contest was "sharply played" with the Reds prevailing, 7–4. Former University of Pennsylvania star Sumner Bowman

• • •
Tom Brown came East with Monte Ward in the spring of 1882 to try out for Providence. He failed to make the Grays but connected with Columbus in 1883 and went on to enjoy a long but very uneven career. Surrounded by a strong supporting cast, as he was in 1891, Brown excelled. With a weak Louisville team three years later, he hit .254 when the average player in the majors—ptichers included—was hitting .309.

• • •

After winning 22 games as an NL rookie in 1887, Kid Madden could not stay healthy again for a full season until 1891. Sent to Baltimore by the Boston Reds early in the 1891 campaign, he bagged 13 wins for the Orioles, including the final championship game ever played under the AA's auspices.

took the loss for the A's. It was the last game Bowman ever pitched at the major league level. Darby O'Brien, who finished the day in the box for Boston and got the win, was also working in his last game. He died over the winter of pneumonia.

But the last official Association game of the 1891 season and, though no one could then know it, the final championship contest ever to be played by the Beer and Whisky League, came at Washington's Boundary Field, where the Nationals put on a fielding exhibition that one reporter on the scene judged "the worst ever seen in this city." After dropping the first game to the Orioles 15–3 and committing nine errors, Washington racked up another six miscues in the nightcap, which was called, mercifully, after just five innings with Baltimore ahead 15–11. The Orioles' winning hurler was Kid Madden, who, like Bowman and O'Brien, was also destined never to pitch another game in the majors.

On October 9, Phelps issued League president Nick Young a formal challenge to a World's Series, but Young said it was unacceptable because the Association had broken the National Agreement. The League began to take an even harder line with its rival, when Charles Prince made it known that he wanted to sell his interest in the Boston Reds and get out of baseball. Association moguls realized that they were in deep trouble if Prince sold his stock to the Beaneaters and the two Boston teams were consolidated, yet could not themselves muster the capital to buy the Reds. Throughout the fall of 1891, Association chieftains continued to put on a brave front, but Harold Seymour has depicted them as "behaving like young boys whistling in the woods when dark approaches."

Faced with the unappetizing prospect of having to back several weak franchises in order to keep the Association going, Von der Ahe, in October, found himself listening to John Brush's plea that a single 12-club league was the only way to save the game. Meanwhile, Henry Von der Horst was turned over to Cleveland owner Frank D. Robison to convert to the 12-club plan. The two beer barons were considered by the League to be all that stood between it and victory.

At first Von der Ahe scoffed at the notion of consolidating and encouraged his Association compatriots to continue the struggle. The League then revised its strategy and began to woo the Association's players. Second baseman Bill Hallman of the Athletics was the first big-name performer to jump from the Association to the League after the 1891 campaign ended. Association teams made a few conquests of their own, including Phillies pitcher Kid Gleason and Giants shortstop Jack Glasscock, both of whom signed with the Browns, but the Beer and Whisky loop's losses far outweighed its gains. The *coup de grace* came on October 29 when all of the Browns stars, led by Comiskey, Tip O'Neill, Jack Stivetts, Tommy McCarthy and Denny Lyons, announced that they would play with League clubs in 1892. Reportedly, this mass desertion stemmed from growing animosity between Von der Ahe and Comiskey, who had been allowed to run the team during the 1891 season in name only, while Von der Ahe really called the shots. Shortstop Shorty Fuller was the sole Browns regular who would not publicly admit to "giving Chris the goose," but before long he too defected, joining Lyons and catcher Jack Boyle on the New York Giants.

Now that his team was decimated and his chief lieutenant had jumped to the League, Von der Ahe became almost putty in the hands of the forces pushing for consolidation. Indeed, the lone voice that was still ardently opposed to a 12-club merger belonged to Brunell, one of the linchpins behind the Association's new Chicago entry. Brunell argued that a circuit with 12 teams would make for too many also-rans by June and would cause fan interest in most cities to dwindle accordingly, but his doomsaying fell on deaf ears.

On December 12, 1891, the headlines of *The Sporting News* trumpeted:

THE REAL SOLUTION
The League and the American Association Likely to Consolidate
Four of the League Clubs Willing to Play Sunday Games

A week later, *The Sporting News* confirmed that the League and the Association had officially consolidated on December 18

• • •
The 1895 St. Louis club, with Tommy Dowd, top row center. In 1891, Dowd lived a rookie's dream when he opened the season in right field for the defending PL champion Boston Reds, only to be shipped to Washington a few days later after Hugh Duffy took his job. It was Dowd's last brush with respectability until his coda in 1901. During the intervening ten years, he played for some of the worst teams ever assembled, and his best club—St. Louis in 1894—managed to win just 42.4 percent of its games.

ST. LOUIS BASE-BALL CLUB 1895.

• • •

The 1891 Boston Reds, the last AA champion. Top (left to right): Bill Joyce, Morgan Murphy, Bill Daley, manager Arthur Irwin, Hugh Duffy, Charlie Buffinton, Tom Brown. Middle (left to right): John Irwin, Hardy Richardson, Paul Radford, Dan Brouthers. Bottom (left to right): Darby O'Brien, George Haddock, Cub Stricker, Duke Farrell. Arthur Irwin capped a long career as a shortstop by managing for several years. In 1921 he disappeared while traveling the Atlantic on an ocean steamer. The presumption that he jumped overboard was given weight by the revelation after his disappearance that for years he had maintained two separate conjugal homes. In May 1891, Irwin had to quell an insurrection when he replaced the injured Richardson with his brother, John. The Boston Reds, said *The Sporting News*, were "completely disgusted with this act of nepotism."

at the Bates House hotel in Indianapolis, after executives from both loops had met in closed session all week. St. Louis, Baltimore, Washington and Louisville were formally accepted into the League and representatives of the other Association clubs were called before the executive committee of the new 12-team loop separately and asked to submit their buyout prices. After a great deal of haggling the Athletics, Columbus, Milwaukee, the Boston Reds and the embryonic Chicago club were awarded around $135,000, with each of the 12 surviving major league clubs committed to contribute 10 percent of its gate receipts until the amount was obtained.

Though the Association's beacon, which had glowed and sputtered for a full decade, was now extinguished, its aura still glimmered. Not only were fully two-thirds of the franchises in the new big league spawned by the Association, but its influence on the game permeated the constitution adopted by the 12-team federation.* Paramount among the amendments the consolidated loop ratified were: (1) a 25¢ admission price in all cities that demanded it, though a minimum 50¢ grandstand admission charge was urged; (2) Sunday ball in all cities where it was allowed, though no club would be compelled to play on Sunday; (3) each club to have the right to decide for itself whether to sell alcoholic beverages in its home park.

Thus it was that three of the Association's founding principles came to be a universally accepted part of the framework of our national pastime in 1892 and remain so today. Actually, at the time that peace was made, the League was willing to embrace almost all of the Association's rich heritage, even its name. After long debate, the fledgling 12-team confederacy was called the National League and American Association of Base Ball Clubs. The unwieldy appellation was used only on formal documents. In 1892 the consolidated loop's standings were carried by most newspapers under the heading "League-Association." Originally, the consolidation committee had proposed a much snappier name for the new circuit, but too many League owners had vetoed it. The stumbling block was that the Association's contribution to the combined name had been put first, which was unpalatable to the old guard. Soon, however, they would be caught in the web of their own chauvinism as another threat to their supremacy emerged that was far more powerful than any that had come before it. They would remember then with bitter irony that, in December 1891, the consolidation committee had recommended the new loop be called the American League.

• • •
Early in the 1891 season, Clark Griffith looked like the Browns' newest pitching find, but he ran into arm trouble and was sold to the Boston Reds. Released when his arm did not respond, he floated around the minors until he was summoned to Chicago by Jim Hart, one of his early managers. An instant hit in the Windy City, Griffith won 240 games—second only to Gus Weyhing among pitchers who debuted in the AA—before finding later success as a manager and owner.

*Of the 12 teams in the new league, only Chicago, Boston, New York and Philadelphia were not sired by the Association.

	W	L	PCT	HOME	ROAD	GB
1. Boston Reds	93	42	.689	51–17	42–25	
2. St. Louis Browns	86	52	.623	52–21	33–30	8.5
3. Milwaukee Brewers	21	15	.583	16–5	5–10	22.5
4. Baltimore Orioles	72	63	.523	44–24	27–40	21
5. Philadelphia Athletics	73	66	.525	43–26	30–40	22
6. Columbus Solons	61	76	.445	34–29	27–47	33
7. Cincinnati Kelly's Killers	43	57	.430	24–20	19–37	32.5
8. Louisville Colonels	55	84	.396	39–32	15–51	40
9. Washington Nationals	43	92	.319	28–40	16–51	50

1891 SEASON LEADERS

BATTING

•••
Charlie Buffinton fanned 417 batters and won 47 games in 1884 but was eclipsed by 60-game winner Hoss Radbourn. In 1891 his 28 wins were eclipsed by teammate George Haddock. Buffinton is nonetheless considered by many analysts to have been among the top five pitchers in the last century. His 28-9 mark in 1891 is the best of any hurler who spent just one year in the AA.

BATTING AVERAGE (325 ABs)

1. Brouthers, Boston	.350
2. Duffy, Boston	.336
3. T. Brown, Boston	.321
O'Neill, StL	.321
5. Van Haltren, Balt	.318
6. D. Lyons, StL	.315
7. McCarthy, StL	.310
8. Wood, Phila	.309
9. Donovan, Louis-Wash	.305
10. Milligan, Phila	.303
McGuire, Wash	.303

ON-BASE PERCENTAGE

1. Brouthers, Boston	.471
2. D. Lyons, StL	.445
3. Hoy, StL	.424
4. Seery, Cinci	.423
5. Duffy, Boston	.408
6. O'Neill, StL	.402
7. Welch, Balt	.400
8. Wood, Phila	.399
9. Van Haltren, Balt	.398
10. Milligan, Phila	.397
T. Brown, Boston	.397
Taylor, Louis	.397

HOME RUNS

1. Farrell, Boston	12
2. Milligan, Phila	11
D. Lyons, StL	11
4. O'Neill, StL	10
Duffee, Colum	10
Larkin, Phila	10
Canavan, Cinci-Mil	10
8. Van Haltren, Balt	9
9. Duffy, Boston	8
McCarthy, StL	8

SLUGGING AVERAGE

1. Brouthers, Boston	.512
2. Milligan, Phila	.505
3. Farrell, Boston	.474
4. T. Brown, Boston	.469
5. L. Cross, Phila	.458
6. D. Lyons, StL	.455
7. Duffy, Boston	.453
8. O'Neill, StL	.447
9. Van Haltren, Balt	.443
10. Larkin, Phila	.441

TOTAL BASES

1. T. Brown, Boston	276
2. Van Haltren, Balt	251
3. Brouthers, Boston	249
4. Duffy, Boston	240
McCarthy, StL	240
6. Werden, Balt	234
7. O'Neill, StL	233
8. Larkin, Phila	232
Duffee, Colum	232
Milligan, Phila	232

RUNS

1. T. Brown, Boston	177
2. Van Haltren, Balt	136
Hoy, StL	136
4. Duffy, Boston	134
5. McCarthy, StL	127
6. D. Lyons, StL	124
7. Welch, Balt	122
8. Brouthers, Boston	117
9. McTamany, Colum-Phila	116
10. Hallman, Phila	112
O'Neill, StL	112

HITS

1.	T. Brown, Boston	189
2.	Duffy, Boston	180
	Van Haltren, Balt	180
4.	McCarthy, StL	179
5.	Brouthers, Boston	170
6.	O'Neill, StL	167
7.	Hallman, Phila	166
	Duffee, Colum	166
9.	Hoy, StL	165
10.	Wood, Phila	163

STOLEN BASES

1.	T. Brown, Boston	106
2.	Duffy, Boston	85
3.	Van Haltren, Balt	75
4.	Hoy, StL	59
5.	Radford, Boston	55
6.	Stricker, Boston	54
7.	Wheelock, Colum	52
8.	Crooks, Colum	50
	Welch, Balt	50
10.	Werden, Balt	46

RBIs

1.	Farrell, Boston	110
2.	Duffy, Boston	108
	Brouthers, Boston	108
4.	Milligan, Phila	106
5.	Werden, Balt	104
6.	O'Neill, StL	95
	McCarthy, StL	95
8.	Comiskey, StL	93
	Larkin, Phila	93
10.	Duffee, Colum	90

PITCHING

WINS

1.	Haddock, Boston	34
	McMahon, Balt	34
3.	Stivetts, StL	33
4.	Weyhing, Phila	31
5.	Buffinton, Boston	29
6.	Knell, Colum	28
7.	Chamberlain, Phila	22
8.	McGill, Cinci-StL	20
9.	Dwyer, Cinci-Mil	19
10.	Foreman, Wash	18
	O'Brien, Boston	18

LOSSES

1.	Carsey, Wash	37
2.	Knell, Colum	27
3.	McMahon, Balt	25
4.	Chamberlain, Phila	23
	Dwyer, Cinci-Mil	23
6.	Stivetts, StL	22
7.	Foreman, Wash	21
8.	Weyhing, Phila	20
9.	Gastright, Colum	19
10.	Fitzgerald, Louis	18

INNINGS

1.	McMahon, Balt	503
2.	Knell, Colum	462
3.	Weyhing, Phila	450
4.	Stivetts, StL	440
5.	Carsey, Wash	415
6.	Chamberlain, Phila	405.2
7.	Haddock, Boston	379.2
8.	Dwyer, Cinci-Mil	375
9.	Buffinton, Boston	363.2
10.	Foreman, Wash	345.1

COMPLETE GAMES

1.	McMahon, Balt	53
2.	Weyhing, Phila	51
3.	Knell, Colum	47
4.	Carsey, Wash	46
5.	Chamberlain, Phila	44
6.	Stivetts, StL	40
7.	Dwyer, Cinci-Mil	39
	Foreman, Wash	39
9.	Haddock, Boston	37
10.	Buffinton, Boston	33

STRIKEOUTS

1.	Stivetts, StL	259
2.	Knell, Colum	228
3.	Weyhing, Phila	219
	McMahon, Balt	219
5.	Chamberlain, Phila	204
6.	Carsey, Wash	174
7.	McGill, Cinci-StL	173
8.	Foreman, Wash	170
9.	Haddock, Boston	169
10.	Buffinton, Boston	158

WINNING PCT. (25 DECISIONS)

1.	Buffinton, Boston	.763
2.	Haddock, Boston	.756
3.	Weyhing, Phila	.608
4.	Stivetts, StL	.600
5.	McMahon, Balt	.593
6.	O'Brien, Boston	.581
7.	McGill, Cinci-StL	.571
8.	Knell, Colum	.509
9.	Crane, Cinci	.500
	Ehret, Louis	.500
	Madden, Boston-Balt	.500

ERA (140 INNINGS)

1.	Crane, Cinci	2.45
2.	Haddock, Boston	2.49
3.	Buffinton, Boston	2.55
4.	McMahon, Balt	2.81
5.	Stivetts, StL	2.86
6.	Knell, Colum	2.92
7.	Mains, Cinci-Mil	3.07
8.	Weyhing, Phila	3.18
9.	McGill, Cinci-StL	3.33
10.	Ehret, Louis	3.47

LOWEST ON-BASE PCT.

1.	Buffinton, Boston	.281
2.	Haddock, Boston	.293
3.	Knell, Colum	.300
4.	McMahon, Balt	.301
5.	Weyhing, Phila	.306
6.	Stivetts, StL	.310
	Ehret, Louis	.310
	Sanders, Phila	.310
9.	Fitzgerald, Louis	.314
10.	Stratton, Louis	.317

THIRTEEN

• • •
Harry Stovey reverted to
Stowe, his birth name, after he
retired from baseball and settled permanently in New Bedford, MA. For years he served
the town as a policeman,
walking his beat, answering to
"Officer Stowe." After a while,
most people had no inkling
he'd once been a famous ballplayer. In 1936, he received
six votes for the Hall of Fame,
twice as many as Kid Nichols,
and six more than Jim
O'Rourke, both of whom were
later inducted. The following
year Stovey, or Stowe, died,
and he's never received a vote
since.

REQUIEM FOR A RENEGADE

THE NATIONAL LEAGUE AND AMERICAN ASSOCiation of Base Ball Clubs officially opened for business on April 12, 1892. Of the four surviving Association teams, all but Louisville fared badly in their inaugural contests. The St. Louis Browns lost 14–10 on Opening Day to Cap Anson's White Stockings at Chicago. In the nation's capital, the defending League champion Boston Beaneaters belted the Washington Nationals, 14–4. The Baltimore Orioles, which also opened at home, were trounced 13–3 by Brooklyn. However, Louisville not only topped Cleveland 5–2 at Eclipse Park behind Jouett Meekin, but ended the first week of the season tied for the lead with Boston and New York at 3–1. Seven days later, after the Colonels had raced to a 7–2 mark, only a game off the early pace set by Boston, *The Sporting News* judged that "Louisville's chances [for the pennant] are now considered very gilt edged."

But the Colonels' fast start was as delusive as it had been in 1891. By the final day of May, Jack Chapman's team resided in

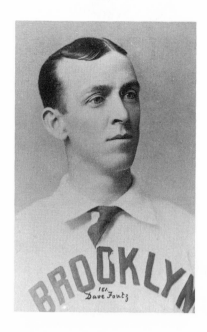

ninth place, trailed in order by Washington, St. Louis and Baltimore. Indeed, the four Association adoptees were destined to bring up the rear of the new 12-team loop in 1892, with the Baltimore Orioles a sorry last as they had been ten years earlier, their first year in the Association. Baltimore would soon develop into a power, winning three consecutive pennants between 1894–96, but so dreadful did the other three Association teams remain throughout the 1890s that it became hard to argue that the League had not been superior all along. Yet there was an explanation, if not an excuse, for the poor showing the Association graduates made against their League brethren.

Washington and Louisville had been the two weakest teams in the majors in 1891 and could hardly have been expected to perform much better than they did the following year. Baltimore, though a first-division team in the Association's last season, had made a serious miscalculation before consolidation occurred. Afraid he would lose his players to League raiders, Henry Von der Horst hastened to sign them all to 1892 contracts. Inasmuch as they already had a full roster, the Orioles were then unable to bid for players a special committee designated for distribution to clubs needing help. After his stars deserted him, Chris Von der Ahe, in contrast, signed very few players, thinking he could pick up talent on the cheap once the dust settled. But this strategy backfired, largely because the Browns had too many holes to fill and the League clubs had carefully locked up most of the better players by the time peace was made.

Von der Ahe's plight only worsened over the years, and the tale in Washington and Louisville also grew more and more doleful. Baltimore speedily escaped the nether regions, however, after Von der Horst hired Ned Hanlon to run the Orioles. Hanlon was everything to Von der Horst that Comiskey had once been to Von der Ahe. He gave the Orioles what they had always lacked: a mentor who not only could recognize talent, but also knew how to nurture it. For Von der Ahe, it must have particularly galling when Hanlon built Baltimore, a perennial Association doormat, into the only former Association team that was ever able to hold its own in the combined National League and American Association of Base Ball Clubs.

By 1899 the Browns' ownership had passed from Von der Ahe to the Robison brothers, who also still held a controlling interest in the Cleveland Spiders, and virtually all of the Spiders' regular players were transferred to St. Louis when the Robisons grew disenchanted with continual poor attendance in Cleveland. Bereft of talent, the Spiders replaced St. Louis, the 1898 cellar-dweller, in the loop basement. So bad, in fact, were the Spiders in

1899 that they could win just 20 of 154 games and finished a record 84 lengths behind first-place Brooklyn.

At the close of the 1899 season, Cleveland was targeted for elimination along with Washington, Louisville and Baltimore when the 12-team experiment was finally adjudged a failure and the lone major league loop again cut back to just eight clubs. So it happened that the same four franchises, with the substitution of Cleveland for St. Louis, which had been infused with Cleveland's (and thus "National League") blood, were jettisoned that had been absorbed from the American Association. Whether the four were earmarked for extinction by eerie coincidence or by clever and malevolent design is impossible, at this long distance, to gauge, but whatever the case, when it grew apparent that the old Association clubs were history, John McGraw, who was loath to play anywhere but in Baltimore, threw himself into an abortive effort to revive the American Association.* Also involved were Cap Anson, Al Spink, editor of *The Sporting News*, and the editor of *Sporting Life*, Francis Richter. Formally organized in Chicago, McGraw's brainstorm sought franchises in Boston, Milwaukee, Louisville, Providence, Detroit and Philadelphia, along with Chicago and Baltimore. Philadelphia was viewed as the cornerstone, and when backers there had trouble landing a playing site, the venture ran aground.

In hindsight, National League moguls must have regretted their opposition to the attempt to resurrect the Association, for if it had been successful, Ban Johnson almost certainly would not have had room to maneuver little more than a year later, when he renamed the Western League the American League and endeavored to transform it into a second major league. Moreover, many of them must have questioned long before then what they had gained by killing the American Association in 1891. The hope had been that, with the Association dead, salaries could be shaved to a pittance, since players no longer had any option but to take what they were given. In March 1892, Frank Brunell prophesied that the Brotherhood would resurface if the owners tried to implement a proposed $2500 salary limit the following year, but he was wrong. When several teams trimmed salaries a few months into the 1892 season, so that the war debt owed to the Association clubs left out in the cold could be more swiftly paid off, Charlie Buffinton, for one, refused to accept a pay cut and quit the game, but most of the other players affected com-

---

*There had also been a try at resuscitating the Association in 1894, led by Billy Barnie and Fred Pfeffer. The Association was finally successfully revived in 1902 as a minor league and still exists as such.

• • •
Silver King's pitch was a side-arm crossfire that he started in the back left corner of the pitcher's box and finished by stepping to his right and firing the ball over his left shoulder. His move was so sudden and so extreme that batters continually argued that he was out of the box when he pitched. King's pet delivery was eradicated by the introduction of the pitching rubber in 1893 and a rule that a hurler had to stand on it as he released the ball. He had 143 wins before his twenty-third birthday but was back working for his father as a bricklayer by the time he was thirty.

• • •

Cincinnati's outfield for most of the 1892 season had Tip O'Neill in left, Pete Browning in center and Bug Holliday in right. Toward the end, Curt Welch replaced Browning. That's three of the AA's best hitters and its best flychaser in the same outfield. Sadly for the Reds, all but Holliday were just about played out by 1892. Welch and Browning had become hopeless alcoholics, but O'Neill had another problem. As long and lean as Gary Cooper in his early years, he had begun to suffer from the most lethal malady for a ballplayer back then. It was not consumption or even paresis. It was corpulence.

plied meekly. Yet the return to one major league during the 1890s, rather than restoring a financial equilibrium and promoting a higher quality of play, led to baseball's least economically and aesthetically successful decade in history.

But if the National League's ceaseless desire to eliminate its most formidable challenger in the last century is difficult now to fathom, it has never been hard to understand why the American Association ultimately succumbed. The eight most prominent reasons, in order of their significance, were:

1. The failure to replace Denny McKnight with a strong president. After Pittsburgh defected to the National League in the wake of McKnight's dismissal, the Association sorely needed a leader who had vision and panache. The best that was ever said about Wheeler Wyckoff was he was an able and honest clerk. Opie Caylor might have been the ideal president if he had not been so despised and distrusted for his vitriolic pen and ferocious ego. For he had vision, along with a flair for self-mockery, and could charm his critics when he put his mind to it. It is probably significant that after he left Cincinnati, the Reds were never again a serious contender until well into the 20th century. Brunell was another who might have made an able president if he had not been similarly distrusted because he was a writer, and Boston Reds owner Charles Prince might have been the best candidate of all had he not withdrawn from baseball, as if he foresaw that it would be a poor arena in which to make money during the 1890s.

2. The mishandling of the New York Metropolitans situation. Even after John Day transferred Jim Mutrie and the Mets' two biggest stars, Tim Keefe and Dude Esterbrook, to the New York Giants, the Mets could have recovered with help from the stronger Association clubs like the Browns and Brooklyn. Instead, Charlie Byrne stripped the Mets of most of the rest of their better players. He seemed unaware that, down the road, having another strong team in the New York area could only enhance his Brooklyn franchise, and Von der Ahe too seemed oblivious to the value of keeping the Mets alive and healthy.

3. Entering into an unwritten agreement with the National League to bar black players. After being the only major league in the last century to allow blacks, in 1885 the Association joined the League in buckling under to threats from several League players, led by Cap Anson, to boycott the majors if they were not kept lilywhite. In so doing, the Association lost not only a large talent pool of players but also a vital piece of its autonomy, as well as an opportunity to alter baseball history in a way that would have indebted the game to it forever.

4. Allowing Brooklyn and Cincinnati to bolt to the National League. Replacing the Bridegrooms with another Brooklyn franchise in 1890 more or less showed that the Association immediately realized its mistake, as did putting a new team in Cincinnati in 1891. Both clubs, but especially Brooklyn, considered returning

to the Association before it collapsed, suggesting that neither would have deserted in the first place if more effort had been put into keeping them happy.

5. Treating Cleveland and Kansas City so cavalierly. Both were good baseball towns and would have stayed in the Association if they had been made to feel a part of the inner circle rather than like stepchildren. Lost too, when both teams departed, were stars in the making like Ed McKean, Chief Zimmer, Billy Hamilton and Herman Long.

6. Ignoring the deteriorating situation in Philadelphia until the Athletics' franchise had become almost unsalvageable. The A's strong play in the early part of the 1890 season may have disguised the havoc in the front office, but someone, nevertheless, should have noticed that things were coming apart and sounded the alarm. Instead, the A's were allowed to become the only major league team ever to hire its players on a game-to-game basis like day laborers, rather than putting them under contract.

7. Von der Ahe's nagging belief that he knew baseball and could run a team without the help of a manager like Comiskey. Always something of a problem, it grew lethal in 1890 when the Browns did fairly well without a real manager as Von der Ahe, rather than replace Comiskey, put the team under a string of playing captains—all of whom were really no more than his puppets. The false appearance of success in a war-weakened season induced Von der Ahe to take on more power, even after Comiskey returned to the team. When he continued to indulge his belief in his acumen

Bid McPhee scored nearly 1,700 runs and set hordes of fielding records for second basemen. He also collected nearly 1,000 walks in an era when few players had as many as 500, got plenty of extra base hits and stole tons of bases. McPhee is seen as final proof that the Hall of Fame is off when it comes to AA players. The thing is there are other neglected middle infielders of his time whose credentials aren't far behind, and then there's Bill Mazeroski.

• • •

Bob Caruthers supposedly had a heart problem that killed him while he was still young. Then some think he died young of paresis. But forty-seven was not so young in 1911 when the great ump rang him up. Imagine a lineup of Caruthers, Mullane, Foutz, Hecker, Jack Stivetts, Scott Stratton, Cannonball Crane, Elmer Smith and Adonis Terry—enough AA pitching greats there to cover every position, and each one a tough out, but it would still have to be Caruthers in the box.

in 1892, disaster resulted, as he ran through no fewer than five different managers and seemed still to be without a clue that he didn't know what he was doing.

8. Dropping the double-umpire system before it was given a full trial. In 1889, when the notion of assigning two umpires to a contest was first tested in regular season games, the innovation was applauded by many observers as yet another way in which the Association was more daring and progressive than the National League. The Association, moreover, had long had a better quality of officiating. But when the double-umpire system got off to a rocky start, partly because Wyckoff hired too many former players rather than recruiting experienced umpires, the Association owners who objected to the additional expense made their voices heard, and the experiment was scrapped. Soon thereafter the Association lost its leadership position in the crusade for improved officiating when several of its stronger arbiters, namely John Gaffney and Bob Ferguson, skipped either to the National League or the Players League.

In the final analysis, though, the Association did well to have lasted as long as it did in the face of a much wilier and better-heeled adversary. That not a single one of its leading stars has been granted Hall of Fame recognition suggests that the game continued to bear a grudge inherited from spiteful National Leaguers deep into the 20th century. It is now extremely unlikely that this injustice will ever be rectified. Not since 1977, when Amos Rusie was selected, has a 19th-century player been enshrined in the Hall of Fame, and few in the last 30 years or so have been given even cursory consideration by the Veterans Committee. Phillip Von Borries argues correctly that the Hall of Fame situation is now such that it is virtually a guarantee that "baseball will always lose more history than it secures." But Von Borries may be too gloomy in maintaining that "as long as the anti-American Association elitism flourishes, the rich legacy that the American Association left to the game so long ago . . . will remain unclaimed." For Hall of Fame recognition is not a be-all and end-all. While every knowledgeable baseball fan wants to feel the game's pantheon contains all of the sport's most worthy contributors and nothing but, even its most sanguine critics have long realized the selection process is too faulty ever to achieve such a lofty goal. So for some of our finest diamond athletes and umpires and executives, alternate forms of recognition must be sought. Certainly it is not only to complete the historical portrait of the Beer and Whisky League that we offer these lists of its career batting and pitching leaders, and then put our heads into selecting an all-time Association all-star team.

BATTING

BATTING AVERAGE **

1.	Pete Browning	.345
2.	Tip O'Neill	.343
3.	Dave Orr	.338
4.	Denny Lyons	.327
5.	Tommy McCarthy	.307
6.	Harry Stovey	.302
7.	Henry Larkin	.301
	Long John Reilly	.301
9.	Cy Swartwood	.300
10.	Oyster Burns	.299

SLUGGING AVERAGE

1.	Dave Orr	.497
2.	Tip O'Neill	.489
3.	Harry Stovey	.482
4.	Pete Browning	.476
5.	Denny Lyons	.465
6.	Long John Reilly	.460
7.	Jocko Milligan	.445
8.	Oyster Burns	.442
9.	Henry Larkin	.441
10.	Charley Jones	.434

GAMES

1.	Chicken Wolf	1195
2.	Charlie Comiskey	1032
3.	Curt Welch	1005
4.	Bid McPhee	911
5.	Hick Carpenter	892
6.	Joe Sommer	887
7.	Henry Larkin	859
8.	Arlie Latham	839
9.	Harry Stovey	824
10.	Jim McTamany	813

TOTAL BASES

1.	Chicken Wolf	1921
2.	Harry Stovey	1654
3.	Pete Browning	1567
4.	Tip O'Neil	1558
5.	Charlie Comiskey	1554
6.	Long John Reilly	1523
7.	Henry Larkin	1511
8.	Curt Welch	1443
9.	Dave Orr	1402
10.	Bid McPhee	1309

HOME RUNS

1.	Harry Stovey	76
2.	Long John Reilly	59
3.	Tip O'Neill	47
4.	Jocko Milligan	40
5.	Denny Lyons	39
6.	Henry Larkin	36
7.	Frank Fennelly	34
8.	Charley Jones	32
9.	Pete Browning	31
	Dave Orr	31
	Oyster Burns	31

RUNS

1.	Harry Stovey	883
2.	Curt Welch	854
3.	Arlie Latham	829
4.	Charlie Comiskey	816
5.	Chicken Wolf	778
6.	Bid McPhee	762
7.	Long John Reilly	703
8.	Tip O'Neill	702
	Henry Larkin	702
10.	Jim McTamany	693

HITS

1.	Chicken Wolf	1438
2.	Charlie Comiskey	1199
3.	Pete Browning	1136
4.	Tip O'Neill	1092
5.	Curt Welch	1069
6.	Harry Stovey	1035
7.	Henry Larkin	1031
8.	Hick Carpenter	1000
9.	Long John Reilly	998
10.	Arlie Latham	975

*Includes only stats compiled while playing in the AA.

**Batting and slugging leaders played at least four seasons in the AA; winning percentage leaders registered a minimum of 100 decisions in the AA.

•••

Tony Mullane not only led Toledo in wins in 1884; he also topped the club in home runs, and his batting average was second only to Sam Barkley's. In his final season, ten years later, Mullane hit .396 for Baltimore before being let go. It was like his pitching. Mullane could do anything on the diamond when he got his mind right, but there were whole years sometimes when it almost seemed he wasn't there.

PITCHING

WINS

1. Tony Mullane	203
2. Bob Caruthers	175
3. Guy Hecker	173
4. Will White	136
5. Dave Foutz	129
6. Matt Kilroy	122
7. Gus Weyhing	115
8. Toad Ramsey	114
Ed Morris	114
10. Silver King	112
Icebox Chamberlain	112

SHUTOUTS

1. Tony Mullane	26
2. Will White	23
3. Ed Morris	21
Bob Caruthers	21
5. Matt Kilroy	18
Jumbo McGinnis	18
7. Dave Foutz	16
8. Guy Hecker	15
9. Ed Seward	13
10. Adonis Terry	12

STRIKEOUTS

1. Toad Ramsey	1515
2. Tony Mullane	1340
3. Matt Kilroy	1088
4. Guy Hecker	1067
5. Adonis Terry	953
6. Ed Morris	926
7. Hardie Henderson	919
8. Bobby Mathews	877
9. Icebox Chamberlain	845
10. Gus Weyhing	829

LOSSES

1. Guy Hecker	139
2. Tony Mullane	134
3. Toad Ramsey	124
4. Hardie Hendeson	117
5. Adonis Terry	107
6. Henry Porter	104
7. Matt Kilroy	103
8. Jack Lynch	96
9. Al Mays	90
10. Gus Weyhing	87

GAMES

1. Tony Mullane	364
2. Guy Hecker	330
3. Bob Caruthers	249
4. Toad Ramsey	248
5. Matt Kilroy	243
6. Adonis Terry	220
7. Icebox Chamberlain	210
8. Will White	209
9. Gus Weyhing	208
10. Dave Foutz	206

WINNING PCT. (100 DECISIONS)

1. Bob Caruthers	.732	(175–64)
2. Dave Foutz	.701	(129–55)
3. Silver King	.696	(112–49)
4. Ed Morris	.667	(114–57)
5. Will White	.663	(136–69)
6. Tim Keefe	.639	(78–44)
7. Bobby Mathews	.634	(106–61)
8. Jack Stivetts	.605	(75–49)
9. Tony Mullane	.602	(203–134)
10. Icebox Chamberlain	.599	(112–75)

ALL-STAR TEAM*

FIRST TEAM		SECOND TEAM	
1B	Dave Orr	1B	Long John Reilly
2B	Bid McPhee	2B	Lou Bierbauer
3B	Denny Lyons	3B	Arlie Latham
SS	Germany Smith	SS	Bill Gleason
OF	Pete Browning	OF	Charley Jones
OF	Harry Stovey	OF	Tommy McCarthy
OF	Tip O'Neill	OF	Curt Welch
C	Pop Snyder	C	Jocko Milligan
P	Tony Mullane	P	Will White
P	Bob Caruthers	P	Matt Kilroy
UTIL	Guy Hecker	UTIL	Dave Foutz
MANAGER	Charlie Comiskey	MANAGER	Bill Sharsig

* Includes only players who performed in the AA for at least four seasons.

•••

Had Pete Browning lived to see Rogers Hornsby play, he might have recognized himself. Browning—like Hornsby—was a great righthanded hitter who was damned for his fielding and his idiosyncratic personality, but he differed from Hornsby on three important counts. He drank, he stared into the sun in the misguided belief that it would improve his eyesight and he played in a time that was a hitter's nightmare. With all the rule changes in the 1880s and the constant tampering with the balance between pitchers and batters, there were a *dozen* regulars each year who hit in the low .200s for every Browning who hit his .340.

THE BEER AND WHISKY LEAGUE

BIBLIOGRAPHY

Alexander, Charles. *Our Game*. New York: Henry Holt & Company, Inc. 1991.

Allen, Lee. *The Cincinnati Reds*. New York: G. P. Putnam's Sons, 1948.

————.*The Hot Stove League*. New York: A.S. Barnes and Company, 1955.

————.*The World Series: The Story of Baseball's Annual Championship*. New York: G. P. Putnam's Sons, 1969.

Axelson, G. W., *"COMMY": The Life Story of Charles A. Comiskey*. Chicago: Reilly & Lee, 1919.

Bready, James. *The Home Team*. Baltimore: privately published, 1958.

Brown, Warren. *The Chicago Cubs*. New York: G. P. Putnam's Sons, 1952.

Coombs, Samm & Bob West, eds. *Baseball: America's National Game 1839–1915 by Albert G. Spalding*. San Francisco: Halo Books, 1991.

Dewey, Donald, and Acocella, Nicholas. *Encyclopedia of Major League Baseball Teams*. New York: Harper Collins, 1993.

Goldstein, Warren. *Playing for Keeps: A History of Early Baseball*. Ithaca: Cornell University Press, 1989.

Graham, Frank. *The Brooklyn Dodgers*. New York: G. P. Putnam's Sons, 1945.

———.*The New York Giants.* New York: G. P. Putnam's Sons, 1952.

James, Bill. *The Bill James Historical Baseball Abstract.* New York: Villard Books, 1988.

Kaese, Harold. *The Boston Braves.* New York: G. P. Putnam's Sons, 1948.

Lanigan, Ernest J., ed. *The Baseball Cyclopedia.* New York: The Baseball Magazine Company, 1922.

Lansche, Jerry. *Glory Fades Away.* Dallas: Taylor Publishing Company, 1991.

Levine, Peter. A. G. *Spalding and the Rise of Baseball: The Promise of an American Sport.* New York: Oxford University Press, 1985.

Lewis, Franklin, *The Cleveland Indians.* New York: G. P. Putnam's Sons, 1949.

Lieb, Frederick G. *The Baseball Story.* New York: G. P. Putnam's Sons, 1950.

———.The St. Louis Cardinals: The Story of a Great Baseball Club. New York, G. P. Putnam's Sons, 1947.

Lowry, Phillip J. *Green Cathedrals.* Cooperstown, New York: Society for American Baseball Research, 1986.

Mack, Connie. *My 66 Years in Baseball.* Philadelphia: Winston, 1950.

Nemec, David. *Great Baseball Feats, Facts, & Firsts.* New York: New American Library, 1987.

———.*The Ultimate Baseball Book.* Edited by Daniel Okrent and Harris Lewine. Boston: Houghton Mifflin Co., 1991.

———.*The Great American Baseball Team Book.* New York: New American Library, 1992.

———.*The Rules of Baseball.* New York: Lyons & Burford, Publishers, 1994.

Palmer, Harry. *Stories of the Base Ball Field.* Chicago: Rand McNally & Co., 1890.

Povich, Shirley. *The Washington Senators.* New York: G. P. Putnam's Sons, 1954.

Rankin, June. *The New York and Brooklyn Base Ball Clubs.* New York: Richard Fox Printer, 1888.

Richter, Francis. *A Brief History of Base Ball.* Philadelphia: Sporting Life Publishing Company, 1909.

Ritter, Lawrence. *The Glory of Their Times.* New York: Random House, 1985.

Seymour, Harold. *Baseball: The Early Years.* New York: Oxford University Press, 1960.

Spalding, John. *Always on Sunday: The California Baseball League, 1886–1915.* Manhattan, Kansas: Ag Press, 1992.

The Baseball Encyclopedia. New York: Macmillan Publishing Company, 1968, 1976, 1982, 1990 and 1993 editions.

Thorn, John and Pete Palmer, eds. *Total Baseball.* New York: Warner Books, Inc., 1993.

Tiemann, Robert L., and Mark Rucker, eds. *Nineteenth Century Stars.* Cleveland: The Society for American Baseball Research, 1989.

Tiemann, Robert L. *Dodger Classics*. St. Louis: Baseball Histories, Inc., 1983.

Turkin, Hy and Thompson, S. C. *The Official Encyclopedia of Baseball*. New York: A. S. Barnes and Company, 1951.

Voigt, David Quentin. *American Baseball, Volume One*. University Park, Pennsylvania: The Pennsylvania State University Press, 1983.

Von Borries, Phillip. *Legends of Louisville*. West Bloomfield, Michigan: Altwerger & Mandel Publishing Company, 1993.

Westlake, Charles. *Columbus Baseball History*. Columbus: Pfeiffer Printing Company, 1981.

Zimbalist, Andrew. *Baseball Billions*. New York: Basic Books, 1992.

PERIODICALS

1. NEWSPAPERS

Brooklyn Eagle, 1889–92
Cincinnati Commercial, 1882–83
Cincinnati Enquirer, 1882, 1884–86
Cleveland Leader, 1882
Louisville Courier-Journal, 1882–85
New York Clipper, 1882–91
New York Times, 1882–1891
Providence Journal, 1884–85
St. Louis Post-Dispatch, 1884–85
Missouri Republican, 1882–83

2. SPORTING JOURNALS

Sporting Life, 1883–86, 1887–91
Sporting News, 1886–87; 1890–92

3. BASEBALL GUIDES

Reach's Official Base Ball Guide. Philadelphia: A. J. Reach & Bros., 1884–92.

Spalding's Official Base Ball Guide. Chicago. A. G. Spalding and Bros., 1882–93.

4. OTHER SOURCES

Chadwick, Henry. His personal scrapbooks on microfilm in the New York Public Library. Albert G. Spalding collection.

Nemec, David. "Last Call for the Beer Ball League." Hot Stove Baseball, Winter 1991.

Thorn, John and Mark Rucker. *The National Pastime: A Review of Baseball History. Special Pictorial Issue: The Nineteenth Century*. A publication of the Society for American Baseball Research, 1984.

INDEX